Jedediah Purdy

BEING AMERICA

Jedediah Purdy grew up in West Virginia and attended Harvard College and Yale Law School. He has served as a fellow at the New America Foundation and the Berkman Center at Harvard Law School.

ALSO BY JEDEDIAH PURDY

For Common Things:
Irony, Trust, and Commitment in America Today

BEING
AMERICA

BEING AMERICA

Liberty, Commerce, and Violence in an American World

Jedediah Purdy

VINTAGE BOOKS
A Division of Random House, Inc.
New York

The Library of Congress has cataloged the Knopf edition as follows:
Purdy, Jedediah, 1974–
Being America: liberty, commerce, and violence in an American world /
Jedediah Purdy.
1st ed.
New York: Knopf, 2003.
p. cm.
Includes bibliographical references and index.
1. International relations.
2. United States—Foreign relations.
JZ1480 .P87 2003
2002116390

Vintage ISBN: 0-375-72755-8

*For Pratap Bhanu Mehta
and Owen Fiss*

CONTENTS

—ɯ—

Contents

—ᴍ—

My first book, *For Common Things*, was about what happens to politics when citizens pay it no attention, or the wrong kind of attention: prurient, crudely cynical, or naively anodyne. This book, too, is about paying attention to—about ways of see-ing—a world held in common but inhabited in fractious and often violent ways. *Being America* addresses a country and a world in transformation. Abroad, the United States is using military power with a new self-confidence, and a new disregard for the opinions of its allies. Its rewards are a new set of allies, neither as reliable nor as formidable as the traditional ones, and widespread resentment of what the world sees as American arrogance. At home, the political indifference of the 1990s has yielded to intense patriotism, but also to a public dismember-ment of the truth that dwarfs the evasions of the Clinton era, and which may be expected to produce its own crop of cyni-cism. After a decade of childlike complacency, the country has embraced leaders who practice the rhetoric of seriousness, maturity, and duty; but the reality may be a different matter.

One telling change of the last two years or so is the status of the term "empire." In the summer of 2001, when I began writ-ing this book in earnest, I was intensely aware that the word was a pariah. It was associated with critics on the far left and right. Otherwise it was not just an unpopular word, but a *for-eign* word, like "petit bourgeois" or "revanchist." Those words don't have a grip on the social or moral imaginations of most Americans. We don't use them in anger or exhortation, or, really, much at all. The reason is not xenophobia, but that such words come from other traditions of political thought, which have never seemed to bear on American conditions. "Empire" was like that—a word used by and about other nations, with histories very different from ours.

That was then. Now, empire is everywhere. The major newsweeklies, big daily newspapers, magazines of ideas and opinion, and book publishers all have trumpeted the rise of American empire. And the tone of discussion has changed. In the months after September 11, some asked, "Are we an empire?" or "Why would others regard us as an empire?" Now such questions are set aside as naive and banal. Of course we are an empire, announce the pundits. As an empire, then, how should we behave? We are treated to primers on imperial policy: how to awe the natives, how to co-opt local power brokers, how to use military superiority to the best political advantage.

The change in our language is a symptom of a profound shift in our approach to the rest of the world. The change is still tentative, but if it goes forward it will have consequences for both international order and our own political culture. Yet on the question whether the change is good, whether we should embrace it, the national conversation is—as Robert Byrd said of the Senate on the brink of the Iraq war—ominously, dreadfully silent. This book is partly an attempt to grapple with those questions.

There are two central ideas in the imperial doctrine (and I mean the term not as an insult, but as a description) that the United States is in the course of adopting. The first is the political inequality of countries—not just the happenstance difference between big Germany and little Andorra, or rich Australia and poor Uganda, but inequality in their competence to govern themselves. That means *practical* competence, including the resources and institutions to secure order within national borders. It also means *moral* competence, that is, commanding democratic consent from the people of the country, or refraining from violations of basic human rights. Countries that lack practical competence are "failed states," such as Somalia. Countries that lack moral competence, such as North Korea and Saddam Hussein's Iraq, we call illegitimate. The basic idea of the new imperial doctrine is that countries that are competent to govern, in both of these senses, can intervene in and, for a time, rule countries that are not.

The political inequality of countries is the first big idea in the new imperial doctrine. The second big idea is that the United States has unique authority, and perhaps unique responsibility, to save others from bad governments and even from themselves. A hodgepodge of reasons lie behind this conviction: that we are overwhelmingly the world's most powerful country, that we have a special relationship to the values of democracy and personal liberty, perhaps that we are divinely appointed. These convictions intermingle and reinforce each other in a manner exemplified in the president's speeches.

This idea can license two kinds of intervention. The first kind rests on the inequality not of peoples, but of *governments*. Such an intervention proposes not that some peoples aren't capable of ruling themselves, but that they need to be rescued from their governments. Governments that can't keep order, or that rule in terribly illegitimate ways, can legitimately be overthrown and replaced to save the people who have to live under them. This was the spirit of the 1999 NATO intervention in Kosovo. It was also one rationale of the American-led invasion of Iraq: freeing Iraqis from a tyrant. Freeing people, however, often brings the liberator face to face with the possibility that the people are not quite ready to govern themselves, at least not in a manner that the liberator finds satisfactory. It begins to appear that some *peoples*, perhaps including Iraqis and Afghans, cannot be left to their own devices. Rather than setting a people free, then, the imperial power assumes responsibility for governing the country. The ongoing exercise of control over another people is a much stronger form of imperial policy than the overthrow of a despicable regime.

Together, these ideas form a radical rejection of the bedrock principles of international order in the twentieth century, particularly in the decades after World War II. The principles of that period were, on the one hand, the sovereignty of nations, and, on the other, the self-determination of peoples. They were as often violated as honored—in the Soviet invasion of Afghanistan, for instance, and the American support for antigovernment guerrillas in Nicaragua. Nonetheless, there was no other set of principles seriously offered to replace them in the law of nations. The new American policy appears intended to supplant them.

What has made American leadership so freshly self-assured in the use of force? Defenders of imperial policy advance three kinds of considerations. The first is global security. In the eighteenth century, piracy was regarded as a threat to all, and pursued wherever it took refuge. Terrorism—politically motivated attacks on civilians by non-state actors—has become the piracy of the twenty-first century. In combination with the technological power of biological and nuclear weapons, terrorism presents the potential of devastating attacks. Although the threat has been used profligately and perhaps disingenuously to defend the invasion of Iraq, in principle it is genuine. It implies that entire regimes, which cannot be trusted to keep certain weapons out of terrorist hands, may be brought to heel in the name of collective security. The attacks of September 11 demonstrated nothing new about this problem, but they mightily focused, and perhaps also distorted, American attention to it.

The second consideration is the protection of basic human rights. Certain actions are absolutely prohibited, say defenders of human rights law, and when they are violated—especially by a government—others have a right and duty to intervene and protect the victims. At the end of World War II, the Universal Declaration of Human Rights was a radical document. Today, groups such as Amnesty International and Human Rights Watch, which try to make good the promise of that and other international rights declarations, are essential custodians of public conscience. Genocide is the outer limit of evil in the Western political imagination, and it is to prevent genocide that we most readily believe intervention to be appropriate. Both the moral status of the Kosovo intervention and the lingering sense of culpable neglect around the failure to act in Rwanda in 1994 demonstrate the power of this consideration.

The third consideration is human flourishing. The most basic and widely shared human interests, such as security, dignity, and material comfort, can support imperial policy if the best way to advance basic human interests is through the domination of one people by another. This was the foremost moral defense of nineteenth-century British imperialism, as expressed by John Stuart Mill and his father, James Mill. On this view, social orders premised on superstition and tyranny should be replaced by the hard-nosed but beneficent tutelage of more advanced nations, which can train "underdeveloped" peoples in liberal and democratic values. At the end of their tutelage, the subject peoples can be expected to emerge into the full historical daylight of self-government, commerce, and reason. Until then, so-called principle of self-determination was, on this view, a pleasing illusion.

Although it was long disdained as the racist legacy of "white man's burden" thinking, this idea is increasingly recognized as the implicit theory of nation-building, which the United States and other powers are engaged in from Cambodia to Bosnia, and which some local populations might welcome in the war-torn countries of western and central Africa. It takes further support from the collapse of state-socialist regimes in Eastern Europe and the former Soviet Union, which seemed to confirm that people everywhere really do want the same things: personal liberty and security, a measure of comfort and opportunity, and the privilege of feeling at home in a "normal country" (in the poignant phrase of post-Milošević Yugoslav leader Vojislav Kostunica).

None of these considerations is mere cynical cover for power or arrogance. All respond to genuine problems: the ever-finer technology of terror, pervasive and terrible violations of human rights, and the total failure of many governments in formerly colonial countries to provide for their people. Moreover, these considerations address deep human interests, indeed, the same ones that the principles of sovereignty and self-determination are intended to protect: security from war, oppression, and chaos, and the chance to live in dignity. Viewed sympathetically, an imperial doctrine based on these considerations is *more* egalitarian than the conventional view that all countries and peoples are politically equal: such an imperial doctrine proposes that powerful countries have a duty to protect the human rights and the interest in flourishing of all individuals, everywhere. From this point of view, the principle of sovereignty is a legalistic excuse for avoiding the obligation to secure human rights, and the principle of self-determination is naive idealism that ignores the work really required to prepare a people for democratic self-government. An imperial doctrine with these claims can be credibly presented as more egalitarian, more humane, and also more realistic than alternative views.

That, however, is not the end of the story. Although Americans have recently been reacquainted with reasons *for* empire, we have not had the same experience of the reasons that counsel *against* empire. The latter part of the twentieth century mostly lost track of the counter-imperial tradition of thought, in favor of a simplistic just-so story: empires were racist and exploitative, and the progress of history has replaced them with a fairer, freer world. True enough, of course, but if those were the only reasons to oppose empire then there would be much less reason for hesitation about our new imperial policy, with its egalitarian foundations and humanitarian aspirations. There are, however, some other considerations to weigh.

To begin with, is the kind of intervention we have undertaken really the best way to promote the values we claim for it? There are several reasons to think it might not be. On the axis of global security, setting ourselves up as the world's law-giver—which we have not exactly done, but which we are lurching toward doing—risks shredding the norms of restraint in the international use of power. What we do now, Russia has already done in Chechnya, and China may well do in Taiwan or its Muslim northwest, or India in Pakistan. When one country puts itself above the law in the name of saving the law, other countries will take the opportunity to exempt themselves as well, and soon there may be no law to save.

Unilateral intervention also threatens global security by strengthening the incentive to acquire nuclear warheads and other devastating weapons. At the time of writing, it seems likely that the lesson to small countries from the American encounters with Iraq and North Korea (not to mention Pakistan, our unstable and nuclear-armed client state) will turn out to be this: we punish those who pursue nuclear weapons and fail, but reward those who succeed. That is a powerful spur to nuclear proliferation.

There are also reasons to doubt that imperial use of American power is the best vehicle for promoting human flourishing. It runs up against at least two competing considerations. The first is the power of nationalism. People everywhere want liberty and security, yes; but they also want not to be overrun and occupied by foreign powers. If their pragmatic interests lead them to welcome American power, their pride is likely to tug the opposite way, toward resentment and resistance. This need not mean that American power will inspire open revolt. It can be enough to bring down institutions that the people living under them do not love them, lend them no passionate loyalty, and feel a secret (or not-so-secret) satisfaction when they fail. A regime installed and overseen by American power, as in Iraq or Afghanistan, risks producing just such citizens.

The second competing consideration is the need for civic institutions that make democratic government stable. When democracy is won over time, as in the United States and Western Europe, the parties, unions, and civic groups that drive it forward are also its bulwarks, keeping it intact in times of crisis, and mediating between citizens and the state. A democracy imposed from outside, even with the best of intentions, will necessarily lack these supports—especially when it comes after tyranny—and so will be all the more likely to succumb to crisis.

There is another question, of broader scope. The exercise of American power cannot be assessed only by its effects in the countries where we intervene. It must be judged by its effect on the status of liberal and democratic values around the world. Here, too, there is reason to worry. When America is viewed as arrogant and "imperial"—using the word now in its insulting sense, which still has great force in postcolonial countries such as Egypt and India—the credibility of American values declines. We have bribed or browbeaten, rather than inspired, nearly all our partners in the Iraq operation—excepting Britain, whose population nonetheless roundly opposed the war. We are increasingly regarded as a country to be "played," not one to be followed: a source of advantage, say, in the jockeying between India and Pakistan, but not an avatar of the values we espouse.

That is saying something, because America, unlike many great powers, has always benefited by its distinctive power to attract and inspire. Even those who resent American force and dislike American foreign policy will often admit, or eagerly volunteer, that they admire American society, and wish they, too, could enjoy American freedoms. American exceptionalism, then, has not been a matter merely of American perceptions: the world has admitted that there is something to it. But the Iraq war, the road test of a new doctrine of foreign policy founded on the preeminence of American power and the authority of American judgment, was seen almost everywhere as hasty, ill-justified, and pregnant with risks. It weakened the hands of America's friends abroad.

But the most basic consideration concerns not the rest of the world, but the United States itself. An imperial America would not be the same country as a nonimperial America. The oldest objection to empire, but the one with the least hold on the American mind nowadays, is that it is bad for a country to become an empire—not so much pragmatically inconvenient as morally dangerous. The basic tool of an empire, whatever its humanitarian goals, is war, and an empire, as a dominating and occupying power, is always actually or potentially at war. War gets into the texture of the public culture. In a climate of war, patriotism is always at risk of degradation, from honoring a country's principles and aspirations to cheering for its victory, right or wrong. In wartime, the call to unity is powerful and dissent comes under automatic suspicion—a fact the Bush administration has used ceaselessly to its advantage. Introspection, criticism, and hesitation, all essential political virtues, are reviled as signs of weakness, or even covert sympathy for the enemy. War is bad for democracy—it may be the worst thing for democracy—and the war climate of empire brings persistent erosion of democratic practices.

I fear this danger is even greater when the declared enemy is nameless, faceless, and placeless: terror, which shifts identities, ideologies, and homelands with each turn of the geopolitical wheel. In a war with such an enemy, every victory is also a potential escalation, an occasion for heightened fear. In such a situation, fear and belligerence feed on and intensify each other.

It is one of the great achievements of liberal modernity to have moved the center of public esteem from military glory and aristocratic display to civilian life: family, home economics, the refinement and silliness of arts and entertainment, personal religion, and a modest form of civic virtue. The achievement is not altogether stable. Some lament the change, and pine after, or try to revive, what they imagine as the heroism of the past. In most people the appetite persists for glory, victory, and violent power—now satisfied mostly in sports arenas and at the movies—and for aristocratic leaders, without the disappointing whiff of ordinariness, whom we can revere. These impulses are intelligible. They may even correspond to something noble in us. But they run contrary to the most humane achievements of our civilization. They tempt us to give up the hard judgments of democratic self-government in favor of the enthusiasm of demagoguery. In an imperial culture, with its natural tendency to become a military culture and to exalt its leaders, resistance to these temptations comes harder.

For now, the eagerness for imperial ideas is an elite thing, broad enough to sweep in policy makers, journalists, and scholars, but not a genuine popular phenomenon. Most Americans are, by disposition, nonimperialist if not anti-imperialist. It will take more than a few televised wars and a drumbeat of fear to overwhelm our civilian and democratic culture.

The intention of this book is to contribute to that culture by showing something about its virtues, its limits, and the way the image of America operates abroad. The mood of the book is liberal above all: it is written in hope of progress, and in the belief that human freedom, both *from* oppression and suffering and *to* act and live as one wishes, is the foremost value by which progress should be measured. The temper of the book is also conservative in important respects, which are qualifications to its liberal commitments. One is the conviction that change brings losses as well as gains, even when the gains much outweigh the losses. Another is the belief that human nature contains many hazards, especially the taste for domination over other people and the resentment that domination breeds: when these get into politics, the danger to liberal values is very great. And *Being America* is skeptical, an attitude on which neither liberal nor conservative thought can claim a monopoly.

Throughout, it explores the perverseness of human judgment, our tendency to assess all the world by our own experience, to imagine that others are either clones of us or inhumanly alien, and to hold to fixed views not because they are true, but because they bring us some (often undeserved) emotional comfort. I do not see any contradiction among these intellectual and political commitments. Indeed, I am fairly convinced that to flourish they require each other.

—꧁—

Once again America is a prophetic nation.

Around the world new ways of life are rising. Aristocracies, priesthoods, and peasants give way to entrepreneurs, migrants, self-inventors, and the wayward and lost. Inherited duty and privilege matter less, and luck, initiative, and ruthlessness matter more. More lives are idiosyncratic, hybrid, and cobbled together. As old certainties melt away, a great space opens up in human life, and fills with new purposes, or bewilderment and loneliness, or violence.

We are the world's image of this future, because we were born that way. The United States is the first modern nation, which is why Alexis de Tocqueville came here to glimpse Europe's next century. This does not just mean that MTV and McDonald's are everywhere. It does not mean, either, that other countries will cease being Indian, Chinese, or Egyptian and become just like America—whatever that would mean. It means that whatever else they are, the world's peoples will live in modernity: amid individualism, mobility, instant communication, and traditions shattered or reshaped. None of these conditions is truly new, and the idea that old societies know nothing about them is a caricature, but they are now wildly intensified, and Americans were the first to found a culture on them. We have experimented more with modernity than any other people, because we have known hardly anything else. Today's world is American because it is taking the shape of the modernity that we pioneered.

Modernity is not the end of history. It is a democratic time when elections in much of the world would bring in fundamentalist Islam or Chinese nationalism. It creates a capitalist world where markets both build and destroy lives, and carry freedom and exploitation together. In this time traditions melt into air, and are revived as new and volatile convictions. Middle classes are developing everywhere—the same class that in the last century produced liberal democracy, social democracy, and fascism.

Little wonder, then, that this is a time of American prominence when America means many contradictory things to many people. Admiration, desire, resentment, and hatred clash and mingle together, born of conflicting ideas of what America is and means. We are onstage at the center of the world, and in others' eyes we are what they want us to be, what they fear that we are, what they want to become, and what they loathe in themselves.

In exploring this tumultuous world I have chosen the compass of Edmund Burke, the defender of the rebellious American colonists, critic of the French revolution, and enemy of British imperialism in India. Burke defined his marriage of liberal and conservative commitment by saying that he loved liberty and hated violence. He meant that we should cultivate the arrangements that enable people to live together in peace and dignity, and should refuse to accept coercion and injury as ordinary features of social life. Sometimes violence is necessary to defend liberty, but the two are nonetheless contrary principles. Enough violence always destroys liberty; mutual respect is the best stay against violence. Moreover, the two appeal to opposite parts of human nature: violence to self-righteousness and the taste for domination, liberty to forbearance and a love of everyday life.

This book asks how today's lives produce both liberty and violence. What is the proportion of freedom to exploitation in an economy? In politics, where do people feel control over their own choices, and where do popular passions flirt with chaos or dictatorship? Which inflections of a culture help its members to live with dignity, and which ones erode it?

These are political questions, in two broad meanings of politics. Politics is one of the ways that people remake their moral worlds, for better or worse. Nothing human is just an objective fact, like a geologic stratum or a physical law. Every place where we live is also shaped by our desires and fears, by emulation and aversion, by pride and humiliation, by the wish for transcendence and the hunger for familiarity. Today these passions express themselves in new forms. Most prominent is the struggle between violent nationalism and nascent liberalism in India, China, the Middle East, Southeast Asia, and elsewhere. These new forms of national life exist alongside other new political communities: long-distance diasporas and networks of international activists. Global communications and global capitalism speed up these new politics and give them the texture of commercial life.

Politics is also an answer to the problem of nakedness: the essential vulnerability of human beings. This is the nakedness that Shakespeare's King Lear contemplates when, exiled, mad, and wandering the heath in a storm, he tears off his clothes and declares: "Unaccommodated man is no more but such a poor, bare, forked animal as thou art"—bent and unclothed flesh over bone, without a kingdom or a bed. Hannah Arendt had this nakedness in mind when she observed that refugees, stateless people, and the victims of extermination camps are at the mercy of others because no community owes them the protection of its law and rights: they suffer from "the abstract nakedness of being human and nothing but human." They are always at risk of individual violence or political exclusion, unpunished murder or uncontestable deportation. They are reminders of what can happen to anyone when social and political life fail. Arendt wrote of them, "It seems that a man who is nothing but a man has lost the very qualities which make it possible for others to treat him as a fellow man."

Membership in a political community provides a claim on the forbearance of others: it clothes members in rights, freedom from fear and want, or, in an older phrase, "privileges and immunities." A changing world creates new vulnerability: dislocation, exploitation, and outright violence. These will test whether we can make a humane world, whether in new conditions politics will still be the redress of nakedness.

I

EMPIRES OF DESIRE

All the super-added ideas, furnished from the wardrobe of a moral imagination, which the heart owns and the understanding ratifies as necessary to cover the defects of our naked, shivering nature, and to raise it to dignity in our own estimation.

—Edmund Burke,
Reflections on the Revolution in France

CHAPTER I.

Where All the Ladders Start

—m—

Those masterful images, because complete
Grew in pure mind, but out of what began?
A mound of refuse or the sweepings of a street,
Old kettles, old bottles, and a broken can,
Old iron, old bones, old rags, that raving slut
Who keeps the till. Now that my ladder's gone
I must lie down where all the ladders start,
In the foul rag and bone shop of the heart.

—William Butler Yeats,
"The Circus Animals' Desertion"

I am reading another verse than Yeats's, this one a text message on an Egyptian medical student's mobile phone in a TGI Friday's by the Nile in Cairo:

SATURDAY NIGHT PARTY
BOMBS IN WORLD TRADE CENTER
SPECIAL DJ OSAMA BIN LADEN
FLY IN COURTESY OF AMERICAN AIRLINES

Sitting with us are a young corporate lawyer and a first-year law student. The three are sisters, from an established but not eminent Egyptian family, and are fashionably turned out in tight black slacks and T-shirts several sizes too small. The medical student's pink shirt, from Naf Naf, reads "Girls Only." They are all giggling, waiting for me to appreciate the satirical phone text. When I am slow to respond, the lawyer, Ingy, takes it on herself to explain: "So, all people in Egypt admire bin Laden, because he is the one who hit the U.S. So, he is like a hero for us, rather than a terrorist."

I have come here trying to understand the attraction and resentment, the imitation and rejection that America inspires everywhere. I am hoping to glimpse the place where ideas and feelings begin.

Ingy is my special friend in Cairo, having adopted me after her employer—a friend of a friend—offered to help me navigate this challenging city. She talks at precipitous speed, with nearly perfect lawyer's English, precise but seldom evocative. Both her thoughts and her tongue run a half-step ahead of her mental translation from Arabic, and she bridges the gaps with "so" if she is expanding a point, "but" if she is refining it. Now she is concerned about my reticence, and picks at her chicken fingers and French fries while she waits for the conversation to repair itself.

We chose TGI Friday's because it is a modish destination for students and young professionals. The Oreo Sandwich and Mocha Madness Cake cost ten times more than a pita stuffed with chicken and sausage at one of the tiny shops that line Cairo's roads and alleys. Because only professionals and aristocrats can afford to hold a table, the sex roles that govern Egyptian street life are suspended here. In Friday's women can smoke the *sheesha*, the elaborate, thigh-high, brass water pipe whose curvaceous design and long breathing tube were the accessory of the mushroom-seated caterpillar in *Alice in Wonderland*. Sidewalk *sheesha* cafés are everywhere in Egypt, but they are the preserve of men. Here, though, stylish Cairenes can alternate between spoonfuls of heaping American desserts and drags of apple-flavored tobacco.

The grimy, oily lanes where blacksmiths and mechanics work alongside food vendors are the ominous "Arab street," which many commentators suppose to be the seat of sympathy for Osama bin Laden and Islamic radicalism. These daughters of a senior civil servant in the regime that has been America's most reliable Arab ally are not part of that street. They are, as we like to say, Westernized. The ensembles and phones are not just veneer. Before her sisters arrived and the conversation turned to politics, Ingy spent more than half an hour describing her attitude to her work, her family, and her Islamic religion. She was one of the top law students at Cairo University, which guaranteed her a place in the public prosecutor's office. In a country where political power is mainly a way of securing private fiefdoms, that prestigious position enables the prosecutor to protect family and friends and punish enemies. The venality of Egypt's civil service is in constant competition with its indolence. A capable person can perform a full-time prosecutor's duties in a few hours a day, a few days a week.

Ingy's father was determined that she should take the prosecutor's job, so she did, and now she puts in her twelve weekly hours, filling out forms in Arabic and shuffling through the cases of accused criminals. Upon graduating, she also took a job with a young German lawyer who had just arrived in Cairo to try his luck in a less staid place than Germany. In his office she leads the working life of a Western lawyer, staying at her desk from eight in the morning until nine in the evening, six days a week, with breaks for visits to the prosecutor's office. She explains to me, "From being a prosecutor you become a judge. That is very prestigious, and very secure. The president appoints you, and only he can remove you. You have immunity, and free health care at the best hospital, and a car and so on. But what you are doing there is really nothing. So it is just doing whatever is set before you. So if I have a master's degree, so if I speak five languages or just one, it doesn't make a difference."

5

Instead, she says, she wants work that challenges and engages her, that makes her learn. She wants it to be at the center of her life. "So work is not just something I do. It has become"—she struggles for a phrase—"my point of stance." "Your identity," I suggest, and she lights up: "Exactly."

Ingy's attitude toward work has the thrill of rebellion against a culture with limited space for professional women. Once when we were in her ground-floor office after dark, she made a show of pulling the curtains "so that the men in the street will not think I am being abused. It is a terrible thing for a woman to be made to work so late." This small performance was a way of letting me know that her staid work has, in its context, a lively hint of scandal.

Her work is also an anesthetic. Of her two closest friends from college, one has died of cancer, and the other is married and living in the oil-rich Gulf emirate of Dubai. "When my friend died," she tells me, "I worked so hard that I had no time to be depressed. So that was something for me." She is just as direct about losing the other friend to marriage: "She is telling me, you should get married and so on. And she is sitting there, pregnant." There is a hint of disgust in her face. "So of course she is telling me this."

A career as stimulation, fulfillment, identity, and anesthetic: a place in the world and an obsessive distraction from one's own life. These are contemporary, Western, and especially American experiences that have become global. But they have not set Ingy against Egypt, or made her one of the frenetic imitators of American manners who can now be found anywhere. She says of those people, "They do not belong in Egypt anymore, but they are not European or American, either. They want to be modern, but they adopt only the superficial things. So, a man and a woman live together before they are married. In the U.S., that is a part of your society; but here, it does not make sense, and they are not happy. And if they go abroad, then when there is terror, everyone will remember that they are Arabs."

Ingy has always prayed five times a day, in the prescribed Muslim fashion, and a few years ago she had a kind of religious awakening: "Now I can feel it, it is what is in me, and it is beautiful." She does not elaborate on this passage from ritual to personal expression, but it is most important to her. It sits comfortably amid the rebelliousness, conformity, perfectionism, and self-seeking of her professional life.

Ingy seems a model for the view, fashionable among commentators on globalized culture, that people combine global trends with their local culture to make hybrid lives. With more options, people become more complicated versions of themselves—as has been true throughout history when cultures have met. Implicit in this picture is the idea that everyone will also become more tolerant and peaceful, as if all diversity had the mood of American multiculturalism.

This optimist's idea is in my mind as Ingy makes another try at elaborating on the text message promoting DJ Osama bin Laden. "Osama is a defender of the Palestinians. Of course, as Arabs we hate Israel. But that hatred for Israel we do not feel for the United States. And of course, people like me think that the way Osama did it was criminal. He should have attacked the White House. Then, no one could have said it was murder."

I let that go unremarked. It is a commonplace among liberal Arabs that suicide bombings against Israeli government targets are legitimate, but that attacks on civilians are morally uncertain. Ingy assumes that extending that logic to the United States will reassure me. Instead of responding directly, I point out that Osama bin Laden has only recently put the Palestinians at the center of the account he gives of his terror campaign. His fatwas from 1997 and 1998 are directed mainly at the presence of American troops in Saudi Arabia. It was only after September 11 that he warned: "Americans will not know peace until the Palestinians know peace."

When I recite this phrase, the young women laugh merrily. Between the American pop music hitting my right ear and the breeze blowing off the river, I think I must have missed something, and I look inquisitive. Ingy's sister, the medical student, explains: "We laughed when he said that." Osama's words placed the collapsing World Trade Center towers in a story of Israeli wrongs and Arab retribution that most Egyptians immediately understand. The same words that reassured Egyptian listeners sent Americans into their most intense alarm after the shock of the attacks themselves.

Almost every major city abroad has a World Trade Center (or Centre), symbolizing its aspiration to commercial modernity. Cairo's is across the Nile, its red neon logo glowing from the top floors. With the young women's laughter like a translucent wall between us, I turn toward the tower. Half the letters have burnt out, leaving only W   T de Ce   re, a nonsense phrase lighting a patch of the night.

This is the first fact of global life. We Americans live in an American world, more than the citizens of imperial Rome inhabited a Roman world or nineteenth-century Englishmen a British one. The sun never sets on us. Where two or more are gathered, we are with them. Wherever one is trying to make sense of her life, we are there.

Beyond our power and wealth, America provides the global language of dreams and the imagery of ambition. We are what everyone, everywhere, might yet be. Ours is the face that has launched millions of planes and billions of migrant journeys, whether from Bombay to New York or from a Tamil Nadu village to Bangalore.

People everywhere want to spend their days not eking out survival, but enjoying the bounty of a rich country. The fantasy of a land of plenty is very old: it figures in Muslim views of paradise, Hindu descriptions of the Golden Age, and the legendary Cockaigne of medieval Christianity, an imagined place of perpetual feasting. Americans live in that place, the everyday tenants of one of the enduring human myths.

Apart from wealth, people are moved by the wish for freedom— which today means American freedom. The ordinary liberty to go through a day or a week without harassment from the police; to choose your own friends and lovers; to speak your mind and come to your own opinions; to have ways of making the powerful answer to you: these are human aspirations, charged with new force in our age of democracy and human rights. For all its failings America stands for them. We live in the flesh and trip off the tongue of anyone, any-where, who desires what it is human to want.

The world's hunger is not exactly a compliment, and we should not take it complacently. We are loved, desired, and resented, often in one breath. Life is full of injury, confusion, and humiliation in a world upset by vast migrations, the rise of huge cities only fifty years old, and the collapse of social orders to which people belonged for cen-turies and millennia. Resentment and hurt, like aspiration, run to America: the country that offers to the mind and heart everything that real life denies the hand and mouth. This is not a question of what attitude we deserve. Admiration and resentment have always attached themselves to the powerful, the successful, the visible.

There is no guarantee of an American future. It is naïve to believe that the migratory icons of American modernity—constitu-tions, regular elections, free markets, shopping malls, MTV—will turn every place to a version of what we already are. What awaits us is not restricted to what we wish for, or even what we can imagine.

The Weapons of History

I spend most of my afternoons and evenings on the Arab street, walking the promenades along the Nile and veering off into the alleys where the industry and commerce of five hundred years live together. Here a tiny, gray donkey harnessed to a wooden cart chews a sheaf of fresh green grass from a heavily scored tree stump—a common object here, put to use as a chopping block, end table, or in this case a manger. Across the alley, workers unload acetylene cylinders from a flatbed truck. A young man in full-dress Tommy Hilfiger uniform walks by with his hand on the arm of an older woman wearing a veil and head-to-toe black robes. In a blacksmith's shop, a powerfully built man jerks a small boy toward him by the collar and, with his free right hand, sweeps a hunting knife into stabbing position. When he catches my eye, his pose collapses and he begins to laugh while holding my gaze. The boy is laughing, too, at the age-old game of sham violence.

Not once, even in slums where I have to dodge garbage heaps and children chase me for the excitement of seeing a foreigner, do I catch a hint of the anti-American passion that is supposed to animate ordinary Egyptians as the bombing of Afghanistan proceeds. So I begin to inquire after it, asking shopkeepers, the owners of tea stalls, and the old men who sit together wherever they can find a bench what they make of the attacks on America and the bombings of Kabul. Some profess to have no political opinions, but the heavyset owner of a bookshop agrees to sit down and talk with me.

He is heavy in all his features, and his short black hair and mustache are not quite clean. His knee-length shirt and loose pajama pants, customary among Egyptian men, have the patchy soiling of long use. No one would pick him out as an educated man, but his shop, the size of a college freshman's dormitory room, is stacked from floor to ceiling with books. All are in Arabic, and most deal with Islam or the politics of the Middle East. When he fixes on my topic, he reaches behind him and pulls down a thin paperback whose cover shows Osama bin Laden's head and shoulders, flanked by Soviet and American flags. He had this published, he explains, to show how Osama emerged from Soviet and American manipulations of Muslim politics, especially in Afghanistan. Osama is not a hero to him.

Then we are off through the gallery of Egyptian political culture. Do I really think it is possible that those pilots could have hit the World Trade Center if they had not flown that route before? They must have been Americans, or Israelis, with experience above the skies of New York. And do I not know that of the more than four thousand Jews who worked in the World Trade Center, not one was in the buildings on the morning of September 11? How do I explain that unless the Israelis planned the attack?

I don't try, and he picks up again. The United States has shown again and again that it puts little value on Muslim lives. Look at the war in Iraq, America's support for Israel, the civilian deaths in Afghanistan, the wars in Bosnia and Kosovo.

Bosnia and Kosovo? But the United States intervened there to save Muslims who were being slaughtered by Christians.

Yes, but they waited too long. That proved they don't care about Muslim lives.

The shopkeeper is enjoying the conversation, glad of the chance to share his views and show hospitality. He insists that I take the thin book on Osama, and will not let me pay him. His wife and daughter have opened dusty bottles of orange soda on the worn copying machine that is the shop's only furniture besides a few chairs, and the daughter hands me one with a shy smile. I have the same dreamlike sense of incongruity that beset me at TGI Friday's. A diorama of anti-American conspiracy theory has been arranged for my benefit, but my host does nothing to suggest that either of us should find this awkward. Hoping to snap out of the dream, I ask, Does he think Americans are a good people?

"Yes, you are a very good people. You are generous and open. But you are all helpless victims of your government, the same as we are with President Mubarak. Every one of your presidents in our generation has been lobbying for Israel. It is the same everywhere."

If Egyptians are political victims, is there anything that can bring true self-governance to the country? The shopkeeper is about to answer when someone shouts out, in English, "The victory of Osama bin Laden!" It is a young man, not past his early twenties, neatly groomed in glasses, slacks, a blue oxford shirt, and black leather shoes. He is leaning on the copying machine, and when he lurches forward I see that he is lame in one leg. He introduces himself with a grin as Ahab, another bookseller whose shop is just down the street.

What does he mean by "victory"? "It is a matter of regaining our pride," he explains. Osama has always fought for Islam, and now he has penetrated the United States. But even if Osama were not responsible for the attacks, the United States would blame him, and that would be enough to make him guilty in the eyes of the West. Now Ahab and the shopkeeper are playing off each other. The United States needed an excuse to maintain its power in this region, says my host. America is a thug. Yes, agrees Ahab, but America will never be number two in the world. It cannot accept that.

Now the shopkeeper asserts his prerogative: he is the older man, and this is his shop. "Once," he begins portentously, "a man decided he would fight a war with God. So he shot an arrow into the sky. The arrow came down with blood on its tip, and the man decided that God had been killed. But God sent down a bug that crawled into the man's nose, and up into his head. It ate his brain, and he died. *Inshallah*, this will be the fate of the American administration."

The story reminds him of another. "Once, when an army of the infidels attacked Mecca, God sent birds with pebbles from Hell to rain down on the infidels. They all died. This will happen again. Perhaps the anthrax that is causing fear in America has been sent by God."

This was the political talk that I found in Egypt whenever I asked about September 11. Always the same inconsistency: we admire Osama for attacking America, but in fact it was the

Israeli secret service that attacked America. Always the distinction between the violent and bigoted American government and the decent, generous American people. Always the suggestion that American leaders hate Muslims. Every time, anger at the American power to control global images, to declare guilt and innocence, to set the official boundary between civilization and barbarism. And always, outside the elite circles where people learn not to say such things to foreigners, the Jews as the wedge between the Americans and their government and the source of evil in the Middle East.

The shopkeeper becomes distracted, and I step outside with Ahab. Would he like to go to America? "Of course I would like to go to America for work. But I am afraid that now there is prejudice against Arabs, and I will not be able to go." He does not appear to connect this concern with the opinions he has just expressed. He gives me the number of his mobile phone, in case I need anything—"anything at all." Also the e-mail addresses that he and his sister maintain at Yahoo. His sister "can give you answers to your questions. She has a very good command of English."

When I prepare to leave, my hosts crowd around for handshakes: "Welcome, welcome, welcome to Egypt." Ahab adds, "May there be peace, for the sake of humanity."

Egypt has not always been home to extremism. One of the early and ambitious Islamic approaches to modernity happened here. For centuries, Cairo was part of the great Ottoman Empire and, like the Ottoman capital Istanbul, an intellectual and cultural capital of the Muslim world. Then Napoleon occupied Cairo between 1798 and 1801, setting off a period of fighting in the country among the French, the British, Ottoman troops, and local mutineers who took the invasion as a chance to grab power. From the Muslim point of view, the French occupation was a barbarian conquest. When an Ottoman commander of Albanian nationality, Muhammad Ali Pasha, took over Egypt in 1805, he set the country on the same course that Istanbul had begun and China and Japan would pursue later in the century: emulating the West to match its strength. Delegations of Egyptian students and scholars from Cairo's great Al-Azhar University traveled to Paris to study European technology, philosophy, and politics. Egypt reformed its army, industry, court system, and property regime along Western lines. In 1878 the country adopted the world's first Islamic constitution, replacing absolute sovereignty with a consultative assembly, which liberal reformers saw as a step toward complete rule of law.

In the 1860s, as construction of the Suez Canal neared completion, Egypt fell into debt and accepted financial receivership under the European powers. In 1882, when Egyptian political strife threatened national stability—and the canal—the British invaded. They ruled Egypt through a series of puppet governments until 1914, made it a formal protectorate when Britain fought the Ottoman Empire in World War I, and finally granted independence with significant British control in 1922. Between 1882 and 1922, Egyptian politicians redirected their energies from reform to the struggle for independence, which took on an increasingly nationalist and Islamicist tone. After 1922, the liberal Wafd Party maintained a strong presence under a constitutional monarchy, but the Islamicist Muslim Brotherhood also grew in influence. In the same period, Egyptian nationalism grew steadily into pan-Arab nationalism, driven by resentment of British imperialism and sympathy for Arab Palestinians in their conflicts with their British governors and then with the new state of Israel. Liberalism, Islamism, and Arab nationalism formed the competing currents of Egyptian politics, Arab nationalism often blending with a socialism borrowed from European leftists.

In 1952, military officer Gamal Abdel Nasser took over the Egyptian government and made himself a leader of pan-Arab hostility to Israel. Five years later, by buying weapons from communist Czechoslovakia, he aligned Egypt with the Soviets. He suppressed liberal and Islamicist politics, although the Muslim Brotherhood survived tenuously. Economic growth advanced, then faltered, while political reform languished. Nasser died in 1970, and in 1971 his vice president, Anwar Sadat, won a struggle for power, relaxed Nasser's political repression, and moved toward friendship with the United States and tense peace with Israel. Islamicist fundamentalists assassinated Sadat in 1981, and his vice president, air force commander Hosni Mubarak, has ruled ever since as a highly subsidized and mostly compliant ally of the United States. Political and civic life has continued to atrophy under Mubarak, who maintains substantial influence over the media, has made political opposition almost impossible, and shuffles outspoken liberals, leftists, and Muslim Brotherhood leaders in and out of jail. The Muslim Brotherhood, which calls itself democratic and advocates government by Koranic principles, has become the only visible and popular opposition to Mubarak. The president, in turn, presents himself to his American benefactors as the gatekeeper who locks out Islamic extremism. To his opponents he is for America what the puppet governments early in the twentieth century were for the British: a convenient tool of imperialism, keeping Egypt from expressing its Arab and Islamic character.

Their theories of September 11 seem patently irrational, but Egyptians have learned that the official story is usually a lie. Mubarak's government teaches Egyptians a lesson in what to expect of politics: deception, betrayal, and occasional satisfaction in public expressions of anger. The government-influenced press uses anti-Semitic and anti-American rhetoric at its convenience to rouse popular passions. Political life is mostly theatrical, a stage for improbable conspiracy theories that suggest the stagnant economy and civic life are the fault of someone other than the corrupt and unresponsive government. None of the public performances of resentment, paranoia, and catharsis are expected to have much effect besides distraction and transient relief. Politics here occupies the role of a night of frenzied dancing in a sober professional life, or an explosive fight in a usually placid relationship. It makes nothing happen except feeling.

The Egyptians who talk with me are displaying civic life as they have learned it. Among their teachers is America. The country that stands for liberal freedom and tolerance is also the sponsor of their government and so is implicated in their illiberal, anti-Semitic political life. For Egyptians America is the country that covertly installed Iran's repressive Mohammad Reza Pahlavi, courted Iraq's Saddam Hussein for years before making him an icon of evil, sponsored the mujahideen warriors of Afghanistan for a decade and then abandoned their country to chaos after they defeated the Soviet Union, and maintains close ties with the deeply illiberal Wahhabi regime of Saudi Arabia. In all of these roles, the United States appears to Egyptians as the successor to Great Britain and the other European imperial powers. For many Americans, September 11 seemed to represent a loss of innocence about the country's place in the world. For most in the Middle East, America's political innocence was lost many decades ago, if it ever existed.

Americans sometimes imagine that we face a battle between the future and the past. The main opposition to American-style modernity comes from various forms of nationalism and fundamentalism. Serbian nationalism in the Balkans, India's Hindu chauvinism, the repressive programs of Muslim fundamentalists, and the new nationalism among young Chinese who imagine reclaiming their country's greatness in a struggle with America: these all look like assertions of lost history. The leaders and rhetoricians of these movements call on past defeats and remembered glory to move their supporters. Sometimes they propose to restore the specific achievements of the past: seventh-century Islamic society, the religious order of an all-Hindu India. More commonly, they invoke an imprecise but potent image of what has been lost and might be regained: the time before we fell, before we were humiliated, when we were kings.

Westerners who believe in the battle between future and past take the self-image of the nationalists and fundamentalists too seriously. These mutinies against modernity are themselves the children of modernity. They are no more resurgences of the past than Timothy McVeigh's attack on the Murrah Federal Building in Oklahoma City was a reassertion of the values of the American founders, whom McVeigh claimed as his guides.

People attracted to today's extremism are reacting to the strains of modernity. Billions of lives are defined by leaving a stable village for a new slum-city, the confusion and threat of women's changing place in society, and images of limitless prosperity and pleasure thrown starkly up against neighborhoods full of foreclosed lives. Such changes sharpen the appetite for belonging to a larger community than one's own cluster of shacks or scattered family, putting one's fragmented life into a story of greatness, decline, and revival that dignifies whatever it touches. Grandiose and millenarian beliefs are most likely to emerge among people who feel lost, humiliated, or undone. This is true equally of apocalyptic religion and of nationalism founded on past glory and drastic revivals. In this sense, nationalism and fundamentalism appeal to the same human needs: the confidence of knowing who one is, and the pleasure of identifying with a great and righteous struggle.

The new atavism depends on new technology. The Ayatollah Khomeni, leader and icon of Iran's fundamentalist revolution in 1979, built his following with audiotapes passed from hand to hand in Teheran and in the Iranian diaspora. Slobodan Milošević turned much of Yugoslavia from a pluralist, semi-socialist country to a nationalist nightmare-state with the help of the government's broadcasting network; in the elections of the 1990s, his party performed much better where there were only official radio and television stations than where there were also independent ones. A critical moment in popular Hindu nationalism was the broadcast of a television *adaptation of the* Mahabharata, *a traditional epic of good and evil that cleared the Indian streets during its Sunday afternoon slot. The readiest source for students of Hindu nationalist thought is a clutch of sprawling Web sites. Osama bin Laden's taped commentary on Islamic culture and the crimes of the infidel West created his Muslim following, and the terrible climax of his career was the most perfect visual image of mass destruction in war since the bombing of Hiroshima.*

The extremists create new kinds of shared identities. In the past, people formed religious and national communities around shared ways of life, rituals, language, and landscapes. There were conversions, of course, but in infrequent waves and often driven by conquest. What people had in common was largely given. Today, technology creates what people have in common. It delivers a shared story and a common iconography, such as the images of bin Laden that spread from Morocco to Indonesia in the weeks after September 11. This is why diaspora populations have been important to the new nationalism and fundamentalism. Almost twenty years ago Sikhs in London and California financed much of the armed movement for independence in the Indian and Pakistani region of Punjab, which the separatists called Khalistan. The Hindu nationalist Bharatiya Janata Party collects funds from Indians abroad, many in the United States. Boston has long been the fund-raising capital for an Irish civil war fought by marginal individuals in the name of mythic histories. All these diaspora nationalists have left the daily texture of life that once bound them to their communities, but are devoted to their long-distance identities.

Fundamentalist and nationalist histories are often fabrications. Muslim demagogues in India recite a litany of violence against their population, neglecting that these incidents are matched by atrocities against Hindus during centuries of Muslim rule. Hindu nationalists offer to restore the unity and glory of a Hindu nation that never existed: Hindu practice was wildly diverse for millennia before it became increasingly unified in response to British imperial rule; now it has become more so under nationalist influence. In Indonesia,

Muslim fundamentalists set aside Java's long history of blending Hindu, Catholic, Muslim, and animist religious culture and, in effect, import Arab history as their own. These movements cannot be called assertions of the past. They are arguments about the future, couched in the language of the past because it is convenient and powerful, but achieved at the cost of violence to history.

History, whether real or imagined, becomes powerful only through politics. There is a popular idea that some countries are trapped in history, forever repeating old battles and reopening ancient wounds. President Clinton cited this view of the Balkans as a reason for his long delay in intervening to stop the Bosnian genocide. One often hears that Muslims, Indians, or the Chinese were forever wounded by the Crusades, British conquest, or the Opium Wars. It is true that stories of age-old bigotry and conspiracy arise constantly in those places: in political rhetoric, today's multinational companies become yesterday's imperial armies, the World Trade Organization is transformed into one of the notorious "unfair treaties" that put China into semicolonial status in the nineteenth century, and so forth. These images rally the same anti-colonial sentiments that once threw off empires, and now draw postcolonial countries into the past.

But if history is a curse, it is one that leaders and their admirers have conjured up, by putting themes of past injury at the center of present political life. The past makes us, but just as surely we make and remake the past. Technology that can carry a new image or story across a country in a flash, and repeat it to exhaustion, has tilted the balance between the generations in favor of the living, who now fashion the dead in their image.

The political movements that are often described as resurgences of the past, then, are instead battles over the future, conducted by the means of the present and dressed in the clothing of the past. Westerners often think of them as alien, but we might recall that, after liberalism, the great product of middle-class Western political life was fascism, which invented and spread national myths through the latest technology and grounded a reign of terror on them. For a few years in the 1940s, fascist totalitarianism seemed poised to take over Western Europe, which was then still the center of the world, and to define Western modernity. Having come so close ourselves, we have no excuse for surprise when other peoples, often under more exigent circumstances, show the same dark impulses.

Such movements are not the enemies of the future. Instead, they are contenders for it. They are the enemies of one version of the future: the liberal one, characterized by tolerance, openness, individual liberty, social mobility, and civil government. Fundamentalism and violent nationalism would cast aside these best possibilities of liberal modernity.

Memory and Hurt

Having seen the public face of the resentment, mythological comfort, and symbolic revenge that have distorted Egyptian politics, I go looking for the more intimate sources of its appeal. One evening I eat dinner at the home of Egyptian Christians—not Copts, whose unorthodox Christianity dates back to the fifth-century schism with the Eastern Orthodox Church over whether Jesus was both human and divine or divine only, but Protestants, peasants converted by British missionaries after Britain's invasion. Their family lived in Upper Egypt, in the hinterlands nearer Sudan than Cairo, and came to the capital city only in the 1970s. The father is a minister in the Holiness Church, and the adult son who comes to meet me on a street corner is carrying a wooden cross, which he flashes to identify himself, then slips into a pocket. He is heavy, especially in the legs and back, but his face has not fattened with the rest of his body. His features are blunt, with a heavy brow and a thick, solid nose.

To reach the family's apartment, we take a taxi across town, then alight near a public courtyard full of garbage. A couple in brightly flowered but filthy clothing are picking over one of the heaps, filling an enormous sack slung over the woman's back. As we make our way, my guide whispers apologetically, "This is a public space. It is very dirty. All Islamic countries are dirty this way."

The apartment is down an alley from the courtyard, past some men who are disassembling old mattresses in their open-air shop. As we walk we attract harder stares than I am accustomed to, although it is possible that they are directed at the bouquet of white irises that I have brought the family. When we leave the alley and duck up a set of stairs by the entrance to a small, bare church, my companion relaxes visibly. The apartment is a living room joined with a kitchen, a small bathroom, and three bedrooms—one for the minister and his wife, one for each of the two grown sons. On the walls hang several portraits of Jesus in prayer, some in the commonplace American rendition of a handsome, long-haired Anglo, one with the golden disk halo of Orthodox iconography. Nearby is a clock whose hands are the head and cocked bat of a baseball batter, set against a field of crushed purple velvet. In one corner of the living room sits a ceramic Nativity scene, several feet square. The sofa and chairs are arch-backed, with the arms and legs carved in floral designs, and I ask if they are old. Yes is the answer: they came from Upper Egypt with the family. They are twenty-six years old.

At the dinner table, only I have both a plate and a bowl, while each of my hosts uses one or the other. The ones with plates go easy on the okra soup, but even a cupful spreads to form a shallow lake across the rice, chicken, vegetables, and flatbread. Those with bowls work in courses: now a piece of chicken, now rice with soup. Between glasses and mugs, we each have something to hold our orange soda. My irises started out leaning against the couch, but have since moved to a small shelf where they lie prone. I realize there is not a bottle or vase large and sturdy enough to support them. Besides the cheap furniture, the apartment is so sparse that my small gift has highlighted the family's poverty.

Over a dessert of fresh dates and oranges, we talk about September 11. They want me to know that the Muslims were ecstatic. "They were laughing and shouting, at work, on the bus. We were afraid." And how did my hosts feel about the attacks? Now the son who met me with the wooden cross steps in: "I was sad, but I was not angry. America deserved this."

Why? "You admitted a snake, and the snake grew to bite you."

What snake? The United States admits immigrants without regard to their religion. It received many Muslims, many bad people. So now it is being punished. Perhaps we do not know the simple technical solution to this problem? He finds his Egyptian identity card, and points out the line where he is identified as a Christian. "You need this on your papers. Then you will know.

"America is a Christian nation, but you have said that you have no religion. Your president, Bill Clinton, has said that men who sleep with men, give them a chance. He must be a very bad man. He must hate God.

"And in America there are many churches to Satan. There men sleep with a woman, and then drink her blood. I do not know: why do you allow this? God has exited from America."

I protest that this is not my experience of America, but he is firm: "My uncle is a minister in America. He has told me this, and also a man from Canada. God has exited from America." His mother nods: "America must cleanse itself."

He concludes, "America has grown weak. Christians are the weakest people in the world. When a Jew dies, Israel kills ten. This is very good. When an Islamic believer dies, the Islamic believers everywhere are angry. But when Christians die in Sudan, or in Egypt, where is the United States? It does not care about Christians. I love Christ, but I hate Christians, because Christians are the weakest people in the world."

After we finish the fruit, my guide wants me to join him in his room. He has three favors to ask. First, he wants me to transcribe a letter for him and mail it to a pair of Israeli Christians. He cannot mail the letter from here to Israel without suspecting that it will be opened, and maybe thrown away. His expressions of friendship are fervid, almost ecstatic, and he eyes my scrawl as if doubting that I could be doing justice to his intensity of feeling.

Next, he has twice been denied an American visa. He wants me to intervene—not to help him to apply again, but to get revenge. "There is a man in your embassy, named David. He is a very dirty man. When I went in for a visa, I said, I am a Christian. He said, We don't care that you are a Christian. He is a very bad man. You must tell your government. Madeleine Albright will know who is in your embassy here."

He shows me two dated stamps in his passport, reading "application received." I don't grasp his meaning, so he elaborates again: "The first man, in 1997, he was a very great man. He said, I am sad to stamp your passport, because you will not be approved. But David, he threw my passport back at me. Through the window. Threw it."

Now he has a scrap of paper and a pencil stub. "I will show you." He sketches a face with square features, large glasses, an abrupt part on the right side, and a trimmed beard that emphasizes the rectangular quality of the face. "There," he breathes with satisfaction. "David."

Last, he wants me to send him treasures to add to his collections. He collects coins, stamps, and telephone cards—all the tokens of communication and exchange. The coins have all been circulated, and the telephone cards are used, but the stamps, the emblems of foreign nations, he likes clean. His collection is rich in images of places he wants to visit: "Christian countries, then India. It is partly Christian, so it is cleaner than Egypt." He hands me two used Egyptian telephone cards as a gift.

Back in the living room, sitting on the furniture from Upper Egypt, we move between national history and family history. "We are Pharaoh's children," they tell me, "and our history goes back more than five thousand years. We were Christians from just after the time of Christ, but the Islamic believers conquered us. How could they do this?"

The question is for effect. "The Egyptians had stopped praying. They grew weak. They lost God's protection, so they were conquered. The Islamic believers destroyed our great civilization, and they burned the library at Alexandria." Ancient Egypt was like America today: weakened by its spiritual corruption; but the eldest son is part of a revival. He is studying Coptic, the last living version of the ancient Egyptian language, which has been preserved as the ritual language of the Coptic Church. The author of his lesson book is a Coptic nationalist, a scholar who makes his family speak Coptic at home, like early Zionists with Hebrew and Irish revivalists with Gaelic. So far he has learned only a few phrases.

What do the Muslims do to them now? Sometimes they throw garbage into the church. And there was another son, Anwars. He was very bright, a good student. But once in school a Muslim teacher saw his cross and told him, Take that off and throw it away. He refused, and he failed the second form that year, and the next year, and the next. "All because of this bad Muslim doctor." Then he left, and went to America. He is living in Allentown, Pennsylvania. "Sometimes he works. Sometimes he doesn't. It is hard for anyone to reach him." He tells them that he cannot call, because "he does not have a national phone." The topic is painful to them. They hope I can do something when I return to the United States—as if I could somehow reassert, in my vast and mobile homeland, the abandoned rules of family and locale. "Pray with him, pray for him."

So America, the decadent capital of Christianity, has taken a son. The Muslims pried him away, but America took him and kept him. No wonder the country is such a dark place to them, so corrupted and hazardous and, by virtue of these qualities, half in league with their Muslim neighbors.

The eldest son takes me back to Zamalek, the neighborhood of embassies, wealthy private villas, and shopping streets where I am staying. Driving, we pass store windows where hundreds of women's shoes are displayed like jewels, and many Western stores: Pierre Cardin, Arrow Shirts, Gucci. It would not be much more difficult to drop a thousand dollars here than in New York. When my companion pays our driver and gets out of the taxi with me, I realize that he is going to spend an hour or more on one of Cairo's crowded buses, or perhaps walk back to his parents' apartment, rather than spend the one-dollar fare. I try to give him money to take the taxi home. He refuses and freezes for a moment, unable to say that he cannot afford the taxi but would not have made a guest ride a bus, trying to think of an excuse for walking off into Zamalek. Then inspiration comes to him: "I want to see about buying some flowers."

The apartment he is returning to, and the bare church downstairs, house a small, vulnerable world. Many injuries enter there, and their sources are often only half-intelligible. With them sometimes come stories about where the injuries began, the sources of poverty, humiliation, and frustration. Ideas about civilization and barbarism, pronouncements on the religious duties of nations, and violent invocations of God begin in daily fears and the dead end of ambition.

Later I have a chance to check the history my Christian hosts recounted. The last library at Alexandria, containing the greatest collection of books and documents in the ancient world, was burnt by Christians in 391 C.E., 179 years before the birth of Muhammad.

Reckless beliefs and evil acts are born of the most ordinary motivations: resentment, ambition, the desire for dignity, and the simple tendency to obey orders. Today, most forms of violent extremism attract a few people actually willing to act on their doctrines. Outside that core, a vast number are more or less sympathetic to the extremists but just as sincerely—and often more intensely—drawn to liberty, personal freedom, and at least grudging tolerance. These ordinary cases are, in the end, more important than the extremists who carry out isolated and spectacular acts of violence. There are always fanatics, but they do not usually set the path of history; whether others are sympathetic to fanatics, though, can make all the difference. Young men who would like to study or buy a gas station in America, yet also admire Osama bin Laden, are ordinary in Egypt. The same young Chinese who listen to ultranationalist hip-hop have hopes of working in Silicon Valley, and some of the Beijing students who stormed the American embassy in 1999 returned home the same evening to study for the Law School Admissions Test and the Graduate Record Examination. An American traveling in the Islamic world during the bombing of Afghanistan in 2001 found equal parts enthusiastic welcome of Westerners and violent denunciations of "America" and "the West" as abstract enemies. We are confronting not two global tribes, but two tendencies within every civilization and soul, one liberal and the other illiberal, one tending, in Burke's words, to liberty, the other to violence. That uneasy proportion of gray, which has not yet split apart into black and white, is what should concern us most.

The United States should approach a gray world knowing the limits of our power. Although we periodically imagine otherwise, we cannot remake the globe in our image, no matter whether it would be good to do so. American power takes a tortuous path and does not always work as we intend. Peoples, like individuals, make their own decisions. Nonetheless, the United States does more than any other country to shape the world in which other people find their way, the landscape where the proportion of dark and light forever shifts. Much of this power lies in example: we are rich, free, and capable, the world's picture of a successful future. When the United States is a source of hope—which it is for individuals everywhere—there is also hope in the future. When we are an object of resentment and anger—which we are for nations and individuals in many places—that future can look fraudulent, impossible for those who do not already enjoy it, or fraught with corrupt and decadent values. We stand in for all the possibilities of liberal modernity. We are judged by it, and it by us—often unfairly, but sometimes decisively.

CHAPTER 2

Empires, Visible and Invisible

—⁓—

In the nineteenth century, the red of the British Empire splashed over maps from London south across the Mediterranean to South Africa, overland to the Middle East and India and Hong Kong, over the Pacific Ocean to Canada's vast tracts of North America, and finally back to the small island off the northwest coast of Europe. The sun never set on that red. America is a continental republic, slung over the broad middle of North America, with a few outposts elsewhere. Some are almost incidental acquisitions from the Second World War, others heirlooms from the brief, eager expansionism of presidents William McKinley and Theodore Roosevelt. We would not know what to do with a traditional empire. If an American empire exists it is a new sort, and invisible to Americans.

Yet no people has ever been so ubiquitous and powerful. There is no rounding a corner in Egypt, or most other countries, without encountering a reminder of America. There is hardly a conversation that does not find its way to the desire for American wealth and freedom, or anger at American power and arrogance. Perhaps for that reason, alien though the idea of empire sounds to Americans, it is much more familiar abroad. Much of the world did not hesitate to declare the United States an imperial nation, even before the global campaign against terrorism put American power back at the forefront of geopolitics. *Frontline*, a major Indian weekly magazine, titled a 1999 cover article on American foreign policy "Ways of Imperialism." A South African journalist writes of living in "the outer provinces of the empire." The French, with special insistence, lament that "we are being globalized by the Americans," and polls suggest that two-thirds of the French think that Americans are a nation of aggressive bullies in world affairs. People on the streets of Cairo, Beijing, Delhi, and Jakarta say much the same, as do citizens of such staunch allies as Germany. In a poll of "opinion leaders" around the world taken after September 11, 70 percent reported that their people thought it good for Americans to experience vulnerability, and more than half reported widespread resentment of American power.

Americans, though, are accustomed to discounting foreigners' overwrought reactions to us. In one decade, Russian teenagers come close to rioting over our blue jeans. In the next, a French farmer drives his tractor through the window of a McDonald's in protest against cultural homogenization— while, we suspect, his nieces and nephews are slurping down a Happy Meal somewhere outside of Paris. Like celebrities, we learn not to get too excited by other people's excitement.

More to the point, we think we know what empire means, and we aren't it—no matter what French farmers think. Empire is bloody conquest. It is what the Spanish did to the Aztecs and the Incas—thousands of people put to the sword in uneven military contests, hundreds of thousands virtually enslaved on plantations, and millions dead from disease and displacement. Empire is forced conversion: the Spanish professed to make Christians of the Indians just before slaughtering them, and taught their descendants to speak Spanish so that their masters could give them orders. Above all, empire is the denial of one people's rights by another, more powerful people: rights to political participation, cultural expression, and self-governance. Surely none of these describes the American relationship to the world? In our minds we are partners, modest yet strong. If we win converts to our ways, it is because we have a better idea. We were founded in resistance to British Empire, and we recently defeated the Soviet one. Yet the accusations persist.

The more productive question is not whether America is an imperial power, but why we appear that way to so many people, and not to ourselves. "Empire" is not a precise term. It applies to everything from the Soviet regime, which governed economic, political, and cultural life in excruciating detail; to the ancient Romans' many protectorates and subordinate allies; to the tributary port cities along medieval China's seafaring trade routes; to Britain's government of India, which stitched together regions of direct British rule with self-governing but dependent kingdoms and other feudal states; to the Congo Free State, later the Belgian Congo, from 1885 to 1908 the brutalized personal possession of King Leopold II. Today, when the idea that every people should govern its own country is one of the first principles of politics, "empire" and "imperialism" express distaste more than analysis. They stand for the feeling that one nation is imposing itself on others, pushing them around, and remaking them in its image. Inquiring into "American empire" means exploring the distance and mutual incomprehension between how most Americans think of themselves and how people around the world see America.

We Americans consider ourselves a nation of law and principle. Large-scale democracy with a written constitution was an American experiment that a great deal of earlier political thought would have condemned to failure. When it succeeded here, it became an American thing. The democracy that Americans pioneered is now the only source of legitimacy that a government can seriously claim today. Almost every state in the world professes to be democratic. Politically serious Islamicists present the idea of an Islamic state as democratic twice over: because it reflects the will of a Muslim people, and because Islam's social teaching can be interpreted as containing ideas of democracy. When a new state that is more than a simple despotism emerges in Central Asia, the Balkans, or Africa, American scholars of constitutional law and political science arrive in planeloads to help write a constitution and design a parliament. American observers—some of them college students who have voted once or not at all—certify the elections of what we gently term "fledgling democracies."

The United States was also the first great market society, where status comes from wealth, and wealth from individual luck and effort as much as from inherited position. This is ever more the condition of the world. That does not necessarily mean that life is becoming fairer, more merciful, or in every way more free. It does mean that lives everywhere are taking on more qualities that we recognize as American.

Most Americans would say that these changes reflect the authority of good principles of government and economics. But all empires have considered themselves principled. The British Empire, in one myopic but popular view, was a vast project in improving the world's civilizations by bringing them into commerce and self-government—albeit slowly, with a certain amount of exploitation in the waiting period. The Bolsheviks founded the Soviet Union on what they considered universal, scientific principles of history and government, although these soon fell on deservedly hard times. Spanish conquerors came to the Americas for gold, but also for God, whose truth they were determined to spread. Writing about the Roman Empire, the scholar Anthony Pagden judges that "Roman law was intended to create not merely political and social order; it was also intended to confer an ethical purpose on the entire community." For those who believed this, Roman expansion was not sheer self-aggrandizement, but an extension of civilized government and freedom to peoples who would otherwise have remained sunk in barbarism. New citizens joined a community of rationality and freedom. Many Americans would say the same thing about our constitutional democracy and market society. That does not mean that we are Rome, but neither does it establish that we are not.

Surely, though, the world chooses us? We do not impose our true principles or our cultural idioms on benighted peoples. They take what we offer and demand more. Surely it is wrong to call popularity "empire"? We are multiculturalists who, ironically, find our particular culture ascendant everywhere.

Reflecting in 1790 that the United States might become the Rome of a new era, James Wilson wrote, "It might be said, not that the Romans extended themselves over the whole globe, but that the inhabitants of the globe poured themselves on the Romans." Wilson noted that this was "the most secure method of enlarging an empire." Attracting subjects rather than overwhelming them is the work of a successful empire, today more than ever.

The fruits of our attraction are many. American pop culture is the world's idiom. Michael Jordan's face was recently the most widely recognized in the world. The Coca-Cola logo is familiar everywhere. *Baywatch* has for several years been the most popular television program globally. Young people everywhere share a cultural patois with Americans of all ages. An elite investment banker will find English speakers among her counterparts in Paris and Delhi and Tokyo, and an American abroad will encounter knowledgeable conversation about last year's action movies, this year's pop star (Britney Spears recently topped the charts in Indonesia), and the current National Basketball Association playoffs. In Bangkok, young Thai men in dreadlocks sing rock and roll on stages in front of the World Trade Center, a downtown shopping mall.

American English is the world's second language. It is the language of global media and business, the badge of arrival into the arenas of power, opportunity, and cultural knowledge. Although only 350 million people are native speakers of English, as many as a billion have already made it their second language by learning enough to strike a bargain or argue about a basketball game. Those numbers will grow enormously in the next fifty years. In Russia, in India, in the Arab world, across Latin America, and even in China and Japan, ambitious young people choose to study English ahead of the language of a neighboring country, a local tongue such as Kannada in southern India, or the language of a regional power, such as Russian or Chinese in Mongolia. Even institutions with few native English speakers among their members, such as the Association of Southeast Asian Nations, use English as their official language. The Japanese president has announced his hope to make English the country's universal second language, as Germany, the Netherlands, and other European countries have already done. Saudi Arabia has decided to begin teaching English in the fourth grade.

Choice and Resentment

How can resentment arise out of free choice? The answer lies in two kinds of power that are almost never discussed but that non-Americans recognize immediately upon hearing them described. These are Microsoft power and the power of seduction.

Microsoft power begins in what economists call network effects, and for that reason the scholar David Grewal calls it "network power."* A network effect is the benefit from using a system that many others also use. The more people use the system, the more benefit each user gets from it. A fine example is e-mail. If only two hundred people in government laboratories around the country have accounts, getting it in your home or office doesn't do you much good. If 10 percent of the country—or every student in a certain college—has it,

---

*Full disclosure: Grewal is a friend to whose unpublished manuscript on network power I am indebted.

then it helps you to communicate with select people. If everyone has e-mail, from your grandmother to the child your brother baby-sits, then your account connects you with all of them. The more people join the network, the more you gain from being a member. The greater the benefit of being a member, the more people will join—and the greater will be the cost of not joining. Those who don't join will be left out of a great deal of communication.

The Microsoft Windows system works the same way. The more people use the system, the easier it is for any user to swap workstations, trade files, and generally perform any task on any computer in the world. Having a different operating system becomes increasingly inconvenient. You may not be able to transfer files. You may not know how to perform a basic function on a borrowed computer. If you spend a lot of time working on a computer and use a Mac OS 10 or another competing system, you have probably been made to feel half a step behind at least once a week. Microsoft—or whoever else arrives first and brings in the most people—can literally squeeze out the competition, not necessarily by being better, but by being pervasive enough to have big network effects.

The choice of one computer program over another is fairly minor. But suppose the choice is English versus Hindi or Magyar or French? A language has this in common with e-mail or an operating system: it gives people access to each other, to information, and to commerce. The more people speak English, the greater the advantage of being an English speaker—and the cost of not being one. The more a language grows, the more it will continue to grow—just like Microsoft Windows. The more it shrinks, the more it will continue to shrink. Speaking a minor language is a luxury for someone who already has the time, resources, or luck to speak a major one. Speaking a major language is on its way to becoming a necessity for people with certain ambitions. English is becoming the global language—the Latin of the modern world.

Language goes to the core of identity: how you describe the world, which jokes are your own, and whose voice makes you feel at home. It can make children strangers to their parents and neighbors to people halfway around the world. Language has been the occasion for innumerable riots, secession attempts, and prolonged political struggles, and it has contributed to the beginning of wars. It is no wonder that English's network effects—its Microsoft power—give some of those who learn it the impression of empire.

Language is just one of many places where Microsoft power is at work. Wherever people need access to each other in a technologically sophisticated world of interpenetrating law and finance, one standard tends to arise to facilitate exchange. So that corporations and their investors can stage international mergers and acquisitions, the world is gravitating toward the fairly relaxed American antitrust law. To make movement across borders even easier for corporations and currency traders, voluntary but pervasive standards are taking shape for accounting and corporate governance, the rules for relations between a corporation's managers and its shareholders. Countries sign on to international rules of patent and copyright so that technology and ideas can flow, or not flow, around the world in a unified system. Governments adopt liberal trade rules, cut subsidies and deficits, and change other policies to get access to international markets and attract foreign investment. Crises in such reformist economies as Indonesia and Argentina have slowed the juggernaut but not reversed the trend. Because belonging means opportunity, those who don't go along feel increasingly like Basque speakers.

Adopting a new standard brings disruption, whether it is the loss of a former language or the rearrangement of an economy. The disruption is much greater if you were doing things very differently before you joined up, and much less if the rising standard is more or less what you already do. Naturally the English language and American law are rather more convenient for Americans than for other people. The perception that America has become imperial partly reflects our exemption from disruption, an exemption we gain because the world's networks are growing in our direction.

All empires protect the interests of their capitals. Although globalization has wrecked some American industries and helped increase inequality here, we have mainly been spared the huge disruptions that have overtaken much of the world. We pay heavy subsidies to our farmers while peasants in other countries leave the land for sprawling new slum-cities. We do not receive visits from Argentine economists who inform us that we will have to cancel Social Security payments because our national debt is unacceptably high. We are not obliged to auction off the public lands and minerals of the West and the oil reserves of Alaska in an experimental program designed by Russian consultants. Young Americans are not learning to converse in aristocratically accented Hindi so that they will have a chance at joining the global cultural and financial elite, at the cost of becoming foreigners to their childhood friends.

It is inconceivable that such things should happen to Americans. Yet we find it unsurprising that the same inconveniences should befall other peoples. Indeed, we would find it strange if those peoples acted differently. Our Microsoft power is so great that it is nearly invisible to us, until we reverse the lens and imagine ourselves receiving the dictates of a new global network. We should not be surprised that much of the world looks at this American-inflected network and sees empire.

But still, as James Wilson put it, the inhabitants of the globe pour themselves onto America. This is the nature of network power. It operates through free and perfectly rational choices that at the same time are hardly choices at all. Not learning English means giving up certain kinds of ambition. Not adopting liberal trade rules means missing entire streams of the global economy. All options except one come to seem perverse. People experience this Hobson's choice as coercive even as they move toward the American-born network under their own eager power. Emulation and resentment are the paired fruits of imperial power, and the stronger the compulsion to emulate, the more intense the resentment is likely to be.

Free choice and yet no choice—but that expression does not capture the whole problem. After the discovery of penicillin, doctors had no real choice but to give up less effective remedies for infection, even if they were familiar with the old ways and took special satisfaction in them. The population of a town faced with rising floodwaters has no real choice but to grab a few precious belongings and run for high ground. Most pedestrians facing a mugger's pistol at night cannot but hand over their wallets and hope not to be harmed. None of these cases presents a real alternative; yet the situations are very different. With penicillin, reason guides all choices to a single destination; in the case of a flood, happenstance events shape decisions; and with a mugging, unequal force settles the issue.

The same three situations occur in the workings of network power. One network's standard can become dominant because it is the best tool available for what everyone wants to accomplish. This is almost certainly true of certain technologies of globalization, such as cell phones and the Internet, which the world is rushing to acquire or join. In this case, there is room to regret what may be lost alongside the gains, but there is no reason to see empire at work. With the English language, chance is more important than reason. English is not a more efficient language than any other, but the dominant financial, cultural, and military position of English-speaking peoples during most of the past three centuries has made it the world's tongue. But of course, the dominance of the English and the Americans has something to do with British empire in India and Africa and U.S. dominance in Latin America and elsewhere. These histories implicate network power in more overt uses of force.

The economic changes of globalization have the same mixed character. The International Monetary Fund, for instance, claims that its free-market policies express a rationally superior approach to economics. Until recently, there was a fair amount of academic support for this belief, and many of its fundamental elements remain intact. The IMF, though, is guided by American-trained economists, in a time when academic economics has lost interest in the political economy of particular countries, in favor of elegant mathematical expressions of sweeping formulas. That academic attitude has affected the IMF's policy decisions: Jeffrey Sachs, prominent trade and development economist and former IMF adviser, has severely criticized the organization for formulaic policies that worsened the economic crisis in Southeast Asia four years ago, as has Joseph Stiglitz, Nobel laureate and former chief economist of the World Bank. And more is at work here than scholarly trends. The IMF's decision to put a single, American-made economic model at the center of its policy everywhere also reflected the arrogance of American power, the belief that a dominant country's ideas must be true for everybody. The whole effect can suggest either a world moving toward better ways of doing things, or a globe submitting to American empire. The same ambiguity exists in all the areas of network power that we have been discussing: trading systems, business regulations, and the English language. The many who are hurt or threatened by the changes are sure to see empire. A world of American-born networks inspires accusations of imperialism at every turn.

The Empire of Desire

Then there is seduction, the sculpting of desire. Desire is the expression of dissatisfaction, the inborn human sense of being incomplete, not yet being all that we should, needing to possess or see or touch something finer than we have yet. The human being is the animal that is not satisfied: this insight is common to the Gautama Buddha, founder of Buddhism, and Saint Augustine. The Buddha was elaborating and purifying Indian philosophy's doctrine of the cycles of death and rebirth in a world of desire, with the goal being eventual escape into a peace free from desire. Saint Augustine was bringing to Christianity Plato's concept of *eros*, the soul's hunger that carries us toward the thing we believe will be perfect and permanent. Augustine would also have known the doctrine of the Roman Stoics, who sought to quiet their desire so that they could live in the world without the torture of need and disappointment, set free from hope and fear. The idea of desire as the permanent, tormenting fact about human life comes from everywhere, because people have found it whenever they have looked inside themselves.

As Augustine wrote, we know the soul by what moves her. Seduction concerns how the soul learns to be moved: where we find dissatisfaction, and how we try to cure it. In the past, religion has been the main response to desire. Believers of all traditions have soothed their appetite for the pleasures of this world and aimed at final oneness with the divine. Desire has also gone into politics and war, where ideals of heroism and honor draw the ambitious to seek perfection in the eyes of others. Sometimes, particularly after the Romantic revolution in Europe, erotic love has concentrated all desire on a single person in hope of winning perfect peace by union with her or him. The idea that we are born incomplete and become whole in another person is at least as old as Plato's *Symposium*, but its present form dates from the new shape that Romanticism gave to European sentiments.

Modern capitalism puts desire at the center of economic life. Before this explosive shift, most people spent their lives fulfilling the duties of their social positions, which were often inherited and typically not open to much change. Peasants grew crops, craftsmen made goods, traders carried them from place to place, and priests, nobles, and lackeys at the court consumed the surplus. High drama belonged mostly to politics, warfare, and great spiritual quests. Commerce was dishonorable and marginal. The French philosopher Montesquieu wrote in the eighteenth century that commerce was bred

> among men who are constrained to hide in marshes, on islands, on the shoals, and even among dangerous reefs . . . fugitives found security there. They had to live: they drew their livelihood from the whole universe. Commerce, sometimes destroyed by conquerors, sometimes hampered by monarchs, wanders across the earth, flees from where it is oppressed, and remains where it is left to breathe: it reigns today where one used to see only deserted places, seas, and rocks; there where it used to reign are now only deserted places.

Capitalism created two new conditions. It disrupted stable social hierarchies. Now luck and ambition might bring a poor man riches or reduce a great man to nothing. Capitalism also set off a constant increase in total wealth, which made it possible to gain riches without taking them from the already rich. Human restlessness flooded into economic life. In production and trade people tried to become richer, better, finer, and more admired—closer to the elusive perfection where fulfilled desires relax into peace. For early students of commercial society such as Adam Smith and Alexis de Tocqueville, this was as interesting a change as any that capitalism brought. This change has become even more important in our economy of consumption, drenched in advertising, where every feeling is for sale.

Now desire is globalized. People compare themselves to images of distant realities—or imaginary realms that were first envisioned far away. *Baywatch* in Iran affects its viewers' sense of a successful life, a beautiful location, an attractive body, and the nature of emotional and erotic fulfillment. So do hundreds of American movies and thousands of television episodes every year. They present objects of desire so far removed from the lives of their viewers that they soar above like skyscrapers in a city of tin shacks. The eye can follow them upward, but the rest of the body remains on the ground. Fantasy takes on a new power to guide and spur—and to hound and torment.

This is not altogether new. Legends of golden cities drew the Spaniards across the Atlantic, conquering an America whose image they took from the tales of Marco Polo and other travelers, or from even more ancient sources. Christopher Columbus noted in his captain's log that the islands of the Caribbean were home to oysters that hung from trees and dropped pearls from their open shells to the ground—a zoological discovery that has never been repeated, but that reiterated the description of fantastic islands in the writings of Roman geographers. What is new is the extent and uniformity of fantasy, the shared visual world that means a stockbroker in Los Angeles and a teenager in Gaza both know the swoop of a basketball player's signature shot and the erotic sheen of a *Baywatch* episode—and in some way both want them.

The attraction of these images is not just the comfort and pleasure they promise. It is also the seduction of power, which always attaches to the most prominent, potent, and infamous in any gathering of individuals or nations. The power of Rome continued to capture imaginations for many centuries after the empire's fall. It influenced the design of Washington, D.C., and the American founders' understanding of their enterprise. Thanks to television and movies, American seduction presses much deeper into the recesses of geography and the social order than even Rome could.

The power of seduction is especially suited to breeding resentment. Seductive power permeates its subjects. It becomes a part of them, and they follow it willingly, even urgently. Yet their desire is still partly foreign, made in America. This hybrid desire guides people's tongues and directs their gazes to its image of beauty and their convictions toward its idea of justice. Shaking it off would be like plucking a disease from your chest and throwing it away. You cannot easily drive out what you have invited into yourself. You cannot escape or destroy what has become a part of you. And so, sometimes, resentment becomes more insistent even as it grows less effective.

Talk of American empire expresses a state of the passions. When people feel reworked and rearranged without their invitation, "empire" captures that perception. There is no need to admire or accept this characterization of American power, but there is no escaping the need to understand it, because we cannot scoff or argue it away. The idea of American empire is a part of the world's imaginary landscape, as familiar elsewhere as it is alien to Americans.

CHAPTER 3

The Universal Nation

—ɷ—

At the same time that we disclaim imperial aspirations, we Americans suspect that we are the world's universal nation. Being French is an affectation, being Russian a perversion, being from the world's poor regions a deprivation; but being American is just being human. As the English political philosopher John Gray wryly put it, we secretly believe that everyone is born American, but that certain people become something else due to bad upbringing.

This idea goes back as far as English settlement of North America. John Winthrop, first governor of the Massachusetts Bay Colony, proclaimed the new land "a city shining on a hill," showing the world faith and righteousness. "The eyes of all people are upon us," Winthrop reminded his fellow settlers. Winthrop imagined the settlers as architects of an earthly community of the just. In the next century, Americans rebelled against their king in the name of self-evident and unalienable natural rights, which were the innate possessions of all men but which Americans were the first nation to name and defend.

Although Winthrop's image has become hackneyed by overuse, most recently in the hands of presidents Kennedy and Reagan, he founded a tradition with many religious and secular successors. In the first essay in *The Federalist*, the revered exposition of the American constitution by some of its framers, Alexander Hamilton wrote that America's fate was in many respects the most interesting in the world. . . . It seems to have been reserved to the people of this country, by their conduct and example, to decide the important question, whether societies of men are really capable or not of establishing good government from reflection and choice, or whether they are forever destined to depend for their political constitutions on accident and force.

It was as grand a proposal as Winthrop's, although the image is secular: it had fallen to America to determine whether reason and freedom, the great values of the Enlightenment, could remake politics and secure well-being for a nation. The future of all peoples depended on American success or failure.

A descendant thought infused Abraham Lincoln's address at Gettysburg, when he called the Civil War a test of the founders' gamble, an experiment in whether a nation "conceived in Liberty and dedicated to the proposition that all men are created equal" could survive or would tear itself apart. "The world," he said—not the nation, but the world—"can never forget" the deeds of the Union dead, because their cause was human freedom itself. They died to ensure "that government of the people, by the people, for the people, shall not perish from the earth"—again, not North America, not the Western Hemisphere, but the earth. These were not chance excesses of rhetoric. Lincoln's speeches a decade earlier show him agonizing over whether the founders' project could survive in the hands of a new generation. Lincoln was addressing a version of Alexander Hamilton's question to his own contemporaries. In his final speeches Lincoln is almost prophetically obsessed by the question of American destiny. In the greatest American statesman of the nineteenth century, the universal mission of the eighteenth and seventeenth centuries was preserved and renewed.

Lincoln's admirer, the poet Walt Whitman, echoed the man he called "My Captain" when he warned in the prose work *Democratic Vistas* that "the United States are destined either to surmount the gorgeous history of feudalism, or else prove the most tremendous failure of their time." Whitman was concerned about the political community, but even more about the American soul—a concern he shared with John Winthrop, although Whitman's American Romanticism would have been alien to the Puritan governor. In his mind, though, he and Lincoln were putting the same question to the nation, and to history: "Is this thing going to work? All of humanity must know."

In the twentieth century, the idea of America's universal destiny was renewed when Woodrow Wilson proposed the American model of liberal democracy, national self-determination, and free markets as the formula for a system of peaceful relations among countries. American destiny reached a global scale. The expansion came naturally; the world had been watching from the beginning.

The vision of national destiny that began with John Winthrop is the grandest source of Americans' belief that we are a universal nation. Another reason is the way we think and talk about our politics. Since Jefferson invoked unalienable rights in the Declaration of Independence, then wrote them into the Constitution as the Bill of Rights, Americans have thought of their rights as natural facts that govern politics. This is not the only way for a people to picture its rights. In a distinguished English tradition, rights are the embedded customs of a nation's politics—not explicit prohibitions, but settled understandings about what must always be protected. "The rights of Englishmen" have been honored as sturdier and more stable than "the rights of men." Putting rights within a national tradition, British conservatives say, prevents the abstract reasoning that has occasionally led the United States Supreme Court to discover new rights, or the heady excitement that spurs radicals to base their programs on updated theories of human liberty. As the English conservative Michael

Oakeshott put it, "Moral ideals are a sediment: they have significance only so long as they are suspended in a religious or social tradition, so long as they belong to a religious or a social life." In this view, abstract rights drain that vital life by leading people to arid and fantastic reasoning.

Perhaps that is true of England, or once was. It is not true of America. American character is paradoxical in this respect. Abstract, universal rights are to us natural, organic, as much a part of the national spirit as American landscapes and highways. The local, embedded moral life of Americans is universalist, and has been since Winthrop and Jefferson. For us to distinguish "the rights of Americans" from the rights of human beings would seem as improper a contraction as saying "ain't." The rights of Americans are, naturally, also the rights of human beings. We are parochial and universalist without inconsistency, because being universal defines our parochialism.

The Innocent Nation

The universal nation is also the innocent nation, or so Americans have come to believe. The national mood has followed Ralph Waldo Emerson's famous exhortation:

> Trust thyself: every heart vibrates to that iron string. Accept the place the divine providence has found for you, the society of your contemporaries, the connection of events. Great men have always done so, and confided themselves childlike to the genius of their age, betraying their perception that the absolutely trustworthy was seated at their heart, working through their hands, predominating in all their being.

What we feel, who we are, is good and true, healthy and just. That is what Americans incline to believe. We do not do harm. Our hearts are pure, and purity expresses itself in our actions. When we follow our feelings, whether of compassion or of outrage, we are staying close to the truth. The danger is not that we will be wrong, but that we will fail to trust ourselves.

On the Sunday following the September 11 attacks on New York and Washington, I drove to a small Baptist church in central Virginia to hear what sense was being made of the week's events. There, after patriotic hymns, the minister told a story about John Birch, the missionary to China whose name the anti-communist movement took up in the 1950s. Birch, he recalled, once delivered a long sermon in Mandarin to a Chinese audience, ending by exhorting his listeners to give their souls to Jesus Christ. Every last one raised an arm to invite salvation. The evangelist thought he must have been misunderstood: such a high yield was impossible. So he repeated his sermon word for word, hoping to make his meaning clear this time. Once again, there were as many raised hands as souls in the room.

At this juncture, something secular in me expected a punch line. There was none. The Chinese had understood. The lesson was that, although even John Birch sometimes doubted, there is no reason for doubt.

A modest Baptist congregation, made up mostly of poor and working people, was an appropriate place for this reminder of American self-trust at the cusp of a new period in international affairs. Like the idea of the universal nation, the belief in American innocence is a legacy of America's Protestant history. It comes from the religious revivals that swept across North America between 1795 and 1858, beginning during George Washington's presidency and driving into the abolitionist movement that helped bring Abraham Lincoln's new Republican Party to the White House. The churches at the heart of those revivals, not the original Puritan congregations, are the lineal ancestors of today's evangelical Christianity.

In colonial America, the Congregational churches that descended from Puritanism were scholarly and doctrinal. Harvard College was founded in 1636, in the wilderness of Massachusetts, to ensure that the American clergy would know Latin, Greek, and theology. Most colonial Congregational ministers held college degrees. These learned preachers taught their parishioners relentless scrutiny of themselves and their corner of the world. Every day was full of occasions for sin, and equally full of lessons in God's grace. One Samuel Sewall recorded in his diary that God led him to drop his cup of drinking water in bed as a reminder that life is fragile and short. This marriage of humility and self-importance (even in clumsiness being Samuel Sewall was an occasion for divine lessons) seems not to have been unusual. There was no avoiding introspection in a Puritan world obsessed with the question of one's personal tie to God.

This spirit of scrutiny influenced even those American writers whose conclusions were more Romantic than Puritan. Ralph Waldo Emerson's exhortations to self-trust always began with the same reproach: around him people were living in the sin of unconsciousness, slumbering and failing to take in life's lessons. He wrote in order to wake them up and bring them to the light of self-awareness. He was descended from a line of Congregational ministers and graduated from Harvard expecting to become another one. Even after he had adapted from Hindu thought the idea of a universal soul of which all individual souls partake, the urgent, reproachful, yet hopeful spirit of his reflection remained Puritanical.

Emerson's friend Henry David Thoreau filled *Walden* with scrupulous balance sheets, weighing his expenditure on nails against his income from beans grown at his pondside homestead. At first a spoof on the fiscal diligence of his spiritually dozing Concord neighbors, the ledger soon became the critical metaphor in Thoreau's project: giving an account of oneself, husbanding energy and attention for good use, and preserving the lessons that every moment taught. Thoreau's distinctly American reflections descended directly from Samuel Sewall and other pedantic diarists.

But while Thoreau reworked his little-read manuscripts and Emerson traveled the growing country as a celebrated orator, American Protestantism was changing. The Great Awakening—the name usually given to the first wave of religious revivals that began around 1795—and subsequent episodes brought a new religious tone to scholarly New England and the Anglican South. Baptists, Methodists, and others set aside the scripted, carefully argued sermons of the Congregationalists and the ceremony of the Anglicans, and instead appealed directly to the passions. They held that not learning but spirit enabled believers to understand divine revelation, and that spirit could touch any man—or, sometimes, woman—at any time. Ministers and lay believers were notorious for their allegedly divine ranting—what is today called "speaking in tongues." Observers from the educated religious establishment described the new congregations and preachers as primitives from the lowest orders of society, and glimpsed in their enthusiastic disregard for authority the peasant rebellions of English history.

These ancestors of today's evangelical Christians married self-trust to the Protestant drama of approaching God through one's own conscience. If the believer's heart were open, the spirit would guide it to truth. The revivalists trusted God to come undistorted into their individual souls as surely as Emerson urged trusting the oversoul. They did not do away with the Puritan suspicion that sin lurked everywhere, but they put self-scrutiny in uneasy balance with ecstatic self-certainty. When they felt God in their hearts, there could be no sin. And nothing was clearer than the experience of God in one's heart.

Innocence and self-trust persist in several American versions. Emerson's own formulation has become popularized as Americans' second nature, and it blends almost indistin-

guishably with the hairier and more pungent phrases of Walt
Whitman, who thought himself a worthy disciple of the master—although the austere and high-minded New Englander
was not so sure. Whitman began his great "Song of Myself"
with "I celebrate myself," and proceeded to declare that

> I know that the hand of God is the elderhand of my own,
> And I know that the spirit of God is the eldest brother
>   of my own
> And that all the men ever born are also my brothers. . . .
>   and the women my sisters and lovers . . .

He called himself

> Walt Whitman, an American, one of the roughs,
>   a kosmos,
> Disorderly fleshy and sensual . . . eating drinking and
>   breeding.
> No sentimentalist . . . no stander above men and women
>   or apart from them . . . no more modest than
>   immodest.

> Unscrew the locks from the doors!
> Unscrew the doors themselves from their jambs!

> Whoever degrades another degrades me . . . and whatever
>   is done or said returns at last to me.

For Whitman, trust in the body and heart was part of the
spirit of democracy. It was also the way to reach God, "the
elderhand" of one's own hand and the source of the heart's sen-
sations. Solidarity and justice come out of this sentiment, an
embrace of one's own rough "fleshy and sensual" character,
and equally of everybody else's. Rules fall away like doors
removed from their hinges, and the only laws are desire and

sympathy. Out of this wild spirit emerges a Christian sentiment pure enough to have stood alongside John Winthrop: "Whoever degrades another degrades me." Whitman's doctrine would have been alien to Winthrop, however, because sin is absent from it. In Whitman's picture of humanity, the great moral failure is to lack feeling, to turn away from the world's richness.

A strong version of this spirit moved the idealists of the late 1960s. Everyone who follows the sensual, anti-authoritarian, and hopeful habits of that period is a child of Whitman. A weaker version is everywhere in the American cult of feeling, which identifies good sentiments with the good life and good intentions with right action. Love, as the song has it, is all you need.

Among conservative Christians, the evangelical habit of self-trust also remains as strong as ever. Although its adherents might balk at being reminded that they are Walt Whitman's nieces and nephews, the inconvenience of the fact does not diminish its truth. George W. Bush's rhetoric gives a good picture of evangelical innocence. In the 2000 presidential election, voters chose between a loquacious polymath given to speculation and a candidly ignorant, intellectually uncurious candidate whose chief appeal was that he promised a pure heart and a strong arm—sound moral instincts and the ability to carry them out. His implicit message was that government did not matter much, but that having a "good man"—one of his favorite terms of praise—at its helm was better than rule by clever rogues. He was the candidate of the innocence tradition in American politics.

His administration still appears devoted to the theory of the pure heart, the idea that good intentions are an inoculation against abuse of power. When civil libertarians attacked his proposal to hold secret military tribunals for non-citizens suspected of association with terrorists, the president responded that Americans—and non-Americans, who had somewhat more at stake—could trust him to use unchecked power fairly. Whether or not that is true of him personally, the idea marked a departure from the rule of law, which rests on the premise that trusting individual leaders is not enough to preserve liberty. That was the view of the American founders. Since their time, though, it has been a recurrent American impulse to set aside the dry constraints of law in favor of the steady hand and the pure heart. Born of the doctrine of innocence and self-trust, that impulse is now once again shaping domestic law and foreign relations.

Belief in our innocence can make Americans oblivious to the violence that is done in our name. We are apt to view whatever the country undertakes—war, diplomacy, or a foreign-aid project—as innocently motivated and perforce innocuous. The news that American bombers killed tens of thousands of Iraqis in retreat from Kuwait did nothing to shake the popular conviction that the Gulf War was bloodless. The question here is not whether the war was appropriate, or whether there was military reason to bomb the Iraqi army as it retreated. The remarkable fact is that, despite those foreign deaths, many Americans believed that they had won a war without human cost. In the same spirit, at the end of the American bombing campaign in Afghanistan in 2001, television anchors and commentators remarked that the beleaguered country was seeing its "first peaceful transfer of power" since before the Soviets invaded in 1979. It was a puzzling locution, coming at the end of two months of relentless air strikes and a savagely fought ground campaign with thousands of Afghan casualties, which ended with the former government plotting revenge in the hills of Pakistan. Again, the point is not to criticize that campaign, but to remark that it was, openly and without apology, anything but a means to the peaceful transfer of power. The phrase sounded right because it fit with ideas of innocence: American violence washes over the world like a gentle rain, and where it soaks into the earth, peace blooms. That view is far from the facts: power changed hands after an American exercise of revenge and self-defense that was both justified and, like all war, terrible for those caught in it and costly in human life.

If the United States was right in Afghanistan, our innocence also helps us to forget the times that have been in the wrong. During the Cold War, America stood for the right values, and our victory served freedom; but our larger rightness does not erase or justify the unnecessary wrongs we perpetrated. In Angola in the 1980s our support for the guerrilla leader and diamond smuggler Jonas Savimbi made us complicit in the deaths of hundreds of thousands in a long civil war that meant almost nothing to the Cold War. In Chile in 1973 we helped to orchestrate the overthrow of the democratically elected socialist Salvador Allende, and installed the authoritarian Augusto Pinochet, whose secret killings and undemocratic rule deeply wounded civil society and violated Chile's long tradition of constitutional government. In Iran in 1953 we thwarted a constitutionalist movement and elevated Mohammad Reza Pahlavi, a pro-American ruler whose repression, anti-Islamic policies, and open dependence on the United States inspired the Islamic revolution of 1979; in a quarter of a century American power helped move Iran from the liberal forefront of the Muslim world to the head of its illiberal Islamicist movement. In El Salvador in the 1980s, we supported death squads that killed nuns, priests, journalists, labor organizers, and other civilians who sympathized with the country's leftists. Anyone who believes that American power has been good for the world in the last century—which I am inclined to believe—has to consider these acts, and admit that they leave us anything but innocent. Believing in our own innocence only suggests to others who cannot believe in it that we must be smug about our guilt.

The Visible Empire

On September 20, 2002, the White House released a summary of the Bush administration's vision of foreign policy. The document, a legally mandated annual report to Congress, expressed a conception of America's place in the world that had taken shape by fits and starts over the previous decade and had begun surfacing after September 11, 2001. As former Chinese premier Zhou En-lai reportedly remarked of the French Revolution, too little time has passed for us to know its significance.

The tone of the document, like that of American foreign policy in the year preceding it, was blithely imperial. I have already noted that "imperial" is used mainly as an expression of distaste, but here I mean it in a more precise sense. The official American position at present may be reduced to a few simple propositions. First, there is one set of principles binding all countries in the world, whether their governments acknowledge or ignore them. These are democracy, free markets, human rights, and peaceful behavior toward other countries. Second, we embody these principles, and we have the last word as to what they mean and where they have been grievously violated. Third, we will enforce these principles with our unparalleled military strength and will not permit competitors to arise and challenge our supreme position. In us, and only in us, power and righteousness coincide.

The administration candidly acknowledged facts that many find discomforting. No other country or combination of countries approaches the military capacity of the United States. Because there is only so much others can do to restrain us, we will inevitably make many of our own rules: Once we have settled on a course, little can turn us away. Moreover, we are in fact the world's picture of liberal modernity, and of a humane future which most individuals, if not all of their governments, would like to join. It is not absurd for us to claim a special place in a world whose language of political legitimacy is defined by democracy, human rights, and free markets. It would be odd if we did not have such a place.

The events of September 11 took place in a world already reworking its international law. NATO's intervention in Kosovo and strikes on Serbia in 1999 violated the principle of sovereignty, that governments do not interfere in the internal affairs of other countries. That principle had hardly retained its purity before then, as the cold war was full of battles by proxy, from Vietnam to Nicaragua, but this was an overt, coordinated action, undertaken for the humanitarian purpose of stopping a Serb campaign of ethnic cleansing against Kosovar Muslims. The intervention implied that, once Serbia's government violated basic human rights, it lost its legitimacy, and that once its legitimacy was gone, others could act against it to vindicate human rights. Although it excited much scholarly debate, the Kosovo intervention stayed mute in geopolitics: It did not produce a new principle, a general theory of when to interfere with—or topple—irresponsible governments.

The Bush doctrine does. It creates a class of countries that are standing candidates for intervention. These are countries that violate human rights at home; disregard international agreements and act belligerently; seek to acquire advanced military technology including but not limited to chemical, biological, and nuclear weapons; sponsor terrorism; and "reject basic human values and hate the United States and everything for which it stands." Assuming that the last is mostly a rhetorical flourish (Saddam Hussein did not hate the United States, but was grateful for its military and political support, until the tables turned after his invasion of Kuwait), this list includes, at a minimum, Iraq, Iran, North Korea, and Pakistan. Any number of countries in war-pocked West Africa might have to go on the list as well.

Here the Bush doctrine hits a paradox. It defines terrorism as "premeditated, politically motivated violence perpetrated against innocent civilians." That definition is not restricted to shadowy bands of guerillas slipping across borders or hiding in urban sleeper cells. It certainly encompasses Russian actions in Chechnya, where troops have leveled whole cities. It arguably includes some Chinese actions in Tibet—or China's jailing and mistreatment of its own pro-democracy activists. What we usually call terrorism is distinguished from these campaigns by the political weakness of the terrorists: They have no army, no tanks or warplanes, and no seat at the United Nations. Terror has become a favorite weapon of the very angry and very weak, because it is the only way they can injure the strong, but it is not a new tactic. Indeed, it is the practice of some of the governments that the Bush administration's document identifies as "the civilized nations."

This is neither an apology for terrorists nor a proposal for an American-led occupation of Moscow and Beijing. There are good reasons for not attacking those countries: We couldn't do it without considerable losses, whatever succeeded the present governments would probably be worse, war is a terrible tool that kills civilians and damages nations regardless of its motive, and—most important—one invasion is license for another, and soon land grabs become routine political gambits under the flag of principle. Such prudent considerations are not just self-interested. Because global disorder takes lives and saps resources, being imprudent in the international use of violence is immoral. The burden of proof, as lawyers say, is on those who are looking for a reason to attack abroad, not those who want to hold fire.

The point of the paradox is that the United States has announced a formula for using international violence that we do not expect to enforce consistently. Instead, the use of violence will continue to be, as it was in Kosovo, a response to specific circumstances, including popular attitudes, military strength and weakness, and the availability of coalition powers. The difference is that the Bush administration has set loose amid this confusion a rule that pretends to say when violence is legitimate—a rule whose meaning shifts depending on where the American government decides to apply it. We should keep in mind some of the dangers of this course.

First, visible empires are expensive. Making ourselves a unilateral enforcer of an international law that we ourselves pronounce costs trillions of dollars in military preparation and foreign operations. It brings keener resentment toward us, ensuring that anyone anywhere who is angry about something will end up being angry at us, since we are more than ever the global emblem of power and authority. The resentment will also be aimed, quite plausibly, at hypocrisy: Those who announce a universal principle should be prepared to deal with the consequences of enforcing it only selectively. Resentment is the seed of terror. As James Wilson suggested, an America on which the world pours itself is safer and stronger than an America that pours itself on the world.

Second, as Edmund Burke insisted, empire has moral dangers. Do we trust ourselves to judge what is right, always and anywhere? Are we immune to the ways in which selfishness, ignorance, and pride blur judgment? If so, we are different from all who have lived before us. The attempts to discipline international violence through the United Nations Security Council and the various doctrines and documents of international relations are sometimes farcical, but they are responses to the dangers of power. Institutions, procedures, and principles put checks, however imperfect, on the solipsism of isolated judgment. Those who set them aside had better be sure they will not need them later.

Then there is the question of what others will do with our new rule of violence—for they surely will not let us be its sole enforcers. We already have a clue in Russia's violent treatment of Chechen rebels and China's actions against its Uighur Muslim populations, both conducted under the rubric of the global war on terror. As it matures, the Bush doctrine has every prospect of becoming a license for large countries to keep small ones in check. The large countries will almost certainly include Russia, which is already reasserting its old claims to Central Asian empire, and China, with its growing ambition to be a regional superpower. This century may elevate a handful of continental empires, each claiming to be the local enforcer of global order. In addition to their intrinsic disadvantages for liberty, such empires have the habit of going to war against one another.

Finally, there is a problem for domestic politics. At least since the end of World War II, critics—some of them cranks, but others as mainstream as President Dwight D. Eisenhower—have worried about the growth of a national security state in America. A huge and costly military, closely aligned with an executive branch that has growing control over both war and domestic security, is at least a cause for worry—especially when its raison d'être, the threat of terror, is a permanent condition.

It is unfortunate that skepticism about American power has come to be associated with the romantic left and the isolationist right wings of politics. There is a realistic tradition, not of hostility but of caution about pronouncing grand ideals and then making oneself their sole enforcer. As the legal scholar Alexander Bickel used to emphasize, large principles forged in extreme times lie around like loaded guns, begging to be put to bad use. I fear that the American government, having loaded for bear, is preparing a dangerous legacy. It might have been better to say less, profess respect for existing rules and institutions, and take care to carve out only the exceptions that circumstances required in the moment. Careful inconsistency can be principled in an arena where prudence is often the highest principle.

None of this can be more than speculation at the time of writing. The meaning of American power will likely take as long to work itself out as the significance of the French Revolution. What one can say, though, is that perfect moral self-confidence is not often a good sign in a lawgiver. The United States has made itself a global lawgiver in the critical question of when one government may use force against another, and our belief in our innocence and universality has given shape to the law we are making.

The best counterpoint to American self-certainty may be another Puritan inheritance: the idea of American sin. This minor theme in national consciousness was the dark aspect of being God's nation. In the same address in which he called the new settlement a city on a hill, the Puritan John Winthrop warned that God's people must be meek, generous, and modest, or lose their divine blessing. If the settlers "embrace this present world and prosecute our carnal intentions, seeking great things for ourselves and our posterity, the Lord shall surely break out in wrath against us; be revenged of such a people, and make us know the price of the breach of such a covenant." Winthrop advised fellowship, modesty, and constant self-scrutiny as the virtues that might keep the new American community in divine favor. Even as he founded the idea of American destiny, Winthrop added an enduring note of caution: too great and powerful a place in this world will destroy what made us good in the first place.

The Federalist, in the quieter tones of Enlightenment, also contains an idea that theologians would call sin: that human nature is so perverse, obdurate, and selfish that any political community must plan to contend with thieves, zealots, and the self-serving. The authors wrote as if aware of Immanuel Kant's remark, made famous by Isaiah Berlin: "Out of the crooked timber of humanity, no straight thing was ever made." They recommended the Constitution as a vessel shaped to accommodate crooked beings. Alexander Hamilton's great question, whether America would prove that freedom and reason could guide politics, received a mixed answer: yes, but only if we understand that freedom will bring some greed, debasement, and irrationality. Allowing for that means not trusting anybody, including oneself, to always be right.

The Puritan idea of a great nation haunted by its own wrongs returned during the fight over slavery and the Civil War. Abolitionists termed the Constitution "a pact with the devil" because it embraced slavery. Abraham Lincoln, in his second inaugural address, described the terrible war as divine punishment for the sin of human bondage. He imagined aloud that the conflict might last "until all the wealth piled by the bondsman's two hundred and fifty years of unrequited toil shall be sunk, and until every drop of blood drawn with the lash shall be paid by another drawn with the sword." The suffering America's ruling race had inflicted would return to it until justice was restored. In this eerie speech, history comes as a bloody redeemer, fulfilling the prophecy that Winthrop issued more than two centuries earlier.

Out of this picture of sin, Lincoln drew a dark but hopeful vision of the country. Little more than a month before his assassination, he noted of the warring sides: "Both read the same Bible, and pray to the same God; and each invokes His aid against the other." Lincoln did not doubt that if there was a God, an idea he identified with implacable judgment after justice, He abhorred slavery. Yet the president observed, "The prayers of both could not be answered; that of neither has been answered fully. The Almighty has His own purposes." The world was too shadowed and creviced a place for either side of a terrible war to represent the forces of light. To imagine that one's own purposes were also God's was presumption and delusion.

Lincoln's call for "a just and lasting peace" began with these famous words: "With malice toward none; with charity for all; with firmness in the right, as God gives us to see the right, let us strive on to finish the work we are in." *As God gives us to see the right.* All the difference in the world lies in that qualifying phrase, so easily lost in the echo of the one that precedes it. Our vision is imperfect, and the ends we believe we serve may not, in the end, prove either just or real. We can have no others to guide us, and we cannot stop believing in them; but it would be sin to forget what imperfect guides they are.

In the last century, from the prohibition movement to today's battles over sex education and gay rights, moralists have addressed only one of Winthrop's two kinds of sin: "carnal" pleasures, the appetites of the body. But Winthrop and his successors also considered "greatness" a sin. Those who seek after power and use it against others risk forgetting their own failings and imagining that they have God always on their side. The thought that power is morally dangerous has almost disappeared from political argument today, yet remembering it adds sobriety to strength. The spirit of patriotic hesitation, which sees circumspection and self-scrutiny as the duties of power, is old and eminently American, and without it we are off our balance.

CHAPTER 4

The American Temper

—ɯ—

Americans' most dangerous quality is our belief in our own universality and innocence. This belief blinds us to our power and the resentment that it inspires. We lose sight of the harm we do. The impression abroad that Americans govern an empire comes partly from our blindness, a parochial self-confidence that the rest of the world takes for arrogance. It is arrogance, too, in effect if not in intention. Assuming that what our hearts tell us must hold true for everyone is neither decent nor prudent.

Americans have other qualities, though, that help us to face the world responsibly and make us attractive in more than wealth and power. These are not grand ideas so much as everyday attitudes, founded in the experience of being American. They are among the better lessons of American life. One can sum them up by saying that we Americans are migrants, merchants, and amnesiacs.

Calling Americans migrants captures a pair of characteristics: we come from elsewhere, and once here we move. We move geographically, but also socially, professionally, and culturally. Already in the 1830s, Alexis de Tocqueville described the American landscape as a tableau of restlessness animated by a churning population—now charging through New England, now filling the South, now flooding into the newly opened Midwest. This churn means that Americans build our identities on different foundations from other peoples. We move much more often than Europeans, and are far less likely than Indians or Chinese to inherit family networks of duty and privilege. In those societies, a large part of identity comes from continuity: I know who I am because of my obligation to my parents, my status in the community, my history in the local landscape, and so forth. Leaving those continuities means surrendering a part of oneself. Americans have never had such a rich set of fixed landmarks. We tend to believe that we are what we find within ourselves and what we make of it. From the beginning we had no other way to think of ourselves.

This individualism has helped the United States to become a great immigrant nation. Becoming American is different from joining any other country. A non-Chinese cannot, legally or culturally, become Chinese. Besides the legal barrier, the density of ethnic identity and social practice is so great that there is no straightforward way to step in and assume a role. Too much learning is required; too much history and social intricacy are attached. And how would an immigrant have joined traditional Hindu civilization? Which would have been his caste, his rituals? Whole communities could sometimes enter and assume special roles distinct from the social mainstream—both China and India welcomed Jewish populations in medieval times and earlier—but integrating an individual foreigner would have been difficult, even unnatural.

America's common identity is straightforward by comparison. You can join us, not just on our tolerance but as an American, if only you consent to do your work and live in your family with a modicum of civility. It is not only that we are quicker than other peoples to welcome newcomers, although that is sometimes true; it is that there is less for newcomers to be kept out of. We are already leading more or less the lives that immigrants arrive here seeking, not practicing some esoteric and elaborate High Americanism that newcomers must master. It is sometimes said that American life is a crude pursuit of wealth and pleasure, lacking refinement and subtle satisfactions. There is something to that, but not much. The critics are looking in the wrong places, in Wal-Mart and faddish television programs. The more intricate achievements of American life are private, in friendships, the families we make as well as inherit, and the complicated cross-stitching of intimacy in lives that were already uprooted when we entered them.

Calling Americans merchants means that we are a commercial society. Our public life, our shared entertainment, and our speech have the shape of business, consumption, and advertising. We devote more energy than any other wealthy people to pursuing, managing, and just contemplating money. This coarsens us somewhat by taking energy away from activities where there are finer and more qualitative distinctions than percentages of return on investment. But commerce, even more than American life in general, is open in principle to anyone. That is why immigrants are so often small-businesspeople: hotel managers, gas station owners, grocers, and dry cleaners. These positions are closed to nobody. Money makes vast inequality possible, because one person can become infinitely rich while others remain poor, but it also produces a form of equality: it has the same worth in anyone's hands. A commercial society has many more entry points than one based on inherited position, aesthetic or spiritual refinement, or martial valor.

Finally, we are historical amnesiacs. Compare the United States to Egypt, China, Ireland, or India, where the wrongs of the past are the ordinary currency of political and cultural argument. Here mentioning Pearl Harbor in discussing trade relations with Japan is considered bigoted, and invoking the Second World War when the subject of Germany comes up is almost unthinkable. In contrast, talking politics in many other countries is an invitation to relive injuries that date back a century, a millennium, or longer. The East India Company, the

Crusades, and the Opium Wars are all part of living political memory. It is inaccurate to believe that those countries are cursed by history. Rather, with help from poverty and imperialism, they have made their histories a curse. Building identity around shared wounds is a political choice. Politics shapes memory for its own purposes, sometimes with grim effects. (The American exception proves the rule. The division between North and South that is still fading was long sustained by Confederates and racist northerners who cultivated the imagined memory of an idyllic antebellum South and its heroic resistance to "Northern aggression.")

Forgetfulness keeps a people open to the world. Many Islamic countries are now poisoned against Jews. Around the world Christian, Muslim, and Hindu sectarians are developing a politics of fatal aversion to each other. The memory of imperial violence, cultivated by political opportunists, cannot win back the past but can pervert the present. Forgetful America is poisoned against no people, and looks to the future in the expectation that, no matter how the country changes, it will remain itself. We will hardly remember—as we hardly remember now—having ever been anyone or anything else.

These are modern, unheroic virtues, but they help a civilization to absorb movements of peoples and changes in culture without believing that it is being violated or overrun. They make American civilization easy to join. In this sense, Americans are indeed a natural people, and others are born with more capacity to become American than to become anything else. This is a historical fact, not a natural one, but it fits our moment in history. It gives some weight and decency to the conceit that we are the universal nation.

The Liberal Temper

America is sometimes accused of not having produced an authentic conservatism. The critic Lionel Trilling once described American conservative thought as a clutch of "irritable mental gestures which seek to resemble ideas." Despite right-wing political success, the very idea of American conservatism is still awkward. The word shares its root with "conservation," keeping alive what is best about the past and present rather than sweeping everything aside to hasten a hoped-for future. What, though, does that mean in a land of constant motion? Should we preserve the virtues of the New England farmers who abandoned their holdings in the nineteenth century and rushed en masse to the Midwest; the excellence of the Midwestern yeomen who took off for Seattle and California after the Second World War; ancient communal traditions in a country where people move from state to state often enough that an e-mail address is often the only way to track down an old friend after a year out of touch? As if to acknowledge the contradiction, most of the American right embraces the free market, which, with the constant change it brings, is the least conservative practice short of war.

The value of European conservatism is its mistrust of clever and ambitious people who design futures without regard for tradition. Presented with a plan to restructure social life or improve human nature, conservatives such as Edmund Burke would ask, in effect: Are we so wise that all the experience of past generations means nothing to us? Does all knowledge begin with us? At its best, this conservative prudence checks illusions of omniscience and the arrogance of power. Burke attacked the French Revolution because he believed its leaders' radical ideas were incoherent, and that their absolute belief in those ideas portended violence and suffering for the French people. Burke also dedicated years of his life to defending India against British imperialism because he believed that when one people takes arbitrary power over another, it will fall into looting and cruelty, debasing itself and deeply wounding the people it claims to govern.

In the United States, mistrust of power and ambition is as much a liberal impulse as a conservative one. Liberalism is a concept that has fallen on hard times. In popular American use it refers to politicians who favor modest economic equality and tend to the interests of unions and organized minority groups. In Europe, "liberalism" means a decorous version of what Americans would call "conservatism": an emphasis on individual liberty and free markets. These uses of the word obscure liberalism's more distinctive meaning. The liberal spirit, as the great judge Learned Hand remarked in 1952, "is the spirit which is not too sure that it is right." He did not mean weak-kneed skepticism, but the opposite. Liberalism is founded on clarity about core moral values: individual dignity, political equality, and abhorrence of cruelty. Liberalism's skepticism, a hesitation about judging any situation too quickly, comes from respect for those values. There are so many ways to do wrong as well as right, and humanity is such a flawed vessel, that we should not trust our judgments too confidently. If moral clarity is necessary for liberty, it always risks becoming moral arrogance, which courts violence.

As a political doctrine, liberalism implies certain limits on the power of the state. The government cannot jail people for their opinions, take property without compensation, or discriminate categorically against members of any race or religion. Access to political power must be shared broadly enough that no group can make the government its private instrument. Within these boundaries—no abuse of individual rights and no shutting groups out of the political process—a modern liberal state must also be democratic. These constraints on state power express a wariness of authority that is a cornerstone of liberal politics. Because power corrupts, when people concede power to a government they should build in as much protection against abuse as is compatible with effective governance.

The success of a political regime depends on whether it suits the temperament of the people who live under it. Liberal temperament is not the same thing as liberal government, of course. There are liberal people in all countries, and illiberal people in liberal countries. But liberal government will not last without liberal temperament among its citizens, and people without liberal temperament will not care for liberal government, anyway. My description of liberal temperament will not, of course, fit everyone who has been called a liberal. In important respects it will not, for instance, describe even so important a liberal as John Stuart Mill, whose version of liberalism made him an adamant imperialist. I am describing a strain of liberal attitude that I perceive as part of the American temper and one of the better versions of the liberal spirit.

Temperamentally, a liberal is disinclined to impose the particulars of his customs and beliefs on other people. This modesty may have many sources: the skepticism of the essayist Michel de Montaigne, who claimed no confidence that his own judgments were right; the loyalty to the constitutional culture of the Bill of Rights that some Americans feel; the particularism of many Jews, who do not seek to bring others into their special relationship with God; the ecumenicism of most Hindus, who believe that religions take various routes to the same destination; and the shrug-and-a-smile tolerance of contemporary America, where a colorful but shallow diversity is welcomed. Liberal people will not struggle to seize government, or exercise their superior social influence in a community, to foist their attitudes wholesale on others. Liberals should not be supremacists for their cultures, or theocrats on behalf of their gods.

A liberal temperament also means not dwelling on the past or nurturing a sense of injury. Indeed, liberalism can be a positively forgetful disposition. People who never forget are not likely to live together for long. On scrutiny, almost every history reveals enough brutality and exploitation to fuel a campaign of retribution. If we were determined to vindicate all the wrongs of the past, the task would fill many lifetimes and generate many new wrongs. The Chinese sense of thwarted greatness, the feeling of civilizational injury that the new pan-Islamic politics cultivates, and the Hindu right's stories of Muslim conquest and repression in India are assertions of memory against both peace and progress.

To advise forgetting asks people to let go of past wrongs in order to live in the present. This can seem gracelessly expedient coming from those who have suffered little, as mainstream Americans have. But what seems expedient is not therefore wrong. Precisely because human history is long and ugly enough to fill the world with resentment, we should not help it to do so. Liberal forgetfulness, although it is compatible with intellectual sloppiness and moral indifference, inadvertently achieves a kind of greatness.

Tolerance and forgetfulness can both be passive virtues: we can let difference wander by and memory slip away without lifting a finger. Independent judgment is a more active liberal quality. The liberal temperament is not quiescent. It does not assume that an act is right just because it is done in the name of the government, the national interest, or some other authority. The Chinese government has a slogan for its mammoth Three Gorges Dam project, which will flood a vast area and displace more than a million people: "Give up the little home to embrace the great home." The great home is the nation, as defined by the government. A liberal is temperamentally inclined to mistrust the claims that the great home makes on the little home, and to suspect that she needs a little home in order to live in the great one. The little home of the independent mind may be the most important one.

The other essential quality of the liberal temperament is a sense of justice, which presses against both forgetfulness and, at the limit, tolerance. The sense of justice insists that people should be treated fairly no matter who they are, and that wrongs should be redressed. It resists accepting the world as one finds it, objects to repressive traditions, and insists that wrongs not be casually forgotten. After his definition of liberalism as principled skepticism, Learned Hand added that "the spirit of liberty remembers that not even a sparrow falls to earth unheeded, the spirit of liberty is the spirit of Him who, near two thousand years ago, taught mankind that lesson it has never learned, but has never quite forgotten; that there may be a kingdom where the least shall be heard and considered side by side with the greatest."

So, when liberalism's cardinal qualities are all present they make for an inconsistent turn of mind. The sense of justice presses against forgetfulness and tolerance. Independent judgment can do the same. Nor is it simply a matter of a happy balance of complements. A commitment to justice strong enough to attack the circumstances of injustice may nearly always require the edge of anger, born of the memory of injury. Any unjust situation also contains, like the American South before 1950, many familiar comforts, and all the accommodations people make with each other in order to live peaceably. Struggle puts those in jeopardy. It is not undertaken on a lark or sustained by a spell of optimism, at least by those who expect to live with its consequences.

Besides inconsistency, every liberal virtue comes with a matching vice. With tolerance come sloppiness and ignorance. The companion of forgetfulness is the complacent sense of innocence that buoys the American conscience. Faith in independent judgment can become arrogant idiosyncrasy, the confidence that one has nothing to learn from other people or from the past. The spirit of justice is linked to obsession and fanaticism, which is why a "crusader" may be the most admirable or the most alarming of men. In their bad forms, forgetfulness and moral arrogance combine to make Americans a universal nation in our own minds.

Sometimes the most important liberal virtue is making good use of inconsistency. The liberal view of political and moral life is full of tension: competing values strain against each other with no neat resolution. The world cannot be made perfect; yet we should try to improve it, even though every change also brings loss and danger. That is a liberal attitude. It is not entirely satisfying, but one liberal insight is that politics is the wrong place to seek the satisfaction of flawless consistency, and that people who understand this will do less harm than those who want a politics without contradiction or confusion. To be at home with dissatisfaction is a mark of liberal character.

Liberal Circumstances

The liberal temperament developed through concrete problems, not abstract dogmas. The skeptical Montaigne, a pioneer of the liberal spirit, served as a magistrate, minor statesman, and a widely admired mediator in the sixteenth century's destructive Wars of Religion. When the Protestant challenge to Catholicism fractured European Christendom, religious division set kingdoms, villages, and brothers and sisters against each other in disastrous bloodshed. As a Catholic who doubted that human reason could solve theological problems, and as a survivor of theological wars, Montaigne concluded that absolute conviction in politics was a disease of the spirit, an impulse that tore believers away from the complicated reality of human life. Absolute conviction made people inhumane—and all too human—fanatics. Montaigne wrote against the moral arrogance that enabled Protestants and Catholics to slaughter each other as infidels, and Spaniards to slaughter indigenous Americans as savages. He insisted on the duty to doubt, to hesitate, because he saw self-righteousness as the most destructive impulse. It blinded true believers to inconvenient facts and offered them the pleasure of dominating others. In all his work Montaigne responded to circumstances that presented a choice: tolerance or violence.

Another kind of liberal, Adam Smith, sketched the theory of efficient markets that became the foundation of contemporary economics, but he did not claim to describe the best of all possible worlds. In a time poised between a world of nobles and courtiers and one of yeomen and merchants, the market channeled ambition into labor and the pursuit of wealth rather than jockeying for courtly status. Smith thought this shift could be good for both prosperity and dignity, because it created competent, self-reliant entrepreneurs and craftsmen, but he also worried that the uprooting of traditional communities would leave people adrift, that repetitive factory work would make them brutish, and that industrial discipline would sap their courage and civic spirit. That is to say, he endorsed his version of liberalism not because it represented human perfection, but because it was on balance a humane response to his time and place.

Liberalism need not emerge triumphant in the clash of eternal ideas, a kind of Platonic Olympics. A liberal society need not be in every way superior to other forms of life. Rather, liberalism is well suited to certain circumstances: diverse political and religious beliefs, the threat of social and religious conflict, and impersonal forces such as the global market that impose rapid and disruptive changes. Supporting liberalism means judging it better than the alternatives: courtly hierarchy, religious war, authoritarian socialism, a clash of nationalist or fundamentalist doctrines, or pervasive disorder. And it means believing that the personal qualities liberalism fosters—ambition rather than reverence, action over reflection, prudence more than heroism—make up, on balance, the human character we would like to live with today. Today's world, with all its potential for violence and intolerance, needs the liberal spirit.

What would be a properly liberal view of today's world? Arguments about foreign relations are sometimes divided into two schools of thought: idealists favor promoting liberal values abroad, and realists mutter that the world is a dark and dangerous place where the best intentions go awry. Since the idealist program is a good idea, morally and practically, and the realist caution is true, the question is how to act on behalf of liberty and humanitarianism in a world full of their opposites. Since most of this book is a meditation on these questions, what follows here is only a sketch of starting points, concerned with American attitudes more than with reform programs. (Some of those come later.)

We should remember that the desire to live more like Americans is real. The images of guerrillas hacking off children's arms in Sierra Leone, ethnic cleansing in Bosnia and Kosovo, and the fiery plumes of September 11 all tempt us to imagine that the world is full of outright savages. On the contrary, most who sympathize with nationalism and fundamentalism, and sometimes people who propagate those doctrines, are torn between resentment of American power and attraction to everything America represents. The fact that America has become the global emblem of liberal, commercial modernity means that resentment of the United States spills over into resentment of modernity, and desire for modernity becomes desire for America. The incoherence of those who admire yet profess to despise America is evidence of the intensity of the emotions at work in them. Young men who do not know whether they want to fight for the mujahideen or study engineering in New Jersey, and who are as likely as not to put up a mujahideen poster even if they get a dorm room at Rutgers, are not our enemies—yet. They are unformed, and the form they will take is tied up with their attitude toward the United States. We need to be on the side of those parts of divided nations and souls that incline to liberalism.

As John Winthrop forecast, the eyes of the world are on us. When Edmund Burke rose before the House of Commons to assail Britain's imperial rule over India, he told his fellow legislators that the honor of the British nation was at stake. Britain was a great power and civilization, and tyranny conducted in its name debased it while debasing India. Burke's three-day oration against Warren Hastings, the governor-general of British India, was a self-conscious act of political theater that brought Britain to trial before its own highest principles. India, Burke reminded his colleagues, could not put the case herself, for she was half a world away: "The cries of India are given to seas and winds, to be blown about, in every breaking up of the monsoon, over a remote and unhearing ocean." So it was left to him to impeach Hastings, "in the name of the House of Commons, whose national character he has dishonored."

Today there is less need for an American Burke to stage a trial. Every act and utterance of the United States government crosses the world instantaneously. We are engaged in an unending political theater that we cannot script. The world watches with a critical eye. In October 2001, when national security adviser Condoleezza Rice phoned the American television networks to request that they not show a newly released video of Osama bin Laden, the world—particularly, but not only, Muslim countries—noticed. A month later, when George W. Bush announced his plan to institute secret military tribunals for non-citizens suspected of terrorism, people everywhere watched the proposal unfold. Whenever the United States is seen to betray liberal values, world opinion takes note.

Some of the hostile judgment against America is opportunistic, driven by resentment against American power and success. Although Muslims from Egypt to Indonesia claimed in the fall of 2001 that they would accept Osama bin Laden's guilt if the United States proved it by public evidence, their promise sounded hollow after Washington released a video in

December that showed bin Laden discussing having planned the attacks. The so-called Arab street didn't blink: the tape was denounced as a fabrication.

Despite widespread hypocrisy, though, many critics of America's illiberal moments are expressing sincere disappointment in a country that remains a global emblem of freedom and idealism. Many people, at the same time that they scoff at the idea of the universal nation, do expect America to be different: more decent, more honest, and more open. Despite recurrent disappointments, they have not abandoned that idea. Their disappointment reflects a double standard, by which the United States must clear a higher bar than other nations. The double standard is a compliment, though, and a burden we should accept with grace.

Every illiberal American act gives comfort to the forces of resentment. Illiberal behavior makes it easier to believe that our government is not really different from those of, say, Egypt or Indonesia. Illiberal American acts also give those governments license to act illiberally. If the United States cannot resist foreign terrorism without secret military tribunals, we weaken the contention of Egyptian human-rights activists that Egypt's secret executions in military courts are the wrong response to extremism. Condoleezza Rice's phone calls to the American networks undermine a United States diplomat telling Chinese officials that, faced with peasant and worker rebellions and secessionist movements, they should free their press from censorship.

When America acts on liberal principles it makes them more attractive. It suggests that those principles are more than convenient window dressing. Around the world, along with the desire to come to the United States or enjoy some of its wealth, there is genuine respect for American achievements: we get things done, our government more or less works, our entrepreneurs are dynamic, and we share some opportunity with immigrants from around the world. More than once justice has moved our national politics. These combinations of principle, achievement, and generosity contribute as much as prowess at long-range warfare to America's status as a great nation.

We should put our own house in order. As a great nation the United States is a source of persistent disappointment. We have the highest murder rate among rich countries, suggesting to the world that we are a more brutal civilization than any in Europe or East Asia. We are the source of the most popular iconography for the killers of Sierra Leone, who have themselves photographed in the distinctive poses of East Coast and West Coast gangsta rappers. The economic differences between black and white Americans, the life prospects of children born in the underclass, and the inequalities in American education and medicine are all notorious. At the beginning of the twenty-first century the richest American corporations were revealed to have engaged in systematic dishonesty to benefit their managers and largest stockholders. None of these facts does honor to our advertised principles.

Whatever else we do, Americans should be circumspect and not expect gratitude. As George F. Kennan has noted, in the relations of peoples the power of example is greater than the power of precept. What we do well will speak for itself, but what we advertise will be turned against us in the form of resentment and charges of hypocrisy. It is better not to speak too loudly of one's own principles. As for gratitude, if we can induce other nations to adopt some of our liberal values, that is all the tribute we should expect. If others accept the best American ways under their own power and forget the taint of foreign origins, then liberalism has a better chance than if we trumpet it as our American contribution to the future. Our greatest power is in our choice of what we display: principle, generosity, and modesty, or opportunism, selfishness, and the pretense to innocence. Our actions teach others what to expect from the future.

II

THE MEMORY OF WOUNDS

—m—

It is possible that there is no other memory than the memory of wounds.

—Czeslaw Milosz, *Nobel Prize lecture*

CHAPTER 5

The Diaspora Soul

—⁘—

In a Gujarati cultural center near Danbury, Connecticut, a few days after an earthquake crushed much of the northwestern Indian district of Kutch, women in saris mix with men in dark slacks and light shirts. Then someone steps to the front of the room, moving lightly on thin, strong legs, a hint of an urban sway in his step. He wears the stylish sports gear typical of young black men. His head is shaven, and he sports twin gold-hoop earrings. Stopped with a question, he will respond, "Yeh, that's phat," "Mm-mm, I sweat her," or "No man, I can't flow with that." It is not an affectation, but dates from years before the suburbs adopted inner-city speech.

When he reaches the front of the room, Vivek Maru begins to speak—in precise English or in Gujarati, as the moment requires—about conditions in Kutch, where his parents were born. Vivek has fresher memories of the region than anyone else in the room. He recently spent a year there, teaching girls in a women's craft collective and helping in a quixotic attempt to shift a planned industrial port away from a mangrove forest that sustains thousands of fishers and farmers. His hosts asked him to stay, and he almost did. But now he is back in New Haven where, among other activities, he teaches middle-school students about what he calls "the legacy of Gandhi and Dr. King." He habitually uses the term "black people" to include himself.

Asked where he comes from, Vivek has to say that it depends on what you mean. Although his family comes from Kutch, he was born in Chicago and grew up in Danbury. There he made the choice—unusual but not unique among first-generation Indian Americans—to identify with the black side of the American color line. He is at home in formal and vernacular English, Gujarati, and Kutchi. He has lost sleep over decrepit schools in southern Connecticut and droughts in western India. A gifted dancer, he knows steps from North America, India, and Africa.

About a year before the earthquake in Kutch, the Brooklyn division of the Kosovo Liberation Army set out for battle. The several hundred volunteers who left the New York area to fight the Serb-dominated Yugoslav Army included a seventeen-year-old high-school girl and men of seventy. KLA commanders in the homeland reported that most of their Americans weren't much help—many had never handled a gun before beginning a month's training in Albania—but they made their neighborhoods proud. Returning veterans were said to have more requests for dates than they could accept. One young soldier accommodated the overload of romantic interest by making back-to-back appointments with prospective girlfriends. KLA fund-raising was openly advertised in the Albanian-language newspaper *Illyria* until Western troops moved in and the KLA ostensibly disbanded. After that, the Kosovar gatherings officially became fund-raisers for humanitarian relief. One of the more popular events was a kickboxing tournament held in Brooklyn.

Fifteen years earlier, when a military insurrection tore apart the Indian state of Punjab, where many people follow the Sikh religion, the rebels who called themselves Khalistanis got much of their financial support from Sikhs living in London and California. Car dealers, real-estate brokers, and shopkeepers sponsored secessionist militias. Most Sikhs in the Punjab wanted an end to the fighting, so that they could return to the farming and manufacturing that have made the state one of India's richest. Long-distance loyalties, though, can override local prudence. For decades, the Boston Irish sustained the Irish Republican Army, whose extremist politics and terrorist methods had alienated almost everyone in Ireland. Early in the 1990s, when war broke out between the former Soviet states of Armenia and Azerbaijan, there were widespread reports that wealthy Armenian Americans were sending not just humanitarian aid, but millions of dollars for weapons in a destructive and senseless war. Very few of these migrant patriots would have welcomed ethnic warfare in their suburban American neighborhoods, but contributing at a distance felt righteous.

Diaspora Lives

Migration is today's great demographic fact. In the United States, more than twenty-eight million people were born elsewhere, the highest number ever and the greatest percentage since the 1920s. Fifty-six million Americans are either immigrants or the children of immigrants. In Europe, countries that have not absorbed substantial immigration since the Germanic peoples displaced the Celts in the later Roman Empire are receiving floods of families from different continents, races, and cultural worlds: Indonesians in Holland and Denmark, Indians in England, Turks in Germany, North Africans in Spain, France, and Italy.

Often migration begins in hope, following globalized desire. To come from India to the United States is to see the homeland of some of your own acquired fantasies, from malls and minivans to Broadway and Mickey Mouse. Global desire calls people to its centers, and they come as people have always come to richer lands and promised lives. There are also migrations of terror and despair. With refugees numbering an estimated fourteen million, the world is more than ever a home to the homeless, who run from civil war, ecological catastrophe, and ethnic cleansing. Bosnia, Kosovo, Ethiopia, and Eritrea are dispersed around the world, as Armenia was nearly a century ago after the Turkish genocide, and as Jews have been since they fled ancient Israel. Peoples with fewer resources are concentrated in the least desirable tracts of their home regions: Afghans in Pakistan, Tibetans in Indian slums, Somalis and Congolese wherever someone will feed them and try to keep them safe. The world is folded in on itself many times over by every motive strong enough to move people from settled lives.

Migration has never meant the absolute surrender of one life for another. Many would-be immigrants to America in the early twentieth century changed their minds in New York and returned to Italy or Ireland or Greece. Others, like American Armenians and Irish, have kept the memory of the homeland alive in the new country. Today migration is more partial than ever. On-line newspapers, chat rooms, and other technologies provide information about the old country and help to sustain a transplanted community in the new place. In the West, particularly the United States, a new cultural openness welcomes traditional languages, food, dress, and religion among people who also learn English and participate in American life. Many migrants maintain several centers of attention, imagination, and loyalty.

People who have never left home also discover loyalty to remote places. Students and other activists working for a new AIDS policy in South Africa, democracy in Burma, or improved labor conditions in El Salvador are motivated by a blend of experience and myth about countries many of them have never visited. Evangelical American Christians who call on the United States to arm Christian rebels in southern Sudan against their Islamic government have decided that the global community of Christ—what Augustine called the City of God—has direct implications for the political communities that form the City of Man. These global, half-imagined communities bespeak a change in how we become who we are. Inherited religious and social attitudes are constantly interrupted. Children move far from their parents' and grandparents' beliefs, sometimes in circles rather than straight lines: many of today's most intense Christian, Islamic, and Jewish believers have revived traditions that their parents neglected or rejected.

For much of history, such changes were hardly imaginable. In traditional Hindu caste society or feudal Europe, for instance, social, economic, and religious life formed a single fabric of identity. One's social position and daily work were the same—serf or untouchable, Brahmin or Catholic priest, ksatriya warrior or martial noble, merchant or banian trader—and changing profession either was impossible or implied a change in status. A merchant in France might buy a title, but he would then cease to be a merchant. A noble who took up selling trinkets became a commoner, at least in theory. Hindu caste distinctions were often even less flexible.

Today emigration, movement from villages to cities, wars and revolutions, and commerce and entertainment have pried apart old connections, setting individuals loose to assemble identities from inherited ideas, new images, intuition, and ingenuity. Although this is less profoundly true, say, in village India than in urban China, let alone Manhattan, the shift is on a tectonic scale. Asked to identify themselves, most people throughout history would have given an answer set for them at birth, as unalterable as a blood type. Now our answers are more akin to ensembles of clothing: restricted by the items in the closet, shaped by the neighborhood and the workplace, but still something we assemble ourselves, from among more alternatives than we could wear all at once.

All of this gives new meaning to an old idea: "diaspora," the name attached to the wandering Jewish nation bound together by the memory of a lost homeland. The word has come to refer to all populations set adrift. One hears of the Indian diaspora, the Persian diaspora, and the Chinese diaspora. Diaspora has never been about a literal home country, because after the founding departure any diaspora is made up of the memories that a people cultivates. That is why Israel, Babylon, and the river Jordan could become the imagined geography of African slaves in the American South, the language of their prayers for deliverance. A diaspora is a community of imagination lifted out of any particular place and connected by phrases, rituals, memories, and hopes. In this sense, diaspora is increasingly an ordinary form of political community, because we are all partly migrants.

Choices of Inheritance

Vivek and the KLA's Brooklyn volunteers exemplify two directions that diaspora communities can take. When an identity, such as "Hindu," spans lives as different as those of a Gujarati peasant and a Los Angeles neurosurgeon, they become less definite but, often and paradoxically, more adamant. A villager whose identity is confirmed by everything in her daily life may be fixed in her caste position, for instance, but at the same time her Hinduism can be flexible precisely because she can do little to change anyone's idea of who she is. This is one reason that, in villages and cities across India, Hindus for centuries have dropped by the shrines of Catholic Christian and Sufi Muslim saints to pay their respects, or have included the Virgin Mary in the corners of their homes devoted to iconography and prayer. Reciprocally, Christian Indians have often continued to offer devotions to the lesser or more local Hindu deities, or have sent friends to propitiate even the great gods Brahma, Shiva, and Vishnu in times of crisis. According to people who have lived in such communities, being Hindu is so natural a fact, so entwined with everyday existence, that a visit to a saint does not threaten it, and even nominal conversion to Christianity does not root it out entirely.

In contrast, a person who asserts her identity against constant uncertainty has something to prove. Because daily life challenges rather than confirms her sense of who she is, identity can take on some of the hardness of armor, or even the edge of a weapon. Hindu nationalism in today's India has no place for Christian or Muslim imagery. Armies of young thugs drawn from the slums of the new Indian cities burn churches and start fights in Muslim neighborhoods, while their ideological guides patiently explain that the country must unite around its common Hindu heritage. To the east, in Indonesia, a strict and sometimes militant form of Islamic practice among the urban middle and lower classes of Java is stripping away the elements of Hindu and animist religion that have been part of the country's village Islam for centuries. Its adherents look west, to Mecca, and think of the Middle East as their spiritual homeland and Arabs as their brothers. In Egypt and Saudi Arabia, the young men who became the terrorists of September 11 or volunteers with Afghanistan's ultrafundamentalist Taliban came mostly from middle-class homes, with enough education and exposure to the larger world to make them wonder, then decide, what they would believe and be. The impulse expresses itself in new forms of nationalism and passionate but sometimes ignorant diaspora ties. These new identities always carry the possibility of violence, the struggle to purify an imagined homeland half a world away or in the Muslim quarter of a slum in Bombay or Ahmedabad.

These adamant doctrines of identity are one response to the vertigo of freedom, the uncertainty that comes when traditions that have been unquestioned become optional, then impossible, in the course of a few generations. The competing impulse is the one Vivek exemplifies: accepting more than one identity, having more than one kind of experience running through an ordinary day. This attitude has a bit in common with the stance of traditional villagers to Hinduism: it requires having enough comfort in one's divided individuality to visit more than one shrine or speak more than one intimate language. The difference is that one attitude comes before modernity's great disruption of tradition, and the other comes afterward and assembles something partly new.

Identity is a back-and-forth between wholeness—which no one achieves, since we are mixed creatures from the beginning—and openness, which can never be complete, because we would dissolve into it. Out of balance, the need to know who we are can become destructive. Today the movement of people and images across the globe has made new imbalances.

CHAPTER 6

Blood Memory

—⧖—

"Islam is founded on rejection, injury, and resentment. It is founded on the rejection of Ishmael and his mother by Abraham. Rejection has poisoned them.

"I always say that Judaism had two bastard children. Christianity is mercy without justice, and Islam is justice without mercy. India is under attack by these two Abrahamic daughters. No one can deny this."

My companion for bottles of watery Kingfisher beer at the Bombay Press Club is Ashok Row Kavi. He is perhaps the country's most prominent advocate for gay rights and AIDS treatment, an outspoken journalist and a regular at international conferences on AIDS and sexuality. During our conversation, his mobile phone rings several times with calls from his "children," the many young men he counsels as they struggle with their sexual orientation.

He is also an impassioned Hindu chauvinist. His colorful garb, the scarf around his thickening neck, and his locutions—"my dear," "that ignorant little bitch"—suggest the intercontinental gay man he is, but his nationalism has an unmistakable penumbra of local violence. "Hinduism needs to cleanse itself. It needs a whip. The Muslims got their country, Pakistan, in 1947, and we got ours. If the Muslims make trouble for us now, that is their problem." When the departing British split the subcontinent into India and Pakistan, the riots and ethnic cleansing that followed left perhaps a million people dead and many millions more displaced. The long-established Muslims of Delhi fled northwest to Pakistan, and the Sikhs of the Pakistani Punjab ran southeast to Delhi. The violence was India's birth trauma.

"India threw off British imperialism, but what about Muslim imperialism? They, too, conquered us. When the Muslims first invaded northern India, a Hindu king rode out to meet them in battle. Six times he drove them back, but he declined to destroy them. He said, 'There is enough here for all of us.' The seventh time, they defeated him, beheaded him, and used that king's head as a pot to piss in. The Muslims say they are so refined, and in some ways they *are* refined; but you can know them by the way they conduct war."

He orders another bottle. "This Afghanistan thing is bringing out the truth about the Muslims. The Muslim mind has split apart. On the one side, they say they are a religion of love, a religion of peace. On the other side is all this violence. Go tell Hamas that Islam is a religion of peace! Don't tell me, I know. I have already been told."

The Press Club has the shabby tweediness of a profession that belongs to gentlemen and the educated sons of the lower middle class. There are no women here. The bar is an enclosed verandah, and every half hour or so some liberal journalist crosses the scuffed, stained floor to greet his nationalist colleague. Ashok shakes their hands, then shudders theatrically as they turn their backs. "Hey," he shouts at one, "now is the time. It is me or the Taliban. You will have to choose!" The thought plainly delights him.

Besides the six victories that preceded the Hindu king's defeat, Ashok's story is mostly about Indian weakness. It is from that weakness, he wants me to understand, that the country needs to renew itself. "The British royal family requested their papers from the Indian archives some years back, and the government refused. A few months later, the papers disappeared. I went to a government official and said, 'Look, I'm not going to report anything, just tell me what happened.' He said, 'They offered me five lakhs'"—five hundred thousand rupees, more then twelve thousand dollars. "With five lakhs he will buy a house. Why should he care? This country is corrupt and filthy, and the papers would have rotted anyway.

"It is always like that. No fort in India has ever been taken by force. India always falls by bribery or deceit."

This is the refrain of the Hindu right: India is soft, passive, defeated ever and again because it takes no pride in itself, gives its Hindu people no sense of belonging to a great civilization. It is apologetic rather than assertive, quiescent instead of defiant. "It is," in Ashok's words, "the country of filth and piss, of killing fetuses, of shitting in the street." This sense of national abjection spurs Ashok's call for Hindu revival.

This disdainful idea of Indian character began not with the nationalists, but with the country's English rulers in the eighteenth and nineteenth centuries. Many British imperialists were not bloody-minded white supremacists, but high-minded liberals such as the reformer James Mill and his son, the philosopher John Stuart Mill. Both worked for the East India Company, and the senior Mill devoted a large share of his mature intellectual life to completing his massive *History of British India*. Here are a few of his judgments on the people of the subcontinent:

> No people, how rude and ignorant soever, who have been so far advanced as to leave us memorials of their thoughts in writing, have ever drawn a more gross and disgusting picture of the universe than what is presented in the writings of the Hindus. In the conception of it no coherence, wisdom, or beauty ever appears: all is disorder, caprice, passion, contest, portents, prodigies, violence, and deformity.

. . .

In point of manners and character, the manliness and courage of our ancestors, compared with the slavish and dastardly spirit of the Hindus, place them in an elevated rank. But they were inferior to that effeminate people in gentleness, and the winning arts of address. Our ancestors, however, though rough, were sincere; but, under the glosing exterior of the Hindu, lies a general disposition to deceit and perfidy.

. . .

There was, in the manners of the Mahomedan conquerors of India, an activity, a manliness, an independence, which rendered it less easy for despotism to sink, among them, to that disgusting state of weak and profligate barbarism, which is the natural condition of government among such a passive people as the Hindus.

There, in outline, is much of Ashok's story. Hindus are passive, unprincipled, deceitful, easy to bully and to buy, and "effeminate." In Mill's eyes, this made Indians—whose homeland he never visited—inferior to both his own European ancestors and India's Muslim conquerors from Central Asia. The superior peoples were known by their "manliness," Indians by the softness that would keep them degenerate until a stronger people elevated them to robust civilization. The Mills, father and son, believed the British mission in India was to impart the manly liberty that a modern nation required—a process certain to take time, during which India would unavoidably remain under British rule.

The Hindu nationalists have adopted the British diagnosis and the British cure, in the name of anti-imperialism. They see one long history of subjugation in centuries of Muslim invasions from Arab lands and Central Asia, and some two hundred years of British rule rising to Queen Victoria's coronation as

Empress of India in 1878. The nationalists present Hindu pride as a necessary part of decolonizing not just India's government, but her mind and spirit. Yet they learn their self-contempt from the conquerors they despise, and their solution is the conquerors' own: become a nation as hard as the one that broke you.

Ashok continues: "When I was young, in our family shrine we had images of the Hindu gods, of course. We also had pictures of the Muslim Sufi saints, and of the Virgin Mary. As far as my mother was concerned, they were all divine. But then, after Pakistan split apart from India with all the bloodshed of Partition, she took out the pictures of the Sufi saints. Then, when the Christians marched through our neighborhood singing 'Onward Christian Soldiers,' she said, 'What is this if not communalism?' "—the Indian term for chauvinist religious politics. "She took out the Virgin Mary. Since then, all the images are Hindu.

"Now a Christian church meets in the apartment below where my mother and I live. When they start to sing, she puts on the stereo and blasts Hindu prayers. She wants to call the RSS"—a street-fighting Hindu nationalist group that might break up the church meeting—"but I say, no, that is too much. Violence is too much. But I tell you, in our building we are all becoming Hindu. We are Bengalis, Punjabis, some of us are Jain, but that is all dissolving into being Hindu."

Is the violence that he will not invite at home necessary to the Hindu renewal he wants for the nation? "I am fifty-four. Who am I to say what will be necessary? A great civilization has been humiliated."

The change Ashok describes is one of the stories of modern India. Although it is not an immigrant society, having traditionally had little room for individual mobility and self-invention, India has always had a genius for absorbing other peoples and traditions without ceasing to be itself. Many Persian Zoroastrians fled to northern India when Muslims conquered what is today Iran; they still live in Bombay and elsewhere in northern India, where they have strong traditions of commerce and civic involvement. Some of the great city's skyscrapers have been specially designed to avoid overlooking the towers where the Parsis (as they are called, meaning Persians) give their dead "sky-burial," waiting for the elements and birds to consume them. The Jewish populations of Bombay and Cochin are ancient beyond memory—some say they arrived after a shipwreck as many as two thousand years ago, others that they are among the lost tribes who slipped out of history after the Assyrians conquered northern Israel in the eighth century B.C.E. The Christians of Kerala and Tamil Nadu claimed to have been converted by the apostle Thomas, and even historians are satisfied that they were practicing before 600 C.E., maintaining relations with the patriarchate of Baghdad. When Portuguese Catholics arrived in southern India in the early sixteenth century, they found Christians whose churches were often indistinguishable from Hindu temples, practicing elements of Hindu devotion in their rituals, and observing caste distinctions to the point where Brahmin Christians occupied different churches from lower-caste believers. The newcomers were incorporated into the caste system, and fragments of their rituals and iconography entered broader practice, while Hinduism—Indianness not as a nation but as a civilization—remained the backdrop of social and religious life. Hinduism had no unifying doctrine, no proselytizing edge, no single hierarchy of spiritual authority. Even the term "Hinduism" was introduced by British writers around 1830 to designate the religious traditions that had sprung up in the Indus Valley about two thousand years earlier. It encompassed a common body of myth describing the doings of a pantheon of gods over many ages of the world; a high tradition of metaphysical speculation about the nature of reality and the destiny of the soul; and devotion to minor gods who might be variations on the heroes of the common myths or purely local figures. Hinduism also meant, in practice, the whole set of social relations that stitched together the peoples and regions of the subcontinent, of which the most complicated was caste: the largely hereditary assignment of occupation, status in religious rituals, social duty and deference, and even ideas of pollution that prohibited a Brahmin from touching a member of the lowest, literally "untouchable" castes. If they had been asked to identify themselves, inhabitants of the subcontinent in the early nineteenth century might have mentioned their families, their caste status, their language, any devotional cult (oriented to a particular god) they followed, and perhaps—depending on their neighbors—that they were not Muslim or Christian. It is extremely unlikely that anyone would have answered, "I am an Indian Hindu."

This plurality, along with a penchant for losing battles to conquering armies, helped to inspire James Mill's portrayal of Hindus as a passive people sunk in disorder and lassitude. In response to that picture, a movement emerged in the nineteenth century to unify and purify Hindu doctrine. In Bengal, a northeastern state where traditions of learning and the arts were particularly strong, two families that would produce a pair of Nobel Prize winners in the twentieth century—the Tagores and the Sens, whose Rabindranath and Amartya received the prize in literature and economics, respectively—became intellectual leaders in an effort to replace traditional "idolatry" with universal religious precepts, such as the existence of God and the duties of ethical behavior. Some of the movement's thinkers acknowledged that Christianity was their inspiration, and welcomed the British as liberators who had saved India from both Muslim dominion and its own primitive habits. Keshub Chunder Sen called for a new church, "thoroughly national" and "essentially Indian." It would combine the Hindu philosophical tradition's refined idea of the divine, the energy and aggressiveness of the Muslims, and Christianity's concepts of love and brotherhood, along with its status as the religion of the world's most powerful nations.

By the end of the nineteenth century, a new form of religious and cultural revival had arisen. It was less apologetic about Hindu custom and owed less debt to Christianity than the earlier, syncretic efforts. It had much in common with European nationalism's cultivation of solidarity around language, common belief, and folk practices. The great figure in this new event was Swami Vivekananda, a high-born disciple of the holy man Ramakrishna. Vivekananda preached robust, self-confident Hinduism as the basis of a revived national identity. Idolatry, he said in defense of ordinary believers, was not degradation; one just had to understand that idols were imperfect representations of a single divine spirit, and that simple worshippers required palpable images to envision God. Vivekananda aimed not to replace Hindu practice with Christian doctrine, but to give Hinduism the proselytizing edge of the revealed religions. Hinduism should be the adhesive and catalyst of a nation that could hold its own among the peoples of the world. "We must," Vivekanada told an audience in Madras, "conquer the world through our spirituality and philosophy. There is no other alternative, we must do it or die. The only condition of national life, of awakened and vigorous national life, is the conquest of the world by Indian thought."

He taught that India was trapped in a diminished and apologetic form of its own traditions. Instead of asserting their Hindu identity, educated Indians slavishly followed the fashions of the West, condemning idolatry, caste, child marriage, and other customs that offended Victorian British sensibilities. Vivekananda harked back to an imagined history of greatness that was the opposite of James Mill's picture of Indian disorder and indecency: India's past displayed "unsurpassed valor, superhuman genius, and supreme spirituality, which are the envy of the gods—these inspire [India] with future hopes."

With this image of the past and confidence for the future, the Hindu should "proclaim: 'I am an Indian, every Indian is my brother . . . O Thou Mother of the Universe, vouchsafe manliness unto me! O Thou mother of strength, take away my weakness, take away my my unmanliness, and—*Make me a Man!*' "

Important as the soul's agonies are to political life, one cannot reduce politics to psychology. Hindu nationalists are at the center of Indian politics for more reasons than the rhetoric of manhood and the frisson of historical resentment. In recent decades, growing literacy and voting rates among poor and low-caste voters have produced a wave of parties based on regional languages and caste groups. Their influence has helped to produce a massive affirmative action policy that makes public-sector jobs and university seats inaccessible for many otherwise qualified members of the upper castes. These changes have put upper-caste Hindus and the new middle class on the defensive. Many supporters of the nationalists hope that a strong, common Indian identity can keep the country from collapsing into regional fragmentation or a caste-based spoils system. Not surprisingly, Hindu nationalists have often exaggerated these dangers to make themselves seem indispensable. This dance of conviction and self-interest is to be expected in a young democracy.

But nationalist politics is also about identity, and there is no getting the soul out of it. Ashok shifts in his wicker chair and puts on a rueful expression. "There is an old expression in Sanskrit that any deviance is simply the essence of what exists. How did we forget that, and fall into these desert religions, with this little Jewish queen on the cross?" His manner is still animated, but it is a thin mask over sadness. The Hindu revival that he supports does not embrace deviance, and it has learned some of its intolerance from the traditions of desert monotheism: it cultivates a unity strong enough to break enemies. Nationalism compresses Bengalis, Punjabis, and Jains into a composite Hinduism in order to cast out impurity. The banner of Hinduism today belongs to people who want not deviance but unity to be the essence of what exists, even at the cost of violence.

Blood Reckonings

Hundreds of miles to the north, in the largely Muslim streets of Old Delhi, the Jamia Mosque sits in a crowded, chaotic district choked by smoke and thronged with pedestrians and three-wheeled auto-rickshaws. It is also a neighborhood of butchers and slaughterhouses, enterprises left to Muslims because most Hindus consider them unclean. The Jamia Mosque is the largest in Delhi, which was the capital of the Islamic Moghul Empire that preceded British rule in much of India.

Hindu nationalists like to say that when the Jamia Mosque's imam, or religious head, visited Mecca, he was greeted as "a great Hindu leader." The story seems improbable, but it captures an idea that pleases them: that Indian Muslims are in essence low-status Hindus who have adopted foreign rituals to try to escape their social position. Perhaps it is this pair of worries—being too Muslim for much of India, yet not quite Islamic enough for some fellow Muslims—that the imam is attempting to tap. He is trying to set himself up as the political leader of Indian Muslims by creating a party that will be a counterpoint to Hindu nationalists—and, not incidentally, make him extremely powerful. He already exudes an air of power here in the inner offices of his enormous mosque. He has a thick, strong build and a crushing handshake. He wears a heavy beard and dark glasses over blunt features. He speaks as he moves, slowly, in a deliberate way that gives the impression of strength held in reserve. Sometimes he nearly growls. His occasional smiles are broad but strictly controlled; they do not open up his face.

Some of India's Muslims, especially educated ones, have long considered themselves part of an international Islamic community. In India's independence struggle, Mohandas Gandhi had to negotiate with Muslim allies who were as concerned about the fall of the Ottoman caliph—notionally the leader of Sunni Muslims everywhere—as with events in Westminster. Today Indian Muslims take their civil cases to *sharia* courts that parallel the ordinary court system, and their continuing distinctness has made them targets of the Hindu right. In the imam's story, India is a country with "two majorities," Hindus and Muslims, but the political elite has consistently failed to protect Muslims: riots still take Muslim lives, the affirmative-action system favors low-caste Hindus, and court cases have gone forward challenging the authority of *sharia* law over Indian Muslim women. Muslims have waited long enough to be handed an equal place in India: the time has come to demand it. "I tell them," he says, "do not be the one who is defeated. Be the one who is able to inflict defeat."

He also believes that a global battle of civilizations is afoot, driven by the Christian West's disregard for Muslim lives. The so-called war on terror is an exercise in hypocrisy. The United States is itself a terrorist nation: its wars in Vietnam, Cambodia, and especially Iraq; its long domination of Iran; and its support of Israel—a state founded and maintained by terror against Palestinians—make it unfit to judge or police others. Moreover, Americans have never spoken against the non-Muslim sources of terror in India: the Christian and animist Nagas who fight for independence in their remote northeastern state, the Sikhs who killed prime minister Indira Gandhi in the course of a civil war in the Punjab, or the Hindu and Buddhist Sri Lankans whose civil war spilled over into the assassination of Indira's son, Prime Minister Rajiv Gandhi. "This proves that the real purpose of the campaign is not capturing Osama bin Laden. It is animosity against Muslims, and imperial designs on the Muslim world.

"I have no sorrow for what happened on September 11, because of all the Muslim blood that has been shed in the past fifty years and is being shed in Afghanistan today. When no sorrow is expressed for us, we will express none. Sorrow comes from the heart, and not just from the tongue. I am not one of those who say one thing in the drawing room, and another in public. The expedient sorrow of the Muslim leaders is just to protect their kingdoms and their self-interest."

Candor is a demagogue's great weapon. Some of what the imam says is undeniable: the rulers of the Muslim nations are self-serving and hypocritical in playing off their American allies against the fundamentalists among their own people. No one in the Bush administration will be sorry if our military presence in Central Asia increases American power. America does have a history of violence abroad, some of it wretched. All of this is too inconvenient for the leaders making decisions in the global anti-terror campaign to admit, but others recognize it nonetheless. Having pointed out the unacknowledged facts that blemish the public compromise of the moment, the imam can then speak for unacknowledged emotions as well: the resentment and anger that the official political culture disowns. As a truth-teller, he authorizes himself to speak the language of vengeance and blood, the concealed passions that can seem to be the truest.

"I can tell that the heart of Bush is poisoned with hate for Islam. When you look at his face, you see a barbaric personality. To people such as him, the blood of Muslims is no better than water. We are saying, The blood of all the people in the world is the same: it is blood."

A Muslim party, he tells me, would seek "a life of honor." What does he mean by that phrase?

"I will give you a brief account. In the name of religion, our blood was shed in this country. We were cut to pieces and thrown into the river. Our houses were set on fire, and our girls were placed on mirrors and ordered to dance.

"Our honor was destroyed. Our places of worship were destroyed. Our children were thrown into the air and impaled on swords as they fell. Women were raped in front of their parents. Brothers were forced to rape their sisters. This is a brief account of what has been done to us.

"No civilized nation can allow such repression, such repression of the religious freedom guaranteed by the constitution. It is time for Muslims to stop begging."

Despite its larger tradition of tolerance, India has seen much religious violence. Partition and periodic clashes between Hindus and Muslims since then are only the most recent and visible. The imam's selective picture draws attention to the most outrageous moments of anti-Muslim violence. The Muslims who conquered northern India visited many abuses on the local Hindu majority during their centuries of rule, including massacres. After President Indira Gandhi was assassinated by her Sikh bodyguards in 1984—in revenge for her suppression of the Sikh rebellion in the Punjab—Hindus stormed Sikh homes in Delhi and killed more than a thousand people. Today many Hindus dislike the Muslim minority: they consider Muslims unclean for slaughtering animals and eating meat, and they fret over the high fertility rate of India's Muslims.

In the spring of 2002 more than six hundred Muslims died in religious riots in the western state of Gujarat—the strongest confirmation of the imam's version of modern Indian history since anti-Muslim riots in Bombay at the beginning of the 1990s killed thousands. The violence began when Muslims attacked a train full of Hindu nationalists returning from a pilgrimage to Ayodhya, a flashpoint town where in 1992 Hindu nationalists destroyed a mosque that had been built in the sixteenth century by the Muslim ruler Babur. The nationalists claimed the mosque stood over the birthplace of Ram, a Hindu god, and so represented Hindu India's subjugation beneath Muslim conquest. Observers reported that the 2002 riots had political motives. Nationalist activists were said to have stirred up the riots, then protected the Hindu rioters, to sharpen

Hindu hatred of Muslims and promote the nationalist Bharatiya Janata Party, which had recently lost several state elections.

Liberal Muslims around India abhor the imam. When I last visited late in 2001, a typical week brought an opinion piece in at least one national newspaper denouncing his extremism. His critics point out that he has been unable to deliver votes to the political candidates he favors, even in the district surrounding his mosque. They also report that he has the sponsorship of Hindu nationalist politicians, who hope he will succeed in drawing Muslim support away from the traditionally more secular Congress Party, which Muslims have historically viewed as their protector. They usually neglect to mention that his vivid picture of Muslim suffering has drawn tens of thousands to his rallies.

Rank-and-file nationalists and fundamentalists are fired by the passions of injury and resentment. In places such as the imam's inner chamber, those passions take a shape, learn a language, and acquire a program. Every pause and growl is measured and premeditated. The imam, like the most effective nationalist politicians, is a calculating man. But he makes his calculations in blood and the memory of blood.

The Necessary Danger

Faced with nationalism upon nationalism, humiliations revisited in search of pride, it is tempting to see nationalism as a perversion. We Westerners hear enough about Serb nationalists, who slaughtered and deported Bosnian and Kosovar Muslims through most of the 1990s; Chinese nationalists, the wild-eyed students who stormed and almost overran the American embassy in Beijing in 1999; Russian and German nationalists, throwbacks to the fascist and totalitarian traditions in those countries; and the "tribalism" that moved Rwandan Hutus to murder more than half a million Rwandan Tutsis in 1994. There is an inevitable impulse to exile nationalism to the wasteland of history's recurring evils and watch diligently against its return.

The difficulty is that, to live freely under a common government, people need some idea of a shared fate, a bond at the level of who they are and what they hope or refuse to become. There must be some way that an injury to one can be taken as an injury to all. Without that emotional tie, political institutions and laws cannot do enough to keep a people together.

That may not have been true under kings and emperors, when political power depended less on the sentiments of ordinary people. National feeling was less important when most people inherited their religious, social, and economic roles and fit like puzzle pieces not into the life of a nation-state, but into the lives of their respective communities—and when governments did little but extract taxes and fight wars. Today, though, governments are susceptible to popular opinion, hybrid and migrant people must determine who they are, and there must be some common terms for arguing about education, the building of dams and roads, and what the wealthy owe to the poor. We do not know another way of gathering disparate human energies in a world of democracy, migration, and complex government.

Yet national feeling is as volatile as it is necessary. The political life of India is just one reminder that both lack and excess of national spirit can be dangerous. The Hindu nationalists have too much national feeling, much of it the wrong sort. At the same time, a lack of principled patriotism saps Indian public life—reinforcing the nationalists' complaints. The country suffers from corruption at all levels of government. Political office is often treated as a private fiefdom. Elections become fights over the fruits of power among parties representing various castes and language groups. All of this is compounded by sheer variety in a country with twelve major languages (one recent prime minister acquired a pained and halting version of Hindi, the nearest approximation to a national language, only after his election); a persistent caste system (ministers from low castes have been known to kneel and touch the feet of high-caste officials during public ceremonies); and a democracy that has only gradually penetrated social life since 1948, when universal adult suffrage arose amid a feudal social order. The constructive side of the nationalists' argument, the part that is not about effeminacy, manliness, and historical injury, is that patriotic spirit is the only way to overcome such political dysfunction.

Nationalism's dangers accompany the unavoidable modern task of defining political communities. Nationalism is potentially violent because it tends to direct anger and vengeance against those who are outside the community. It is also intrinsically violent, because it suppresses the variety of the human world, turning people with complex histories and identities into Indian Hindus on the one hand and, on the other, Muslims identified with the history of the Arabs. The achievement of nationalism is to create a shared memory, a common sense of purpose, and the belief in a linked fate, so that a person can declare "I am an Indian." These achievements are also its crimes.

Ways of Being Who We Are

Because national identity is a condition of modern life, the question is not whether to have it but how to cultivate it. Like capitalism it is a feature of modern liberty that is also a source of modern violence. What kind of national sentiment runs more to liberty than to violence? There will be almost as many answers as there are countries to provide them. The best version of American identity, for instance, is the principled patriotism whose loyalty is to constitutional government and personal freedom, and which tends to accept and even honor radicals and dissenters while holding on to a national center.

This patriotism is the opposite of what we Americans usually mean by nationalism: a violent attachment to one's own people not because they are principled or good, but because they are one's own. The best American patriotism has more to do with letters on parchment than with blood. The blood it involves is what Abraham Lincoln once invoked as the basis of patriotic feeling, the blood of revolutionary ancestors. That blood marks not whose ancestors those revolutionaries literally were, but what principles they fought for, and it is honored by loyalty to principle.

In India, the hard-edged nationalists who speak of Hindu cleansing represent one form of shared feeling. There is also another, more fluid attitude among some of the subcontinent's young people. They are at once more Westernized than their elders and, in their own minds, every bit as Indian. For them being Indian is as much about being flexible as about becoming hard.

On a train between Madras and Bangalore, I sit next to Ganpat Amarnath, a slim, earnest young man—still almost a boy—wearing spectacles. He is on his way to a technology conference. He is a programmer with HCL Technologies, an Indian company that, he tells me, has sixteen thousand employees worldwide, ten thousand of them in India. How is the work? "Many people do it just for money, and that is not good. I love it. I would be doing it for free. But my dream is to go the U.S. and work for Microsoft."

Why Microsoft? "Because it is number one. Whatever they produce, it is always number one. It is the operating system on 95 percent of computers in the world." When I suggest that it is a kind of universal language, he agrees and seems pleased by the observation.

What did he make of the World Trade Center attacks? "My friend has a cousin who works on the second floor of Tower One. He could not get through on the phone, so we were all watching television. We were very worried.

"Now we worry that the jobs will not be there. Already there is the slowdown. A year ago, everyone wanted to go to the States for work. Now they are all getting second master's degrees, waiting for the economy to improve." He wants to know, Are people in the States worried about job cutbacks?

When I ask what he thinks about politics, he is confused for a minute. "There is no politics in IT. There is lots of politics in other industries, but in IT if you are no good you must get out." When I explain that I meant electoral politics, he goes blank, then tells me that he and his friends are not very interested.

On the surface, he is perfectly integrated into the outpost of the global economy that has emerged in southern India's software industry. In one sense he was as close to the World Trade Center attack as I was: like him, I knew no one in the buildings, but plenty of my friends did. His fears about an economic downturn are a world away from the conspiracy theories I heard in Egypt, but in line with many Americans' concerns after September 11. Microsoft's corporate campus is the capital city of his provincial aspirations.

But the topics he raises, other than asking whether I know anyone at Microsoft, have a different tone. Do I know about the sage Vivekananda? I do, and mention his importance in the development of Hindu nationalism. Vivekananda was also a kind of pan-Hindu proselyte to the United States, eager to show that his tradition could join in a contest of equals with the religions of the book. He founded several American centers of Hindu practice that still exist.

That is not Ganpat's interest, though. He wants to tell me about Vivekananda's capacity for knowledge. "He read all thirty-two volumes of the *Encyclopaedia Britannica*. He read them without sleeping or pausing for food and water." Now he wants to know, have I heard of Srinivasa Ramanujan? Yes, he was the mathematical prodigy from an Indian village who was discovered doing the most difficult problems of calculus in his head, and who ended up at Cambridge. "He used to stay up for two days, working on a problem. Two days, on a single problem!" Ganpat is pleased again when I suggest that he probably does the same thing for his programming assignments. "Well, yes, for the final couple of days," he admits.

Hinduism has taken many forms to meet many needs. Now it is a source of inspiration for young code writers. The match is less novel than it might seem. The Brahmin tradition of metaphysics, the old attention to mathematics and astronomy (the concept of the zero is said to have been invented in India), and the austerities of an ascetic tradition all echo in the life of a young programmer who, like everyone, wants to feel himself connected with greater and deeper facts than his own life. Is it betrayal or continuity? He is hungry to see continuity, and this is where he has found it.

Now I am in Spencer Plaza, Madras' ambitious new mall. Its three stories stand on the site of an older Spencer's, the department store of choice for Madras' imperial governors and their successors in the Indian elite. India has few malls, and Madras appears to be leading the country with a handful of shiny, midsized emporia. Spencer Plaza has yet to fill all its store space. When I come in one rainy morning, the atrium has allowed six inches of water to leak into the main entrance, and low-caste cleaning women are using dustpans to shovel the water into plastic buckets. Off the main aisles where the fashion brands cluster, the salesmen of fabrics, clothing, and crafts have not yet learned that mall etiquette does not permit aggressively soliciting pedestrians. And most of the strollers are here just to look: the growing Indian middle class has learned to appreciate the display style of American retailing, but not many people will regularly pay the markup on a Spencer Plaza product over the same item in a backstreet shop.

Nonetheless, on a dry evening the mall gives the impression of success. Boys and girls in little clusters eye each other or talk quietly among themselves. Young men in Western clothing strut in pairs or groups of three, while parents guide their small children with hands on their shoulders. I strike up a conversation with a group of three boys and two girls, all in their late teens. The boys are wearing jeans, slacks, and T-shirts, and one has a thin gold chain around his neck. Both girls wear traditional clothing: the shorter, darker one a simple flowered dress, the tall, fair, and striking one a sari the color of lilacs. The tall girl, Divya, is a student in Madras and is showing around the other four, who are at university in Bangalore. They are all studying variations on computer science.

What do they do when they come to the mall? What are their favorite places? The boys jump in with "Brand stores," and when I ask which ones, they begin a list: "Lee for jeans; Jockey for undergarments" (this to laughter at the daring response). But Divya, who is turning out to be their guide in more than the geographic sense, steps in: "It isn't really about brands. Ten years ago, maybe, everyone wanted brands, and especially American brands. Then, if a shampoo made your hair fall out, but it was American, people would buy it. Now I think we know what we are looking for. Look at what I am wearing: it is all Indian sewn, none of it is American." She lifts her arms and turns a bit to show off her sari. Divya's pronouncement goes unchallenged, even by the boy in the K-Swiss T-shirt.

And what do they think about American culture? Is the mall an American sort of place? One boy tries an answer: "I guess America is global culture, basically," but Divya will not take that. She smiles demurely before she begins: "What India is about today is taking the best from all the cultures of the world, but not those things that do not fit with our way of life. We are very open-minded people."

What sort of thing would they reject, then? What would not fit with Indian culture? That stops them. There are several seconds of silence before one boy offers, "Hurting people?"

After a few more seconds, another boy suggests, "Maybe pollution." Divya, who has been thinking about it, announces, "Social distinctions." The shorter girl, consolidating a few responses, offers a version of Indian values: "Respecting people, basically: mentally, physically, all sorts of ways. And parents come first in that."

Parents. This is the first answer to connect with Indian reality. India is terribly polluted, marked with the world's most refined social distinctions, and as fraught with small acts of cruelty as any mainly peaceful place. The students' version of Indian values are the MTV platitudes of global liberalism. It is true, though, that the ties of respect and obligation between Indian children and their parents remain profound. Children have more freedom than in past generations, though, particularly in the middle classes—freedom to date, to leave home for schooling, to select a spouse. Do these young people feel they are more independent than their parents were? Two boys say yes, definitely, but Divya senses a dangerous question: "It is relative to our options. We have many more options than they had, so it seems we are more independent. But maybe it really is the same." In this picture, change does not mean disruption. Continuity, after all, is a matter of perception as much as fact.

What do they think about American culture? This one is clearly hazardous, so the others hang back and give Divya the first answer. "A lot of hype," she answers. "You brand everything and sell it to the rest of the world; but you are just another country." Once she has set the boundaries, others can express a bit more admiration for America: "You do the smart work. You brand, and let other people do the hard work of making the product." "Someday," Divya adds with a laugh, "India will do the smart work."

In one of India's premier malls, these kids are getting a lesson in consumer consciousness. The hip Western consumer sees through brands and advertising and maintains a wry self-awareness. That is why commercials have adopted an ironic tone about the whole business of selling products. Because everyone is meant to be a player, not just a passive recipient in the brand game, brands exist as much to be scorned as to be desired, and even those who desire them are expected to display a little diffidence. Among her friends Divya is the authority on appropriate behavior in malls—which is to say, appropriate behavior across the landscape of advertising and consumption that the Indian middle class is exploring.

Although putting it this way risks triviality, America is the world's ultimate brand, an image that stands for powerful aspirations: prosperity, independence, personal liberty. But America the consumer culture has taught these students to treat America the brand with a dignified distance: "too much hype," "just another country." This distance, in turn, helps them to feel Indian rather than American, while behaving in a way that strikes an outsider as exceptionally American.

An Indian visitor to the United States might see as many traces of her civilization here as an American encounters upon visiting India. Landing at Logan Airport in Boston or JFK in New York, she could soon find Hindu temples in the suburbs of Boston or the Jackson Heights neighborhood of Queens. Indian food would be everywhere, and the Pakistani cab driver might be listening to the Hindi pop music that accompanies Bombay films. Boutiques would offer bindis, the dots that Indian women place on their foreheads, and variations on saris and kurta pajamas. Every few miles would bring a sign advertising yoga classes, or even ayurvedic medicine, part of the massive arrival of Eastern traditions into the American pursuit of spiritual and physical health. Here and there a poster would advertise an appearance by a Hindu holy man, and in a public square a Hare Krishna devotee might appear, offering flowers and a devotional portrait of Lord Krishna. As surely as McDonald's, Madonna, the entrepreneurial spirit, and Christianity, Indian cuisine, entertainment, and religious life seem to have permeated the world.

The difference is that none of this—not even Indian medicine and spirituality—promises to transform American life in disruptive or alarming ways. Most Americans expect to absorb new influences while remaining, in their own minds, altogether American. In the nineteenth century we had séances, "mind cures" for disease, and our local version of vegetarianism; today we have yogic diets and imported meditation practices. The trends of both periods are equally American: faddish, experimental, hopeful, likely to flourish if they work and disappear if they do not. They do not stand for basic changes in social life, family order, and economic opportunity—as Americanizing changes in India do. Cultural change does not make Americans feel less American, because it slips easily into a way of life that is already plural and fluid.

The question for India is whether Americanizing changes will make the country's people feel less Indian. Some nationalists hope so, because they stand to benefit politically from resentment and xenophobia. In contrast to that attitude, the middle-class children in Spencer Plaza have adopted what might be called an American way of being Indian: accepting constant change as a part of their identity. In a country with a great syncretic tradition, where deviance was once called the essence of all that exists, this is not a foreign concept, even if its present version comes tinged with foreign colors. It is, however, antithetical to the spirit that the Hindu chauvinists offer, where change requires a firm, unyielding Indian response.

From one point of view, the attitude of the Spencer Plaza students is pernicious nonsense because it obscures India's terrible problems under global fantasy. Perhaps it is also salutary nonsense. In the wonderland of the mall, the children of traditional families play at being global adolescents, cultivating the beginning of loyalty to liberal values—a squishy liberalism, but squishiness sometimes just means a substance is not yet fully formed. Moreover, their partial delusions help young people to see the changes that the mall represents—the influx of global culture, changes in Indian family and social life, the renewed question of whether India can become a successful, modern nation—as additions to their Indian identity, not incursions on it.

There is an old philosopher's conundrum about the problem of identity. Suppose that sailors begin repairing an old boat while at sea, and that by the end of their repairs they have replaced every board, one by one, without ever docking. When they reach land at last, is the boat the same one that began the journey? There is no right answer to the question, but uncertainty is hopeful. Perhaps people who are not sure of the answer will be less inclined to set fire to a boat they suspect is not theirs.

I am still thinking this when I walk out of the mall into the blinding beam of the floodlight that comes on at dark, illuminating the façade of the building. The beggar children chase this Western blind man across the plaza and two blocks into the darkness of the Indian streets, where I can see again.

CHAPTER 7

Birds of Prey and Passage

—⁓—

It is early afternoon when Osama bin Laden comes up.

I am wrapping up a conversation with three members of Telapak, a group of Indonesians in their twenties whose lives remind me of the Hardy Boys. From a suburban house in Bogor, a leafy city about forty miles outside Jakarta, they have made themselves the country's foremost environmental investigation team. They spend about half the year stalking the loggers, fishermen, and miners whose illegal harvests are stripping Indonesia of its ecological wealth. To document the clandestine logging that is rampant in public forests, they camp for weeks in those same forests, posing as birdwatchers and ordinary hikers. When they need to trace smuggled logs to the laundering operations of the Malaysian ports where Indonesian wood is stamped with false documents and sent on to the rest of the world, they hit the bars of harbor cities, asking anyone who will talk to them about the price and terms of timber. The next morning they will be on the docks, watching as logs are loaded and unloaded, feigning interest in buying or selling.

The results of these investigations go into ably drafted reports, which Telapak's Indonesian staffers prepare and distribute with help from a private British group, the Environmental Investigation Agency. Sometimes the intrepid investigators end up in prisons run by corrupt local officials, until allies elsewhere in the Indonesian bureaucracy can place a phone call demanding their release. They relish these adventures, at least in retrospect.

A sense of delight in Telapak's work pervades the crowded office where I meet two squat young men, one solid and the other pudgy, and a woman whose strong features are as formidable as the men's are disarming. They are in jeans and T-shirts that hang or bulge without much design, while she is composed in stylish dirt-faded jeans and a black top. I have the undivided attention of the two men, while she taps at a laptop, smokes Pall Malls, and interjects occasional comments without lifting her face from her screen. They are all playful with me. They are thinking of moving Telapak's headquarters to Manhattan, they joke. Will I take them out drinking and dancing when they arrive? I should know that they are party lovers. "Party animals," she corrects them, glancing up this time.

And one more thing: I must be careful leaving Bogor. It is a hotbed of support for Islamic terrorism. They are full of merriment now. Why, right here in Telapak is "our friend and colleague, a great supporter of Osama bin Laden." When I ask to meet him, one of the men goes to the open window fronting on the office's front lawn and hollers, "Yayat!"

Yayat is the fourth member of Telapak's team that focuses on illegal logging in Java. The others did not call him in earlier because he is the youngest of them, and his English is less precise than theirs. He is good-looking, with clean features, the physique of a strong teenager, and close-cropped hair from which black curls are trying to emerge. He is wearing dark jeans and a gray T-shirt with the North Face logo on the breast. His manner, like his colleagues', is sweet and upbeat.

"I support Osama," he tells me. "He is a very independent man, very rich." He pauses a minute: "Very confident." "Confidence" is a word that comes up repeatedly among young men here when trying to explain their attraction to Osama. "Passion" is another. When did he become an admirer of bin Laden? "It was after eleven September that I became aware that he was important. Before that I had heard of him, but as part of the mujahideen," the Muslim guerrillas who fought the Soviet occupation of Afghanistan, then split into tribal and doctrinal factions and fell on each other. Osama first tasted holy war when he began funding—and occasionally fighting alongside—mujahideen in the 1980s. "I had followed them for several years," says Yayat. How did he discover the mujahideen? Since university he has been a member of the Justice Party, a growing political movement that advocates putting Indonesia under Islamic *sharia* law. "I get information from my friends there." Of his three best friends from the party, two are Indonesian Islamicists. The other is Afghan, here in Indonesia to work with the local Islamicists. They are journalists, and right now all three are along Afghanistan's Pakistani border.

He also follows the Palestinian Intifada. Does he feel connected to the Palestinians, Arabs half a world away from his archipelago, where Hindu and animist legacies still show through Muslim practices? "Of course I feel connected with Palestine. All Muslims are my brothers. There are fourteen million Muslims in America, and they are my brothers, as well." (The actual number is well under ten million, many of them Black Muslims whose practice is not generally recognized as Islamic.)

The other men are enjoying the exchange, while the young woman looks up once and announces sharply, "No comment." Do they argue about politics on their expeditions? I ask. "We argue about women, about love," replies Yayat, restraining a giggle. The pudgier of the two men hoots: "Only you! Only he has a love problem—that he loves women!" Yayat looks shy, but also pleased to have his amorousness acknowledged.

Now the spirit is festive. "You must be careful. We know your hotel. We know your room number. We will have a sweeping!" "Sweeping" is the term for the action that local Islamicists threatened after September 11: commandeering guest lists from hotels and ordering Americans and other Westerners to leave the country or face violence. Very little came of it, but the term remains lodged in the popular imagination.

The young man with the solid build decides to put things in order. "This is the diversity of Telapak," he announces with a grin. "We are religious and not religious. We are Muslim, Christian, and animist. And we are for Osama. It's cool. No problem!" Yayat, perhaps also suspecting that things have gone a bit far, moves to reassure me: "I am anti-American, but also anti-violence. Don't worry."

Now I am leaving, and they say, "When we come to America, you will have to join our team. You will be in West Virginia, country roads?" The John Denver song comes up everywhere in the world—but, no, I will be in New York if they come next year. Yayat lets the grin that moves across his face stay a little too long, so that it becomes pensive. "New York. Lovely city."

Until recently, most of Indonesia has been a hybrid civilization, fashioned from the overlay of almost a thousand years of Islam and roughly five hundred of Christian influence on a Hindu-animist past. It was never ruled by any of the great Islamic empires, but was converted peacefully over many years. The Hindu subsoil has never gone away. The national epics, rendered in puppeteers' shadow shows throughout this region of Southeast Asia, are variations on the same Hindu stories that are told in India. Historically, Indonesia's Muslims have been more relaxed in their observances than the Muslims of the Middle East. The advent of a strict form of Islam oriented to the Arab world dates to the arrival of Arab trading communities on the coast of Java some five centuries ago. Rigorous Islam did not become widespread, however, until the rise of urban merchants and middle classes in the past hundred and fifty years. Urban Muslims abandoned village customs and adopted a sterner and more cosmopolitan Islam. At the same time, new steamships made pilgrimage to Mecca possible for people who previously would never have left Indonesia. Those who completed the pilgrimage returned to found religious schools, whose doctrines were shaped by the stern theology of the Arabian Peninsula.

Islamicist political fraternity with Arabs half a world away adds another step to this journey away from the village and the home country, to a cosmopolitan shadowland of long-distance loyalties. Indonesians cannot be as they have been and also declare that the Palestinians are their brothers. If they take that declaration seriously, they will become something larger and stranger, a nation with an adopted history that makes them more powerful in their own eyes, more frightening in the view of the West.

Less than two weeks after I left Jakarta, Ramadan ended with the traditional parades, feasts, and fireworks. Some of the young men riding trucks and jeeps through the pyrotechnically lighted streets held aloft posters of Osama bin Laden, confident that no one would make them regret their show of confidence.

The City of God

Islamicism is not the only international contender for Indonesia's soul. If you want to find an American expert on the battles between Muslims and Christians in the Indonesian regions of Aceh and the Moluccas, you might want to begin with a few evangelical Christians based in places such as Oklahoma and central Virginia. The Christian solidarity movement, which gained prominence several years ago, has turned the political energies of American evangelicals toward the idea of a global Christian community. Christian solidarity activists publicize abuses against their brethren in Sudan, China, Burma, India, Saudi Arabia, and elsewhere, and carry humanitarian relief to places where the United Nations will not go. They work to redirect American foreign policy in defense of Christian communities everywhere. They divide the world into brethren, the unconverted, and the oppressors.

Their emissaries to the world's trouble spots are Bible-carrying doctors, ministers, and former Green Berets who are rumored to have picked up automatic rifles when in trouble along the Thai-Burmese border. A representative of one group as much as admitted to me that contributions have funded Christian militias in war-infested regions of Indonesia. Like Muslim militants, many in the movement found vindication (along with horror) in the events of September 11. Steven Snyder, of the evangelical activist group International Christian Concern, issued an open letter a few days later: "America is witnessing what Christians in other parts of the world have been enduring for some time. We are at war with an unseen enemy that has demonstrated its resolve to launch a 'jihad' (holy war) on Americans, Christians, and Jews—and will show no mercy for innocent lives. We have turned a new page not only in American history but in the history of the world."

Christian solidarity came into national view in 1998, when pressure from religious conservatives made the International Religious Freedom Act a legislative juggernaut. The new law created a United States ambassador-at-large for religious freedom and required the State Department to issue a detailed annual report on the status of religious liberties around the world. It also directed the president to take one of fifteen specified diplomatic actions against any country named as a severe violator of religious rights, ranging from a public rebuke to trade sanctions. The bill was a top legislative priority for the still-potent Christian Coalition and the National Association of Evangelicals. Congregations heard—and told Congress—about ministers jailed and churches bulldozed in China, Christians enslaved in southern Sudan, Christian tribes slaughtered in Burma, and Christians hounded in Iran and Iraq. Sympathetic observers estimated that in 1997, sixty thousand American congregations participated in the International Day of Prayer for the Persecuted Church, part of the campaign for the legislation, and that a hundred thousand joined in the next year. Millions of prayers also meant voluminous mailbags at the doors of congressional offices. A few Christian solidarity organizations had been working on these issues for decades. Oklahoma's Voices of the Martyrs, California's Open Doors, and Virginia's Christian Freedom International saw their membership grow threefold or more as the International Religious Freedom Act advanced. On the Internet they have become clearinghouses for tales and images of persecuted Christians worldwide.

The present campaign began in 1995 and 1996, when an unlikely pair of activists began meeting with the leaders of evangelical political groups, urging them to make the rights of Christians abroad a priority. Nina Shea of Freedom House, a highly respected organization that documents political oppression around the world, pronounced contemporary Christianity the most persecuted faith the world had ever known. Michael Horowitz, a lawyer at the conservative Hudson Institute, who had been general counsel of President Reagan's Office of Management and Budget, joined her and wrote a manifesto on religious persecution, "A Call to Conscience," which was published by the National Association of Evangelicals. Conservative religious leaders were moved—and knew they had found an issue with resonance. As if to confirm the intuition, A. M. Rosenthal of the *New York Times*, who had long advocated a hard line toward China, pleaded the case of Chinese Christians to elite readers while the Christian groups put out the word to evangelical congregations. It was the first time since the anti-apartheid movement of the 1980s that a popular mobilization for human rights had arisen in the United States.

Christian involvement in American foreign policy is a long tradition. The sanctuary movement of the 1980s, which flourished mainly in liberal Protestant congregations, served as a kind of Underground Railroad for Central Americans fleeing civil war in their home countries. Chaplain William Sloane Coffin of Yale was a prominent critic of the Vietnam War who marched with student demonstrators and whose partisanship lastingly angered the young George Walker Bush. A generation earlier, Reinhold Niebuhr at Harvard presented a Christian case for participation in World War II. All human works were fallible, he preached from the pulpit of Memorial Church, and the search for a final political system in either communism or fascism was an act of hubris sure to produce tyranny and suffering.

The Christian solidarity movement is different because it is populist. Its leaders do not teach or minister to students at Harvard and Yale. Its populism is continuous with the domestic politics of the religious right, which has always insisted that American liberalism is morally exhausted and uprooted from the country's sustaining values. The strategy that comes with this perception is to find an issue where official, liberal values are at odds with the sentiments of the American majority and to keep it unrelentingly in the public eye. School prayer, flag burning, and the posting of the Ten Commandments have been such issues, chosen with keen perception of the fault lines of public life. The government's refusal of special solicitude to Christians abroad promised to be another.

Christianity has always contained the seeds of diaspora sensibility. By Saint Augustine's definition, Christians are citizens of the City of God who dwell in exile in the City of Man, maintaining their loyalty to one realm while passing their lives in another. Like every other diaspora, they are linked by blood ties that exist more in the imagination than in reality. Their bond, though, is a remembrance of blood sacrifice rather than a myth of common descent. Members of the Christian solidarity movement like to cite Galatians 6:10, in which Paul exhorts his correspondents to serve all humanity well, but to give special service to those who share in the body of Christ.

Christian activists feel the same romance of authenticity as traditional diaspora groups. They are inclined to see the moral core of the faith expressed in the trials of remote populations. "The closer a person comes to suffering," says a leader of the solidarity movement about the tormented Christian population of southern Sudan, "the closer they come to Christ. The closer they come to what our lord and savior went through." This theme recurs in much of the literature of Christian solidarity. It coexists uneasily with the more conventional humanitarian impulse to relieve the suffering of fellow believers. The feeling that the distant struggle expresses the heart of the community is an old tendency of diasporas, and its Christian version is as romantic in its way as the Sikh, Armenian, or Boston Irish taste for faraway warfare.

Diaspora solidarity bolsters confidence that one can understand a situation half a world away. Moral clarity can produce the illusion of clarity in all things. American Armenians, British Sikhs, and other diaspora groups have done a great deal of harm in their homelands by supporting violence whose origins and effects they only dimly understand. They lent their support generously and confidently because they were, after all, the same people as their distant compatriots, guided by the same loyalties and aspirations. Ulster, Azerbaijan, and the Punjab are only a few of the places that have bled in consequence. What looks to a Christian activist like a matter of straightforward religious repression is often a complex and unfamiliar ethnic, political, and economic disaster.

One country that has suffered from such mistaken goodwill is Sudan. A cartographic legacy of colonialism, Sudan is divided between Islamic Arabs in the north and black Christians and animists in the south, with considerable overlap between the regions. A southern army of independence has spent the past decade battling a northern army that uses extremely brutal tactics. In the course of the fighting some northern soldiers began taking southern prisoners and offering them as slaves in the north. The practice of slavery had never entirely ended in this region, and now it thrived anew. In the middle of the 1990s, when the Sudanese slave trade came to international attention, estimates of the number of slaves in the country ranged from three thousand to fifteen thousand.

At that time relief workers from the Christian solidarity movement were in the most devastated areas of the south, carrying food and providing medical care. They were horrified by the discovery of slavery and, with vastly more wealth than the locals, decided do something about it. They began buying back, or "redeeming," slaves from traders and returning them to their families. Slave redemption became a popular cause among evangelical congregations in the United States. It seemed morally clear, and it united congregations around a common purpose. One elementary school classroom raised $50,000, enough at the time to redeem fifty slaves—although redemption rates have ranged enormously, from more than $1,000 to a recently advertised fixed price of $35. A Harvard undergraduate went to Sudan just before fall classes began; upon his return journalists reported sunnily that he had "taken a little time off to help free six thousand slaves."

Today Christian Solidarity International, the only major organization that persists in organizing redemptions, reports that over fifty thousand slaves have been redeemed—including twenty thousand in 2000—but that as many as a hundred thousand people remain enslaved. The estimated number of slaves in the mid-1990s, remember, was no greater than fifteen thousand. Disaffected slave-redeemers who remain active in the Christian solidarity movement believe that many of the recent redemptions are fraudulent—that people are rounded up on cue as Westerners approach, then released once the money is in hand. Anecdotes suggest that this is often true, but there is also a grimmer possibility: that Christian solidarity redemptions have swollen a real and violent market for human beings by providing enough demand to soak up a growing supply. It is also probable that the redemption program has helped corrupt the southern leaders whom the Christian solidarity activists consider their brethren. One leader of the movement, who arranged redemptions as recently as 1999 but now denounces the practice, expresses confidence that southern Sudanese leaders share in the slavers' profits and use the money for villas in Nairobi and tuition at private schools— Christians selling Christian slaves to Christians in the name of Christian solidarity.

Another difficulty is the interweaving of Christian solidarity and fundamentalist evangelism. When asked about their organizations, movement leaders are quick to assert that they do not proselytize. That is true, strictly speaking: they do not sponsor American or European evangelists abroad. The disclaimer, though, does not capture the whole story. The same evangelical Protestant churches that support Christian human-rights groups also back the aggressive evangelical ministry that has rushed into developing countries in the past twenty years, converting tens of millions in Africa, India, Latin America, and East Asia. Christian Solidarity International urges its supporters to "pray for the freedom to preach the gospel," and another solidarity group suggests "praying for many Saudis to have significant encounters with Christ." Local converts do most of the proselytizing, but they get substantial funds from fellow believers in the West. Many of the abuses that Christian activists denounce in countries such as India are not expressions of simple anti-Christian sentiment, but retaliation against conversion campaigns. Its defense of proselytizers has put the Christian solidarity movement on the front line of global evangelism.

In India, radical Hindu nationalist groups such as the Bajrang Dal, which is connected with the Bharatiya Janata Party, have reportedly trained fifty thousand young men in crude combat techniques to fight both Muslims and missionaries. The Bajrang Dal describes evangelism as an imperialist technique to destroy Indian (by which they mean Hindu) culture. Many Bajrang Dal members regard as heroes the mob that in 2000 burned a car in which a longtime American medical missionary and his son were trapped. Although mainstream Indians view the Bajrang Dal much as Americans do anti-government militia members, many do not welcome evangelists. People close to the U. S. Commission on International Religious Freedom say that its investigators regularly hear complaints about Protestant evangelists from foreign political and religious leaders, including the heads of established local Christian churches. The Indian press, while typically hostile to the Bajrang Dal, is also critical of evangelists, especially those who practice "mass conversions" at revival meetings and win professions of faith from poor people who sometimes rely on them for food and medical care. Christian television broadcasts in southern India specialize in faith healing and promises of good luck in exchange for donations. Even evangelists fear that some converts do not understand the religion they profess to have adopted.

The evangelists could hardly avoid giving offense, since their premise is that non-believers are lost souls. Some of them refer to India and much of Asia and Africa as the "lost world," or the "unreached peoples." One evangelical group laments that Indians "bow down to more than 330 million gods . . . that can offer nothing to the more than 400 million homeless people, lepers, and tribals." The same group warns that "constant washing, polishing, and offering of sacrifice to idols in effect saps the potential of the world's largest democracy," and announces that "India must shed her heathen attitude." None of this makes violence against Christians—which in India has included rapes of nuns and the burning of churches by Hindu nationalists—any less execrable. It does mean, though, that American Christians who condemn Hindu nationalists may only stir Indian resentment. They might better address themselves to the chauvinists among their fellow American Christians.

Aggressive evangelists have spurred nationalist reactions elsewhere, too. In Russia after the fall of communism, the Orthodox Church won legislation confirming its special place in national life as a direct response to an influx of evangelical missionaries. Robert Seiple, a prominent liberal evangelical and President Clinton's ambassador-at-large for religious freedom, has said that missionaries tried "to do the Evangelical equivalent of the Oklahoma land rush, charging in with Conestoga wagons full of Bibles," and he blames them for the Orthodox response.

Evangelism is an American tradition. Early in the nineteenth century, American Protestant churches sent missionaries with a quarter of a million tracts to seek converts among the Orthodox Christians and Muslims of the Balkans. Not long after the Civil War, Southern black churches began dispatching their own missionaries abroad, exporting the religion of a country that had just ended their slavery. This spirit of universalism has been intertwined with American political universalism from the City on a Hill to the Axis of Evil. The Christian solidarity movement shares in some American virtues: courage, conviction, and magnanimity. It also has American vices: parochialism, moral arrogance, and a streak of romanticism. Its success is a reminder that the politics of diaspora is not restricted to the developing world or non-Christian peoples. It runs everywhere because it appeals to the taste for righteousness and gives a license to act on fantasies about remote places, with no need to answer for or even understand the consequences.

Birds of Prey and Passage

Denouncing Britain's imperial rule over India in the House of Commons, Edmund Burke called his countrymen the most monstrous invaders the subcontinent had ever known. The Persians, Arabs, and Central Asians who overran parts of India came to stay, and their lives became interwoven with the place. As Burke put it, they were "very soon abated of their ferocity, because they made the conquered territory their own. They rose or fell with the rise or fall of the territory they lived in. Fathers there deposited the hopes of their posterity; and children there beheld the monuments of their fathers." No matter how brutally conquerors arrive in a land, once it becomes theirs, they also belong to it. Belonging works against the impulse to despoil the place. The British, because they would not bind themselves to India, arrived in what Burke called "wave after wave of birds of prey and passage," rapacious and transient. Whoever governs a place without settling there is the most likely to destroy it.

Ideas are the same way. The more remote beliefs are from the life of a people, the more likely they are to do harm. They can break apart delicate patterns of tolerance and accommodation and open up new opportunities for violence. This is true of the Islamicist internationalism that has entered Indonesia and India, the pan-Hindu nationalism that consolidates India's many traditions into a single Hindu Indianness, or the imaginative solidarity of America's more extreme Christian internationalists. Such ideas were at work when Hindu nationalists destroyed the mosque at Ayodhya to reclaim the mythic birthplace of Ram for Hindu India. The imam of Delhi's Jamia Mosque is drawing on such ideas by linking Indian Muslim politics to a pan-Islamic movement, and treating India's history of sporadic religious violence as a part of a worldwide story of anti-Muslim bigotry.

Remote loyalties often compensate for the ordinariness of life at home. The faraway conflict or global struggle becomes a tableau of perfect right and wrong, injury and revenge, a place to be a hero in one's own mind. The Muslim immigrant to the United States, the evangelical Christian in a secular office, the Armenian or the Irishman in Boston leads a daily life of compromises, small frustrations, and the constant reminder of not being perfectly at home. The Indian Muslim or the Egyptian Protestant feels the same, and so may the Indian Hindu or the Egyptian Muslim when he catches sight of the Christian family next door. Distant battles and dramatic histories promise a purer life, cleaner line between ally and enemy, all the clarity that everyday life withholds. Civil war in the Punjab and the Sudanese slave trade are the price of loyalty that has outgrown the scale of life as actually lived. Such loyalties are inevitable in a time of diaspora nationalism.

CHAPTER 8

The Memory of Wounds

—ɯ—

Some of the new, globe-spanning communities are defined by religion, language, or national origin. Even in diaspora, these resemble traditional nations, only scattered. Other communities have different bases. Sexuality and even disease, for instance, can cut across race, wealth, and culture to link people over great distances. AIDS has done this, forming a political community that intersects with older politics of memory and loyalty.

AIDS has always been political. When it arrived in America in the 1980s, it deepened a conflict between liberals and cultural conservatives and helped spur a revolution in attitudes toward sexuality. Ten years later, it became a raw nerve in globalization politics. The disease is an emblem of how much people everywhere have in common: every human body can follow the same pleasures to infection and surrender to the same invisible virus. AIDS also highlights the world's divisions. The infected man in Manhattan, equipped with drugs, a solid income, and private medical care can correct the weakness of his body—for decades, anyway. The South African shantytown woman with no medicine, no money, and no trained doctor has to wait for her body to fail.

AIDS is the first epidemic to attack wealthy societies since the triumphs of twentieth-century medicine. When HIV infections first appeared in the United States, progress against disease had begun to seem ineluctable. Old killers were now historical terms: polio, smallpox, measles, tuberculosis. AIDS reversed the balance between humanity and disease for the first time in decades. Unsurprisingly, many began looking for someone to blame. Some, especially on the Christian right, took AIDS as a rebuke to sexual license and homosexuality. Secular Americans thought they had conquered death and made sex a plaything, and God was punishing them by joining sex and death in a terrible way. There was talk of a plague sent against the homosexuals. President Ronald Reagan remained silent as the death toll rose, convincing some that he favored the idea of divine retribution. Funding for medical research on AIDS arrived with painful slowness.

The response came when ACT UP, the AIDS Coalition to Unleash Power, attacked indifference and hostility to people with AIDS. ACT UP began in New York, and its campaign was full of urban sophistication. The tone was outraged and terrified, but also cool, insistent, and aesthetically adept. ACT UP's propaganda was mass-produced and austere, and its message was stark. SILENCE = DEATH read the white lettering on a black field. Above the letters floated the pink triangle, used by the Nazis to label homosexuals.

Artists and activists worked to exhaustion to get the word out, and soon unaffiliated guerrillas were throwing up the same slogans wherever they lived. In the last years of the 1980s, SILENCE = DEATH was ubiquitous in New York: plastered on a wall, stenciled on the sidewalk, or (breaking with the strict aesthetic code) scrawled on the windows of subway cars in permanent marker. Other posters were less bleak: an Andy Warhol–style rendition of President Reagan's impish face, smiling indifferently; a towering image of a penis accompanying a call for education and condom use. They were arresting reminders that people were dying.

The spectacle of ACT UP drew attention to the underlying message of the campaign: in the words of a 1988 poster,

ALL PEOPLE WITH AIDS ARE INNOCENT. That was a direct response to the idea that AIDS was the wages of sin against divine law or the natural order. There was no sin here, the protesters insisted, just illness. The only appropriate endeavor was to direct money, research, and sympathy toward AIDS and people sick with it.

The liberal mainstream embraced that view of AIDS, and it won. Ryan White, the young hemophiliac and AIDS victim whose life and death became a television movie, was one milestone in the victory march. Another was *Philadelphia*, the 1993 movie that won Tom Hanks an Academy Award for his portrayal of a gay lawyer dying of AIDS. Red ribbons, expressing sympathy and a call for increased research funding, became ubiquitous. Carpers complained that *Philadelphia* bowdlerized gay life to avoid offending middle-American viewers, but that was just the point. America didn't need to think about promiscuity, anonymous hookups, or sadomasochism. It only had to know that people with AIDS—gay people no less than others—were innocent. That AIDS is just another disease with innocent victims became a premise of public conversation.

In the middle of the 1990s, medical researchers developed a combination of several drugs that suppressed the symptoms of AIDS in many patients. People who had seemed months from death came back to health, and stayed alive. This small revolution changed the politics of AIDS. ACT UP and other activist groups were already beset by the usual splits over tactics and personalities, and now they went into a fade. Many people who had entered AIDS politics because it seemed a life-or-death struggle welcomed the chance to return to their former lives, now extended by the new treatments. And, some critics said, the tenor of gay life changed. AIDS had produced a solidarity of suffering, whose touchstone was the dying body. Now gay men revived their fixation on fitness and beauty. Advertisements for AIDS medicine featured amateur athletes and mountain climbers with the slogan "I'm positive"—upbeat, and infected with HIV. Those who responded poorly to the drugs or were debilitated by side effects reported feeling that they were dying alone and ignored.

It was the story of any political movement for recognition and acceptance. A small core sees itself as fighting against inequality in general, and if it wins one battle it sets out in search of the next. But for most participants, victory means arriving at the promised land of a comfortable American life, where they settle down to tend their private attachments. To the activist core, settling down looks like a betrayal of the fight. They seek new places to take the battle.

While America seemed to have fought AIDS to a draw, the disease was devastating Africa. At the turn of the millennium, conservative estimates had twenty-five million people infected with HIV in sub-Saharan Africa, up to 30 percent of adults in some countries. The disease was infecting at least a million people every year. This was a plague, and because HIV takes five to seven years or more to turn into AIDS, Africa was only beginning to feel its full effect. Soon as many as half the healthy adults in countries that were already struggling would be struck down. AIDS promised not only an epidemic, but also an economic crisis as workers, teachers, doctors, and everyone else fell ill. Economists predicted that South Africa's economy would soon begin contracting as the death toll rose.

Medical advances meant that people with AIDS could live, but Africa might as well have been caught in 1986, when AIDS was incurable. The drugs belonged to the large pharmaceutical companies, such as Merck, Bristol-Myers Squibb, and Pfizer. The companies' advertisements presented them as great service organizations, bringing better lives to everyone. Were they also responsible for the deaths of tens of millions of Africans who could not afford treatment? Activists thought so, and believed they could convince enough others to make the pharmaceutical industry uncomfortable.

Patents give the company that develops a new drug exclusive rights to manufacture and sell it for twenty years. The theory behind patents is that this monopoly encourages companies to invest in useful research. Developing drugs is hugely expensive, and no private company would invest tens or hundreds of millions of dollars if it didn't expect to earn even more from its new product. If other companies could immediately copy the drug and sell their own version, there would be no advantage in having invested the money to invent it.

In the past, patents and other forms of intellectual property—control over words, images, and ideas—have had inconsistent protection beyond national borders. Taiwanese and Japanese manufacturers reverse-engineered American electronics to make knockoff stereos and televisions in the 1960s and 1970s. Today you can buy pirated copies of American movies, music CDs, and software in Bangkok or Manila for a small fraction of their original cost. But in the late 1990s, the World Trade Organization brokered an international agreement to enforce intellectual property rights worldwide. In principle, a company that invents and patents a new technology in the United States can now control it not just here but nearly everywhere. Music and software were already long gone; although corporations and American diplomats are trying to crack down on the so-called pirates in those industries, it is difficult to put a cage around information that can be stored on any CD. Drugs, though, are not pure information. They must be manufactured somewhere and carried from place to place. The pharmaceutical companies were determined not to let them get away.

In 1997 South Africa passed a law allowing the ministry of health to revoke patent protection and permit inexpensive, copycat drugs when "the health of the public" was at stake. The pharmaceutical industry, which had opposed the law, urged the Clinton administration to press South Africa for repeal. A group of forty-two drug companies also filed suit in

South African court, claiming the law was unconstitutional because it gave broad and vague powers to the minister of health. Drug company representatives warned that the South African initiative represented the thin edge of a wedge designed to break apart intellectual property rights.

That was not quite an honest portrayal of the issue. World Trade Organization rules allow countries to lift patent protections through a mechanism called "compulsory licensing." A government can let local companies manufacture a product that someone else has patented, so long as they pay the patent holder a royalty and do not make a profit themselves. For many years Canada created local versions of foreign-patented drugs through compulsory licensing, while paying modest royalties to the mostly American patent holders. Germany and Japan, among others, have used compulsory licensing for decades. South Africa itself had a law that allowed compulsory licensing, but with generous provisions for legal challenge that were expected to tie up any initiative for years. There was nothing novel about the idea.

Still, the new South African law was vague, and drug companies imagined a runaway ministry undermining intellectual property rights. The ministry would have had ample temptation to do so, because AIDS drugs were prohibitively expensive for South Africa. The number of HIV-infected South Africans was then about five million. The annual cost of the full AIDS treatment regimen in the United States stood at $10,000. The average annual income in South Africa is $3,170, and many of its AIDS victims are much poorer than that.

The law was a test case on the future of intellectual property rights in countries that are now poor but, in a few decades, may become lucrative pharmaceutical markets. Brazil's government was already outraging drug companies by supporting a large and successful domestic industry in generic medicines, many of them patented elsewhere. When South Africa suggested that it might do the same, it threatened to lead the developing world toward disregard for the patent rights of companies from rich countries.

Back in the United States, all of this caught the attention of Alan Berkman, a deliberate and soft-spoken doctor who, with his wife, treats poor people and AIDS victims in the South Bronx. His references to a history of "anti-racist and what I would call anti-imperialist activities" indicate the legacy of 1960s activism, but he has the steady realist manner of many doctors—especially those who deal with the poor and the dying. In the spring of 1998, he was in South Africa with the Columbia University Mailman School of Public Health, advising the government on the country's mental-health system. There he saw incarcerated patients with AIDS, and doctors and nurses who were just beginning to succumb to the disease. Having been in New York in the worst days of its AIDS crisis, he knew what South Africa's rate of HIV infection would soon mean for the country. "It seemed to me," he says, "that no one there understood the gravity of what was coming."

There was hardly a sign of the new American medicines in South Africa. Those medicines were on abundant display, though, at the International AIDS Conference, which Berkman attended later that year in Geneva. The tone in the Swiss mountains was celebratory, even triumphant. The new drugs meant long-term survival for patients who could afford them, and the drug companies were spending the profits with self-promotional generosity. Company yachts took doctors out on Lake Geneva, and celebrities performed at their hotels. The nominal theme of that year's conference was "Bridging the Gap" between rich and poor countries, but, Berkman recalls, "I saw no one come forward to do that."

When he returned to New York, he drafted a letter to the leaders of the remaining AIDS activist groups. He proposed a transnational campaign focused on getting AIDS drugs to the thirty million or so people worldwide who couldn't afford them. The facts were stark: there were ways to keep people from dying of AIDS, but people were dying nonetheless, and would die in much greater numbers in the next decade. There was a perfect villain: pharmaceutical companies who seemed to value their profits over the lives of sick people. Populist campaigns often fail in the business-friendly United States, but in 1999 there was already complaint about drug companies' generous profit margins and the effect of medicine prices on elderly Americans. Moreover, the drug companies weren't making any money in Africa; the profits they might fight to protect were purely speculative. Berkman argued that a campaign against the drug companies might convince them to change their policies and release AIDS drugs to South Africans and other poor people.

About thirty-five activists met in January 1999, including representatives of ACT UP from New York, Philadelphia, and Paris. They named their coalition Health GAP, for Global Access Project, in a wry echo of the unbridged gap that had troubled Berkman in Geneva. They began to study global trade rules and intellectual property law. Then, in February, they got their hands on a memo sent from the State Department to a New Jersey congressman. The memo reassured the representative that the Clinton administration was doing everything in its power to support the interests of several New Jersey–based pharmaceutical companies by preventing South Africa from producing generic AIDS drugs. It was the stuff of which conspiracy theories are made—but there it was in black and white.

The memo provided the hook that the activists needed to revive ACT UP tactics. Soon Al Gore, presidential candidate and second-in-command of the offending administration, was a target. Protesters disrupted campaign speeches and fund-raisers in New Hampshire and Tennessee and blocked the entrance to Gore's official residence in Washington. Meanwhile, other members of the coalition met with the United States Trade Representative's office to explain exactly what was troubling those colorful people in the street. Media coverage followed, and ordinary Americans began to perceive that there was a problem about AIDS drugs and South Africa.

In numerical terms, the Health GAP effort never amounted to much. At one point, four hundred protesters marched in front of the White House. Four hundred people makes a mid-size high-school class. Symbolically, though, the campaign was brilliant. AIDS yoked together the first and third worlds within the same moral community. The fact that between three and five million poor children die every year of diarrhea which can be prevented with an oral rehydration formula that costs eight cents per dose has not inspired a movement to rebuke the United States government and American companies. Neither has the failure of rich governments and countries to fund research into malaria, which kills between two and three million every year. (There is great commitment to these issues in leading humanitarian organizations.) When European drug companies began manufacturing a cure for the always-fatal African sleeping sickness—only after the same drug proved effective in preventing the growth of facial hair in women—American newspapers reported the development as a macabre irony. These were all diseases of poverty, far from the American imagination.

But AIDS had been a banner in a cultural war. Caring about it was a mark of being a decent person, and indifference was a sign of brutishness. This, at any rate, was the view of opinion makers, not least the elites of policy and journalism. AIDS was a reminder of the unity of humanity and the universality of human suffering. Poor, distant countries had it in common with us. Once Americans were reminded of AIDS abroad, it was harder to put out of our minds than the other ways that poor people die.

South Africa, too, had a hold on the American moral imagination. The anti-apartheid campaign of the 1980s was the largest American mobilization for human rights abroad ever. At its high point it was a festival of righteousness. Senators, mayors, and celebrities went gaily to be arrested by friendly police officers in front of the South African embassy in Washington, D.C. Under pressure from students, universities pulled their investments out of countries that operated in South Africa, and many prominent companies withdrew their operations from the country. Eventually Congress overrode a veto by President Reagan and prohibited American corporations from doing business in South Africa. When the racist white government surrendered control and national elections brought Nelson Mandela to power, millions of Americans felt as if they had shared in his victory.

South Africa's appeal to Americans came, like the appeal of the AIDS campaign, from its seeming familiarity. The battle over our own version of apartheid in the 1950s and 1960s defined a generation's political experience. By the middle of the 1980s, racial equality was an unassailable American ideal, although hardly a reality. South Africa provided a crystal-clear case of right and wrong, and a chance to be on the side of both history and justice. It had special attraction for white Americans who felt they had missed the battles of the civil-rights era or who wanted to revive the moral spirit of that time, and for American blacks who thought of the South African majority as brethren. It may also have provided some compensation for those who felt uncomfortable with the compromise and retrenchment that followed the heroic civil-rights era in this country.

Nelson Mandela, who was still in power when the AIDS controversy began, belongs alongside Czech president Václav Havel and former Polish president and Nobel Peace Prize winner Lech Walesa in the generation of long-suffering dissidents who around 1990 brought down tyrannical governments in a wave of democratic liberation. Mandela spent years in

South African prisons, and emerged with wit and grace intact. When he spoke out against the drug companies, he exercised the considerable moral weight that he will carry until he dies.

And so, although Health GAP was never quite a movement, it became an event. The *Wall Street Journal* and the *New York Times* ran frequent front-page stories on the cost of AIDS drugs in Africa and the pharmaceutical companies' reluctance to make them available cheaply. The companies began to respond. In August 1999, Bristol-Myers Squibb announced that it would donate $100 million over five years to help South Africa and a handful of neighboring countries develop strategies to fight AIDS—a decision probably unrelated to the Health GAP campaign but made in awareness of spreading discontent. Almost a year later, in May 2000, five American drug companies announced that they would begin offering steep discounts on AIDS drugs in several African countries. The moves were expected to bring the cost of the drugs to 10 or 15 percent of their American levels.

That was the first in a wave of price cuts. The next year Merck and Bristol-Myers Squibb, two of the five companies that had announced the earlier discounts, offered to lower the price of AIDS drugs to the cost of production or less. A week later Abbot Labs said it would offer its drugs at the cost of production. A month after that, Merck and Bristol-Myers Squibb pulled out of the companies' lawsuit against the South African government. Within two days, the rest of the companies abandoned the suit. Both sides declared victory. The companies said they were reassured that South Africa would maintain conventional patent policies in the future, and activists claimed "a dramatic shift in the balance of power between developing countries and drug companies."

In the United States, the widespread impression was that the problem had been solved. According to newspapers and television, there had been two problems: high prices and the suit that kept the South African government from doing something about them. These fit the classic American picture of an abuse: an aberration in a broader pattern in which everything is more or less okay. Someone is doing something wrong, and once the wrongdoer is stopped, things will right themselves.

Things have failed to right themselves. From the beginning of the debate over AIDS drugs, American conservatives had been pressing a pair of pessimistic arguments in the business press. First, they said, the real problem in southern Africa was not that drugs were expensive, but that the cost of distributing them was prohibitive in a region with poor governments, bad roads, and few doctors. Sixty percent of South Africans were "poor," which in Africa means very poor indeed. Forty percent were officially unemployed, and the actual number was higher. Fifteen percent were illiterate. Millions lived in makeshift, unsanitary squatters' camps, without even clean water. Even if two billion free doses of AIDS medication were deposited in Johannesburg—enough to treat every HIV-positive person for a year and then some—that would only be the beginning of a solution. At the cost of production, which to Americans sounded like a giveaway, just purchasing the drugs would cost more than South Africa spends on its annual defense budget. South Africa is the superpower of the region. It is wealthier than its neighbors, and relatively democratic. The numbers in almost any other country would be more disheartening.

Moreover, the conservatives said, most of the governments of southern Africa didn't care to do anything meaningful about AIDS. Although Uganda had cut its rate of HIV infection from 30 percent in 1986 to under 15 percent in 1999 with a campaign of prevention and education, other governments had not made similar efforts. When the United Nations convened a major conference on African AIDS in Zambia in 1999 and invited fifteen African heads of state, none came. Part of the reason South Africa's government relished grandstanding in the suit with the companies was that the high-profile battle excused it from putting its own house in order. The drug companies' mounting offers of discounts and giveaways had found only a few takers, notably not in South Africa.

The skeptics seem to have had a point. The German drug company Boehringer Ingelheim has offered the South African government a free five-year supply of nevirapine, a drug that prevents HIV-positive mothers from passing on the virus to their children at birth. The drug is effective between 50 and 80 percent of the time, and requires just two doses, one to the mother shortly before her delivery date, another to the child not long after birth. The cost of the one-time treatment is about $3, not including the drug itself. The government at first declined to administer the drug, claiming it needed to develop a comprehensive program of mother-child treatment and counseling, which would be expensive and perhaps impossible in shantytowns and rural areas. Critics pointed out that, with or without such a program, it is cheaper to prevent infection than to treat an HIV-positive child. The Treatment Action Campaign, the most prominent South African organization in the battle with the drug companies, sued the government to force it to begin providing nevirapine. The suit succeeded in court, but the government has been uneven in carrying out the ruling.

Everything the government does is suspect because Mandela's successor, President Thabo Mbeki, has staked out a most unconventional position on AIDS. Mbeki, a graduate of England's Sussex University who is noted for his erudition and sophistication, spent years in exile with the outlawed African National Congress, the leading opposition to apartheid. Since the late 1990s, he has repeatedly expressed doubt that HIV causes AIDS. In April 2000 he reportedly sent a letter to President Clinton and other leaders asserting that Africa would not copy Western approaches to AIDS and defending a few maverick scientists who speculated that HIV might not cause AIDS. A month later he created an AIDS advisory panel of thirty-three scientists, including some of those mavericks. One of the senior members called for an end to HIV testing, which he termed "a useless distraction." He went on to note that the illnesses that finally kill AIDS victims, such as tuberculosis, are well-known conditions associated with malnutrition and poverty, and suggested—as Mbeki had done in the past—that these social ills might be the real source of African AIDS. In July attendees angrily walked out of the Global AIDS Conference in Durban, South Africa, when Mbeki opined that scientists should "not blame everything on a single virus."

Although he officially withdrew from the public debate over AIDS in October 2000 and snubbed the 2001 Global AIDS Conference during a state visit to the United States, Mbeki remains head of the country with Africa's largest infected population. Two years ago, South Africa's underfunded public health program left 40 percent of its AIDS budget unspent, partly because local officials were afraid to anger the president with bold measures. The central government has intervened to stop local officials from distributing free nevirapine. Officials insult reporters and activists who question them about AIDS, and the president continues to offer outright lies, such as a claim that murder takes more lives in South Africa each year than AIDS. (The toll from AIDS is ten times that of murder, even though South Africa is one of the world's most violent countries.) Partly because of Mbeki's opposition, South Africa has failed to launch an effective AIDS education and prevention program. After a long silence, Nelson Mandela has denounced his successor's indifference to an impending national disaster.

Mbeki's unsettling pronouncements are an echo of the first debates about AIDS in the United States, almost two decades ago. Wherever it goes, AIDS attracts suspicions about what is *really* wrong with the suffering population. Its resemblance to a biblical plague seems to drive observers to take it as a scourge, an emblem of judgment, and to ask who is being judged. In

America conservatives saw the depravity of homosexuality and drug use, while liberals perceived the inhumanity of the Reagan administration. In Africa, too, AIDS is not permitted just to be, in Mbeki's words, "a single virus": it must also be poverty, racism, imperialism, all the things that Mbeki believes are really wrong with Africa. In Uganda, where education and prevention have cut infection rates in half, President Yoweri Museveni has decided that AIDS is about colonialism: in speeches he harks back to an imagined age of indigenous chastity and sexual fidelity, before Europeans allegedly spread promiscuity and ruined African morals.

Mbeki's case is particularly poignant. Like many leaders of the African National Congress, he is a man of the left in a world where the left is greatly diminished. The ANC took support from the Soviets and from communist trade unions, and many of its leaders considered themselves Africa's last anti-imperialists, determined to end European rule and build a new egalitarian society. In light of the record of Soviet-inspired new societies, history's demurral from their plans is probably to the good, but it is a sharp irony nonetheless. Mbeki, like Mandela before him, has become an architect of Western-style economic reform—cutting budgets, controlling unions, and pressing for laws to ensure generous treatment of foreign investors. Like Mandela, Mbeki must sense that the distance from these reforms to security and comfort for poor South Africans is indecently long. To this historical insult, the AIDS epidemic adds the injury of a senseless natural fact, a new virus come to make everything that is bad worse and take even more of South Africa's history out of the hands of its people.

Mbeki gave a clue to his attitude toward AIDS in an address at South Africa's Fort Hare University in October 2001. There he spoke about the difficulty of being African in a world whose ideas and institutions were created by the same Victorian Europeans who ravaged Africa. Africans, he said, have studied in schools of theology where the Bible is interpreted by those who have justified segregation; law schools where they are told that they belong to the most criminal element in the country; medical schools where they are likewise convinced of their inferiority by being reminded of their role as germ carriers; schools where they learn a history that pictures black people as human beings of the lower order, unable to subject passion to reason.

Mbeki sees Africa's problem as being a legacy of self-contempt, which began with the contempt that European imperialists felt for Africans. In his Fort Hare speech, without mentioning AIDS explicitly, he denounced anti-AIDS activists as bearers of the same racist disdain:

And thus does it happen that others who consider themselves to be our leaders take to the streets carrying their placards, to demand that because we are germ carriers, and human beings of a lower order that cannot subject its passions to reason, we must perforce adopt strange opinions, to save a depraved and diseased people from perishing from self-inflicted disease. . . . Convinced that we are but natural-born, promiscuous carriers of germs, unique in the world, they proclaim that our continent is doomed to an inevitable mortal end because of our unconquerable devotion to the sin of lust.

To Mbeki, saying that AIDS is a South African problem implies that Africans are sinful, uncontrollable animals, unfit to live as civilized creatures. To defy that putative racist vision, Mbeki has denied the scientific view of AIDS and delayed his country's response to an epidemic. To prove that they are human beings, South Africans will be required to die like animals, without even the treatment that is ready to hand.

Accepting the Nobel Prize for literature in 1980, the Polish poet Czeslaw Milosz—like Mbeki a long-exiled child of a tormented land—admitted, "It is possible that there is no other memory than the memory of wounds." Perhaps people can only hold themselves intact by recalling where and how they have been injured, and who has been their enemy. If that is true, then political life will always oscillate between vengeance and confusion, hard-edged anger and indifference. It would be hard to find stronger evidence for this pessimistic view than Thabo Mbeki, an intelligent and cosmopolitan man whose lifetime of political effort is now succumbing to public irrationality, born of the memory of wounds.

In bloody-minded diasporas and nationalisms, the memory of wounds tells people who they are, who is their brother, and whom they ought to hate. At the other extreme, peaceable forgetfulness—the unhistorical goodwill of the Spencer Plaza mall in Madras, and the American tolerance that verges on indifference—may be too forgetful and undisciplined to maintain liberty, let alone advance the kind of justice that Mbeki and the rest of South Africa's leaders fought for over decades. Much of history moves on this short, unhappy spectrum, between those driven to commit violence and those unable to resist it. If liberty lies somewhere between the two, then its best friends are the rare individuals who can look toward the future without forgetting, for whom history's brutality is a memory but not a curse, and who can remember without ceasing to hope or to laugh.

III

LIBERTY AND
COMMERCE

The nations of our day cannot prevent conditions of equality from spreading in their midst. But it depends upon themselves whether equality is to lead to freedom or servitude, knowledge or barbarism, prosperity or wretchedness.

Alexis de Tocqueville,
Democracy in America

CHAPTER 9

The Flow

—ᴍ—

Global capitalism is a triumph of freedom. Markets produce
wealth, disrupt settled customs, and pry open the barred gates
of hierarchical societies. They humble the great, elevate the
lowly, and bewilder those who thought they knew their world.
At their best, they turn personal liberty from a privilege of the
powerful to an everyday expectation of ordinary people; they
overwhelm deference and privilege with a modest but solid
equality, in which titles and ancestors count for less than effort
and intelligence. Every bit as much as wealth, this image of liberty and equality led Adam Smith and other early thinkers to
endorse the market society.

Global capitalism is an abomination of freedom. Markets
sweep across the land like a natural disaster, driving whole
populations before them. They make familiar ways of surviving impossible. Markets tear farmers from their land and fishermen from their nets as surely as drought and disease. They
can topple governments, but cannot replace or rebuild them.
They throw up new inequalities, often abrupt and crass, without even the hint of grace and threads of noblesse oblige that
dignified the old hierarchies. A kind of personal isolation is
possible in commercial societies that hardly has a precedent
in human history. Some souls waste away and societies move
in and out of chaos so that many—but not all—can grow rich.

For the past century, people have become accustomed to choosing between these pictures of the market, for or against. Whether markets are good or bad for freedom was one of the questions of the age. Like interstellar black holes, the poles of the Cold War bent the light of human thought toward them, gathering it around two extremes. For the market's defenders, its critics were sentimentalists, dupes, or communists. The most visible theorists of the market were laissez-faire economists who described a utopia of free exchange that would have rung false to Adam Smith. At the same time, for many of its critics the market was an evil on the same scale as communism. Albert Camus, the courageous French humanitarian and anticommunist, spoke for several generations of left-wing thought when he said, "Choosing freedom today does not mean ceasing to be a profiteer of the Soviet regime and becoming a profiteer of the bourgeois regime. For that would amount, instead, to choosing slavery twice."

Today almost no one believes that communism and capitalism are symmetrical enemies of human flourishing. The market is not an ideological choice so much as one of the background conditions of our lives. We have not, however, recovered the habit of thinking carefully and without prejudice about markets, especially about their power to do both harm and good. Moreover, we tend to forget that "the free market," which both its advocates and its enemies have often treated as a unitary thing, the same anywhere, is in fact a plural thing, with many faces. One might adopt Leo Tolstoy's famous but inaccurate remark about happy and unhappy families to say that, while all unfree societies are unfree in the same way, free societies are free each in their own way. Whether arbitrary arrests, torture, and execution are carried out in the name of the Deutsche Volk or the Soviet proletariat, they soon become the same: the arbitrary, brutal, and unchecked power of some people over other people. However, when people live together with more dignity than humiliation and more liberty than constraint, the achievement takes a distinctive form. Today's Germany is not Japan, which is emphatically not the United States, which is neither Sweden nor Kerala State, India. Democracy and personal liberty link free countries, but habits, beliefs, and important aspects of economic life differ from place to place.

The right way to judge an economic system is not by whether it is orthodox in its market mechanisms or (as ideologists did until recently) its socialist rules, but by simpler yet less tractable questions: Does this economy make people more free, not in some abstract way but here and now among the particular women and men who inhabit it? Does it produce wealth and also protect people from cruel hierarchy? Does it cultivate habits of independence and self-respect, or of sycophancy and fear? Does it create opportunity for people born without much, or does it guarantee that those who choose the right parents will do well from then on? When the market turns life upside down, can the political system absorb the changes, or do they tumble the country into chaos or tyranny? We are only beginning to learn how to ask those questions well.

One place to begin is at a line of tension. What does global capitalism look like? One answer comes in the images of the advertising industry, among the most important visual and emotional ideologues of modern life. Take one advertisement from the *Economist*. The text reads, "Everything that can be bought and sold is getting online." The ad portrays an intersecting, overlapping network of microfibers, infinite in every direction. Glance at them sidelong and they could be blood vessels, nerves, or dozens of highways lit at night by numberless travelers. They are the conduits of impulse, life, and commerce, and they are where these three dissolve into one. Along three of the more remote arcs sit small circles, bits of old-fashioned geometry appended to the flow. Each one marks a commodity: 10,000 CASES OF ENGINE OIL, COPY OF WAR AND PEACE (SIGNED), KHAKIS. The ad is from Corning, which offers the slogan "Discovering Beyond Imagination."

Another full-page ad, also in the *Economist*: a striking blond woman is seated, leaning forward, her impossibly long arms extended to adjust a silver spike heel. Her shoulder-length hair partly conceals one eye as she turns, seemingly startled, to look over her right shoulder. She is edgy but poised, taken by surprise yet evidently expecting to be surprised. The text follows the horizontal line of her thigh, asking, "Who will you be in the *next* 24 hours?"

Ask a conventional economist to name the values of the free market, and you will probably get a set of principles: private property, the power to make contracts, freedom to leave one job for another, and a system of law that enforces the other elements. If you press harder, you may get a broader answer. The free market, she might say, fosters and rewards certain qualities of character: hard work, innovativeness, frugality and self-discipline, and something elusive called the entrepreneurial spirit. That is a common answer among the more politically minded defenders of free markets.

What, then, to make of these images? They are reminders that economies are not only systems of principle. Economies have aesthetics—images of beauty, energy, and impulse. These ads capture today's belief that everything is connected, and all particular differences resolve into flows of information and money. Engine oil and khakis are incidental to these flows; indeed, they are almost flaws. The viscosity of the oil, the stitching and hems of the pants are imperfections in the movement of commercial impulse through the economy's nerves. Plato taught generations of successors to believe that anything particular is a kind of failure, that nothing is wholly good except what is abstract and universal. That is also the aesthetic creed of the new market. It has become the special aesthetic of global capitalism, because nothing is more particular, obtrusive, or seemingly arbitrary than a national frontier. "Border-less Is Rising," one communications company's ad announces over a featureless and limitless landscape.

The inhabitants of a world of flow anticipate surprise. They take revolutions with equanimity and shift with them. Who will you be in the *next* twenty-four hours? It all depends on the flow. There, ideas become reality, spurring small and large revolutions. Like children in a magical world, people learn to sway between terror and delight at an unknown that never stops. "Ideas are capital. The rest is just money," reads the scrawl that occupies most of one white page of an investment bank's ad. People who live in the flow also learn to believe that their choices shape the world. "How would you like the future?" asks Telecom Italia, and the face in each quadrant of its page gives a different answer: the athletic African woman, the pearl-necklaced socialite, the dapper rogue who peers at us over one shoulder, and the beautiful Amerasian woman whose eyes drop with modesty as she takes a phone call, will get the futures they respectively prefer.

This image of the global market is all about freedom. A particular kind of freedom: freedom to communicate, freedom to change, freedom to imagine and to think, to want and to be wanted, to be whoever it seems good to be in the moment. It is sensual and mental, in equal and intertwined parts. If there is an inalienable right here, it is not freedom of contract: it is the right of the imagination to become reality, and of reality to slip back into imagination. That is the freedom of the flow. Over an image of the Berlin Wall coming down, Sun Microsystems tells us: "If history has shown us anything, it's that freedom wins."

So, what about sweatshop workers? What about landless laborers who have lost their farms and come to new slums to try to make a living? Should they, too, appear as Euclidean circles on the arcs of microfibers, patiently labeled: 300 GARMENT SEAMSTRESSES, 2,000 FORMER PEASANTS, ONE TRADITIONAL

PATHFINDER, BHOOMIYA CASTE (NOW PICKING GARBAGE IN DELHI)? How would they like the future—each wish-bearing, impulse-having, landless one of them? Who will *they* be in the next twenty-four hours? Are their ideas—ideas of living in a sound house, returning wealthy to their villages, coming to America—capital, and the rest only money? Has freedom won yet?

To our credit, we are troubled by the problem. It has seemed natural, in many places and times, to believe that the wretched had their lot and the great had theirs, and all anyone could do was try to fill his place graciously. We cannot believe that now: too much, including our own economy, teaches us differently. Commercial societies help to propagate values of freedom, not just in the abstract but also as concrete lessons everywhere. The lessons get into people's nerves and make them sensitive to cruel paradoxes: that some become less free while others become more free, that some suffer while others flourish.

Adam Smith's "If"

There is nothing new about this paradox. It does not mean that capitalism is fatally flawed by hypocrisy. Neither does it mean that those who object to capitalism's injuries and inequalities are sentimentalists who misunderstand the real workings of the system. Both of these cynical views are fatally one-sided. Capitalism makes people free and unfree. It liberates and oppresses, strengthens and destroys. The balance between capitalism's good and bad effects, though, cannot be left to the market alone. Politics is needed to settle the question between clothing and nakedness, dignity and vulnerability.

Adam Smith is the half-forgotten master of this question. Smith believed that the great benefits of the rising modern world were liberty and prosperity. Liberty meant the freedom of the market: to move about, to leave bad situations, and to strike deals that benefited both deal makers. Liberty also meant citizens' right to participate in their own governance. Prosperity came out of commerce: international trade, opportunities for upstart merchants and craftsmen, and chances for entrepreneurs to set up specialized workshops where they could hone production to an art.

Smith did not trust these good things to come about automatically. He was a prophet of liberty and prosperity in an era of slavery, and he saw the contradiction vividly. In his lectures on jurisprudence at Edinburgh, Smith labored to make his students confront the difficulty. Slavery, he began, is a terrible thing. It is not even efficient, because unlike free workers slaves have no incentive except the whip to do their work quickly or well. But that is not even the beginning of the evil. A slave lives in abject dependence on his master, and dependence is the most corrupting condition for a human being. A slave cannot provide for himself or care for and defend his family. A man in these conditions can hardly be called a man at all.

Slavery corrupts the master as much as it wrecks the slave. Slaveholding excites one of the most dangerous passions: the "love of domination and tyrannizing." The slaveholder's great pleasure is to have every whim satisfied. This power rests on the total subjection of the slave. In a curious way, the master is both a tyrant over and a dependent of the slave: without his slaves, he would lose his power and become an ordinary, incapable man. The whole system is wicked, a disaster for human relations and human character.

But the rise of liberty and prosperity will not necessarily sweep away slavery. Instead, it might make the slave's condition even worse. Why is this so? First, a republican government—something like a representative democracy, although Smith did not imagine that the poor would have a vote—is less likely than a monarchy to abolish slavery, because the wealthy citizens and landholders who make the laws will be the same ones who hold the slaves. By contrast, a monarch might abolish slavery, out of conviction or to weaken his political competitors, the landholders. This may seem a whimsical argument, because we are not accustomed to comparing republican and monarchical regimes in our political debates. The loss is ours, because Smith was right. He is describing the policy of the slaveholding American South. He is also announcing a more general principle: when the liberty of some rests on others' subjection, do not count on the powerful to sacrifice their freedom by freeing the powerless. Whether or not slavery is profitable, power is itself such a great pleasure that few will surrender it willingly.

Prosperity, too, holds dangers for slaves. It opens vast social distance between them and their masters. In a poor country, the slave's daily life is not so remote from his master's. The two work in the same fields or shop, eat at the same table, and probably sleep under the same roof. A slave is a slave, but one who shares your kitchen with you also tends to be human in your eyes. But when the wealthy master in his manor glances out on the slave in his distant shack, "he will hardly look on him as being of the same kind; he thinks he has little title even to the ordinary enjoyments of life, and feels but little for his misfortunes." The wealthier the master becomes, the more likely he is to look on his slaves as inhuman. The freer he becomes, the better able he is to keep his slaves in subjection. The blessings of modern liberty are a disaster for slaves.

This paradox was especially poignant for Smith. He saw personal liberty as the solvent that would break up the old ties of feudal and courtly societies. Modern liberty would mark the end of courtiers and supplicants scraping before lords, aping the foolish fashions of the court, and laughing at the bad jokes and idiotic ideas of their social betters. It would eliminate the basest class of men: courtly retainers, the thuggish and obsequious ancestors of the entourages that now surround entertainers and athletes—but who were then near the heart of political as well as cultural power. And it would be the end of lords, those beautiful, gracious, but absurd and incapable characters who had never done a thing to prove themselves, and whose beauty was the jewel of their unmerited self-confidence. Modern liberty would replace these characters with steady, competent, quietly ambitious people, virtuous yeomen and small capitalists.

But here at the heart of Smith's vision, the yeoman was locked in an embrace of mutual dependence with the slave. Before the prophet's eyes, as it were, one man became a tyrant and the other a child. This grim picture led Smith to one of the most arresting passages in all his writings and lectures: "Opulence and freedom, the two greatest blessings men can possess, tend greatly to the misery of this body of men [slaves], which in most countries where slavery is allowed makes by far the greatest part. A humane man would wish therefore if slavery had to be allowed that these greatest blessings, being incompatible with the happiness of the greatest part of mankind, were never to take place."

That "if" is crucial: *if* slavery had to be allowed, a humane man should want to give up prosperity and freedom, not just for himself but on behalf of the whole world. The rising commercial society brings changes, benefits, a heady new concept of liberty: it also presents a choice. In fact, it forces the choice by making the central contradiction of the new economy impossible to ignore. Political choice decides whether freedom or domination, dignity or humiliation, will become the ruling temper of the economy, and how great will be the gap between the most fortunate and the least powerful.

Today activists, capitalists, and rulers are still struggling over Smith's "if." Humane people wince at the contradictions of a vision of freedom, imagination, desire, and flow that turns people into hand-to-mouth laborers or jetsam on a river of displaced humanity. They protest against one version of the market, the unyielding neoclassical vision that—legitimately—claims descent from Adam Smith. But their protest also grows from Smith's tradition, as surely as the liberty he praised made the wrong of slavery more vivid. At the intersection of politics and economics sits that critical "if": economies are systems of values, and values present people with decisions. Markets do not make our history, but only shape the circumstances in which we make it.

Sweatshop Politics

Adam Smith's "if" troubled the students who, beginning in the late 1990s, made Nike, the Gap, and other garment brands very uncomfortable. The trouble began when celebrity Kathie Lee Gifford was linked to dressmakers working in illegal and dangerous factories. Then government agents discovered illegal Asian immigrants living in conditions resembling slavery, sewing for long hours and sleeping in locked dormitories. The students turned these events into a cause.

These were American incidents, involving clear violations of domestic law. The students' first achievement was to extend popular condemnation to factories in the third world, where unions often are shams or do not exist, hours are long and pay is low, and danger and physical abuse are ordinary. The abuses in Los Angeles that aroused indignation had the same power when they happened in Indonesia or Guatemala—even though few people in those countries would have found them surprising. The word "sweatshop," which had dropped out of popular use for much of the twentieth century, returned to everyday speech to describe the supply chains that fed America's boutiques and Wal-Marts.

The students turned out for campus protests, picketed outside stores, and wrote press releases. They succeeded in linking Nike, other athletic shoes, and branded clothing in general to images of exploited women and children. The students were never all that numerous, but they were effective because they intuited the paradox that had devastated Kathie Lee Gifford's reputation: the more elevated and powerful a brand's meaning, the smaller an impact is needed to reverse it. A truck can't crush a rubber ball, but a bent paper clip can bring down a balloon float. Nike and its competitors had spent billions of dollars to associate themselves with images of health, vitality, independence, and authenticity. These ad campaigns had done most of the students' work for them. Once a powerful brand exists, one picture of a child chained to a sewing machine or a woman beaten by her supervisor can contaminate it.

It may be that student strategists calculated this result, but I suspect that, like most successful advertising, it emerged from their own experience of desire and revulsion. A longtime activist who worked with the student campaigns told me, "There was a vehemence about their anger that was astonishing. It was as if they were punishing Nike because they had been lied to and sullied, and they needed to get clean." This seems exactly right. Although the self-consciously savvy don't like to admit it, living in a brand culture means understanding that products evoke emotions, status, and moral values. For a lot of people, putting on Nike clothes felt a little bit freeing. It made a runner feel a little faster, a little stronger, if only for a moment. And then it turned out that our running clothes stood for weak, hungry bodies exhausting themselves to produce our shoes. It is a wretched thought: the minute you have it you want to shake it off. The more perceptive activists must have sensed this response in themselves and set out to induce it in others.

This is why anti-sweatshop activists have mostly harassed high-value brands. Efforts to press the same politics on Wal-Mart have been fruitless, even though it is the world's largest buyer of clothing from poor countries. Wal-Mart denies dealing with sweatshops, activists vituperatively disagree, and since there is no agreed-upon definition of a sweatshop, the battle has proceeded in dim light. Despite the company's profession of all-American values, the core Wal-Mart brand is not ennobling: cheap stuff. Wal-Mart buyers understand that the giant consumption boxes ruin downtowns, are hard on the eye, and aren't always the magnanimous employers they present themselves as being. That is all part of the deal. The hourglass of social sins is dripping sand from the moment we enter the store. Nike's brand aimed for the skies of self-image, both moral and aesthetic, which meant it could be brought down. Wal-Mart built low, but on the solid ground of self-interest. It is invincible to attacks by the purveyors of disapproval.

The students had another advantage: their universities purchased warehouses' worth of sweatshirts, running shorts, and other logo-imprinted merchandise. Few customers worry as much about their public images as university presidents do. As pressure rose, labor secretary Robert Reich convened a working group on sweatshops, to which he invited the activists, representatives of universities, the companies, the major American garment workers' union, and several groups focused on human rights and abuses of corporate power. Many invitees expected the meetings to be mere show, but Reich showed himself genuinely interested in resolving the conflict and helping sweatshop workers. After months of negotiation the group seemed near agreement on a code of conduct for the companies, to be enforced by monitoring. Then the union representatives pulled out, along with the students.

The substance of the dispute covered two issues: whether companies would pay a "living" wage, enough to sustain a family, where the local minimum wage was less than that; and whether activists would be allowed to monitor the companies' conduct, or monitoring would be left to professional auditors hired by the companies and approved by an independent body. The upshot was a pair of competing codes. The mainstream agreement was adopted by Levi Strauss, Polo Ralph Lauren, Liz Claiborne, Adidas, Nike, Patagonia, and several other companies, and a raft of universities that committed to buy only from compliant manufacturers—spurring a new set of companies to sign on, many of them small businesses dedicated to making university gear. The students and unions devised their own code, including the living-wage requirement and a more liberal monitoring policy, and have persuaded nearly one hundred schools to accept it, among them Columbia, Brown, Duke, and many of the large public universities in states such as California, Massachusetts, and Wisconsin. The companies that signed on to the mainstream code have been developing and implementing their monitoring programs, while the administrators of the alternative pact have been compiling lists of factories that serve their member schools, and launching occasional guerrilla monitoring efforts to record factory abuses. Meanwhile, Reebok and the Gap, among others, have established their own codes and monitoring systems, adding to an already confused landscape.

The Gap Among the Khmer

Because I wanted to know how those efforts translated to the other side of the world, I am in Cambodia on a warm November day. It is early afternoon, time for the lunch break at a garment factory outside Phnom Penh. Thirty-five Cambodian women are sitting in the shade of a eucalyptus tree, in a meadow two hundred yards from the factory building. Some of the workers are little older than schoolgirls, and others are well into middle age. The Mekong River runs sluggishly at the bottom of the meadow, and on the opposite bank rises a white mosque, its dome chipped and weathered with flecks of gray. A few emaciated white cows are grazing under another tree not far from us. The women are eating steamed clams and vegetables out of Styrofoam containers, the lunch provided by the union organizers who arranged this gathering.

Jason Judd is talking to the women—90 percent or more of the workers in Cambodian garment factories are female—about why they should want to organize a union. These women are far enough along in the process that the next item today is to schedule a series of organizing meetings, but saying what it is they want is still a challenge. "We can be fired for no reason. We must work overtime," says a woman in brown polyester slacks and a bright green shirt. "And that makes you angry," replies Jason. "Why are you angry, when the same thing happens to someone else, and she isn't angry?" He directs the question to an older woman with gentle features. She grins in panic and buries her face in her hands.

"There isn't a good word for anger in Khmer," Jason tells me later as we pick up the Styrofoam that the women left in the grass at the end of their lunch break. "Anger here is an explosion in response to an insult. You blow up, and that's bad, but it's forgiven, and then you forget you were angry. It's an aberrant moment, and you go back to your life. There's no idea of anger as something that lasts a long time, and keeps you going. Also there's no good word for imagination. We've been calling it 'something that doesn't exist yet.' "

Jason is well over six feet tall and extremely thin, with blond hair that clings ethereally to his lean head. His features are small and slightly crooked—not lopsided, just a slight bend in the nose and another in the mouth. He gives an impression of unprepossessing gentleness, and the theme of anger, to which he returns often, is always a bit of a surprise. He heads the Phnom Penh office of the Solidarity Center, the chief international arm of the AFL-CIO. Unlike most Solidarity Center employees, who are in effect consultants who do tasks from drafting labor laws to training the leaders of new unions, he is a field organizer. He spends most of his days with workers who are trying to create, keep, or strengthen unions.

Politics in Cambodia has followed the cycles of Cambodian anger. Cambodians have mostly gone about their lives, chiefly in rural villages, trying to stay out of the way of grasping and corrupt officials. Now and again explosions have swept over the country like monsoon storms, turning lives upside down without explanation and then ending with a violent change in the wind. In 1975, after some five years of civil war and fero-cious American bombing aimed at communist troops, Phnom Penh fell to the Khmer Rouge, a fanatical group of commu-nists. Their leader, Pol Pot, had developed his ideology among French communists in postwar Paris, and the savagery of his rule exceeded the worst that Stalin and Mao had done. He cleared out the cities and turned Cambodia into a nation exclu-sively of peasants, closing down schools, shops, hospitals, and monasteries, prohibiting private property, and eliminating money. In 1976 and 1977 he tried to double the country's rice production by herding the entire population into forced-labor teams. At least a million people—15 percent of Cambodians—died of overwork or starvation, or were executed by Commu-nist Party cadres. Some responsible historians put the figure at two million. At the end of 1978, the Vietnamese Army invaded, drove Pol Pot into the jungle, and put the shattered country under its tutelage.

Today, Jason tells me, people won't discuss Pol Pot's terror unless they're asked directly. "Someone will say, I had nine brothers and sisters, and four of them were killed. Just like that, no emotion. In fact, there's a real lack of curiosity about the past. My driver"—he gestures at the silent, grim man at the wheel of the car that is taking us back toward central Phnom Penh—"was in the army for twelve years. And he has been liv-ing with the same roommate for ten years now. The other day, I mentioned to his roommate that he had been in the army. The man had no idea. It had never come up. I don't know what they talk about." He pauses. "Maybe you can't afford much emotion—or much curiosity."

Although Cambodia is more stable now, at the beginning of the 1990s it was a fractious ward of the United Nations and the international humanitarian community. The staff members of non-governmental organizations still fill planes to and from Bangkok, the nearest hub, and roam the streets in SUVs. Some are here to consult on democracy and civil society, others to set up a free press, others to cultivate independent unions. They are the last wave: editors from regional American newspapers with funding to spend six months here, NGO entrepreneurs with grants, and people who liked the place five years ago and stayed. The advance guard is already several crises on, moving from the Balkans to Central Asia or West Africa.

Jason professes to disdain all of them: "Seminars and papers," he says. "They come here with their guidance and expertise. It's poisonous." Then he grins ironically. "Of course, I know what *I'm* doing is right." What he's doing is, in fact, a variant of the same effort. In 1998 the United States struck a deal with the Cambodian government: American tariffs would be lowered on garments sewn in Cambodia if, in return, the country would become a model of respect for labor rights in the third world. Jason is here to try to help Cambodian workers make good on that idea in the nearly two hundred garment factories that have appeared around Phnom Penh since the treaty, bringing villagers in from the countryside for factory jobs.

Soon Cambodia will settle into fixed political habits, for better or worse. Today its nascent politics is venal in the extreme. "The labor minister's wife owns a controlling share in one of the major factories outside of town. The governor of Phnom Penh has eight or nine houses, and still when a street gets paved"—most of Phnom Penh's roads are dirt or gravel— "he's a hero in that neighborhood. I figure we have five years before things set, five years before this place turns into India"—meaning corrupt and politically disenchanted, a comparison that is unfair to the subcontinent but expresses a sincere doubt about Cambodia's future.

I want to know what effect the anti-sweatshop activists' achievements are having here. I get a look of partisan contempt when I mention the mainstream code of conduct, but there can be no doubt that codes make a difference. "Some companies are really serious about it. The Gap is the most brand-conscious of all. If you call in a complaint, you can have a compliance officer in the factory in twenty minutes." Jason waits just long enough to draw a breath. "It's a disaster, of course. How can you organize workers who get that kind of treatment?"

Union activists—not Washington bureaucrats or prettied-up spokespersons, but organizers working for low pay in hard places—can be infuriating people. Unionists have their own version of history, centering on the Haymarket Riots, Blair Mountain, the Wobblies, Big Bill Haywood, Joe Hill, the Mineworkers for Democracy, and other heroes and tragedies. They even have their own way of reading literature: one morning Jason comes to pick me up for our day's meetings with Xeroxed pages from Dickens's *Hard Times*, a scathing passage in which the novelist goes after industrialists for resisting reform of labor codes. "Same damned arguments!" he announces with quixotic pleasure. In a world overstuffed with good intentions, where one can hardly open a magazine or turn on a television without being reminded of the earnest benignity of corporations, NGOs, governments, and celebrities, union people believe in combat. They are just about the only people in a world advertised as win-win who admit to believing that there are losers, and that the losers have good reason to be angry.

That is why they are so important. The heart of the union idea is that people get only what they demand, and then only if they fight for it. Once today's Western overseers have left Phnom Penh, that attitude will make some of the difference between a culture of corruption, patronage, and abusive power, and one with somewhat more dignity for ordinary people. That is Jason's point about keeping Cambodia from becoming India, and why the brigades of good intention won't be enough to save the country.

But union people are also violently territorial. They treat any effort to improve the workplace without organized labor as

an attack on workers: not a halfway measure, not a complement to what they do, but a scheme to make organizing harder.
They sometimes oppose civic groups, such as women's organizations, that step forward on behalf of workers where local
unions are corrupt to the point of impotence. Union activists
think that people who attend United Nations conferences,
admire NGOs, and talk amicably with company bosses are
naïve idealists who don't understand how power works.

When I follow Jason to a meeting with a union leader, she
tells a more ambiguous story. Like most labor officials here,
she founded her own union a few years ago, in a factory that
was unorganized before she started working there. She then
led workers in a strike at a Gap factory. After she was excluded
from negotiations between a compliant leader of the local labor
federation and a representative of the garment manufacturers'
association, she had a batch of Gap T-shirts printed and burned
them for television cameras in front of the American embassy.
The next day, she had a seat at the bargaining table. But like
most leaders here, she has followed the pattern of explosion
and indifference that Jason described to me. Last night the
head of a large and growing union aligned with the federation
she heads complained to us that she would not return his
phone calls. When Jason prods her to meet regularly with the
leaders of other independent federations, she demurs impa-
tiently, saying she doesn't believe they are truly independent.

When I ask about the codes of conduct, and about American pressure on garment manufacturers, she is enthusiastic. In
the factories where her union is active, the violation reports go
through foremen to the company compliance officers, so the
union can take credit for enforcing the codes. Moreover, factory managers are much more fearful of American companies
than of local workers. Workers they can fire, and do—especially those who try to organize unions. Foreign buyers are
nearly irreplaceable. "Once," she tells me, "I won a negotiation
just by threatening to go to the buyer. Just by threatening."

Who was the buyer? "I don't know." The specter of pressure from the rich world changes the landscape enough to make a bluff worth the chance. Whoever the buyer was, the local managers—Cambodian, Korean, or Chinese, contracting with an American brand or a middleman—didn't want it to come anywhere near their factory, drawing its train of moral scrutiny.

This seems to be the nature of rich-world politics aimed at helping people in poor countries. The anti-sweatshop activists cannot, on their own, change the lives of Cambodian workers. The distance is too great, in miles and time zones and also in culture and politics: from campus protests and university covenants to corrupt regimes, factory managers who often don't speak enough of the local language to communicate with their line workers, and seamstresses who, at $50 a month, are earning the best wages of their lives. The idea that Nike's adopting a new labor policy would be enough to change workers' lives belongs to the flow-world of infinite microfibers, where thought remakes reality. But the codes of conduct and other innovations do give a new tool to workers. The codes matter when they shift the unequal power between a line worker born in a Cambodian village and a manager sent down from Seoul. Whether they are making their complaints to a compliance officer, going through a union foreman, or using the threat of brand pressure to win some concession, workers learn that principle joined with power is more potent than either principle or power alone.

After dark, Jason and I go to see Nada, a young leader who created a union in his factory just a year ago. We park a few hundred yards from his home, and pick our way around a rubble heap and into a neighborhood of tiny concrete houses built on a reclaimed swamp, where Nada and his wife live. The dirt street and concrete gutters are swept clean, and a few women and men—also factory workers, Jason tells me—are sitting outside, listening to taped music and eating. Nada's house is eight feet wide and fifteen deep. A large bed in the back takes up more than a quarter of the house. There, behind a gauzy pink curtain, Nada's wife is concealed with their two-week-old daughter. A few clean shirts hang from a wire, and a scooter stands in one corner. When we arrive Nada's mother-in-law, who came from her village for the birth, extinguishes the brazier on which she has been preparing to cook and slips outside.

Nada sits with us on a low-slung platform, the height of a kitchen stool and the breadth and width of a large coffee table, which is the only piece of furniture in the house besides the bed. He doesn't have much news to report, and he fingers his cell phone while we visit. A few months ago, the last time he was in touch with Jason, he had been knifed by a fired worker who blamed the union leader for not protecting him. He has healed well, and his union has grown by several hundred members. But, he says, the head of his federation won't return his calls. He is thinking of spinning off his members as an independent union. "Then you won't be independent," Jason tells him. "You'll be alone. Have you been meeting with your deputies?" He has been very busy, Nada says. Someone is sick. There is the baby. They can't get a room. Jason reminds him that he can use a room at the Solidarity Center if necessary. Nada's response is noncommittal.

When we finish, Nada shows me the English phrase book with which he has been practicing. He also has a CD-ROM full of English lessons, but no computer on which to use it. He is hopeful, though. He and his wife will send the child back to the village to live with her grandparents, as they did the last one. That way both parents can work. The house costs just twenty dollars a month, and already they have the scooter.

Jason is both pleased and annoyed. Nada is smart and capable, which is why he managed to organize a union in the first place. He is also—like most union leaders here, and unlike many in the West—an entrepreneur who saw a chance to become a leader in the new world of factories and industrial neighborhoods. People like Nada could easily become strongmen, a much more familiar type of leadership here than the democratic kind that Jason is trying to teach. Five years, he mutters.

As we walk back to the car, Nada clutching my elbow in the manner of the Khmer, we pass a lighted, open building, not much more than a concrete shed. Inside, twenty-five students, ranging in age from eight to twenty-one, are having an English lesson. We step in and, amid the stir we have created, attempt a conversation. The students pay $5 or $6 a month for this nightly lesson—a third of the rent for a livable house. In their sixth month of study, and with the disadvantage of surprise, they still manage to ask me where I come from, whether I like Cambodian food, and if I have a girlfriend. One boy asks how many friends I have and, when I try a figure, shouts in Khmer, "Not many friends!"

Jason and other union people are right: the good intentions of American students won't make life much better for sweatshop workers. Faced with a fragile, corrupt democracy and a budding industrial economy, people who organize themselves will do much better than people who don't—and they will probably live in a better country. They will also have enemies: managers, political bosses, and sometimes other workers and other unions. Jason is trying to help Cambodia to prepare for a messy existence in which bromides about civil society and win-win solutions will not go far outside the conference rooms of nice hotels.

These workers, though, are not likely to decide that global capitalism is their enemy. That idea still lives in the secret emotions of union politics: that with the right combination of anger and organizing we might break through to a purer kind of solidarity, perhaps even socialism. Such remote promises will not have much hold on people who are entrepreneurial, looking out for their own next step, ready to make alliances but not to foreclose their own futures. These Cambodian sweat-shop workers are in the global web after all, and although it is not as utopian for them as in the images of the ad writers, it is the source of the moment's main chance. It is worth hoping that they will reach neither perfect class solidarity nor win-win naïveté, but what Tocqueville identified as the measured generosity of the free man or woman: self-interest properly understood.

CHAPTER 10

Commerce, Reform, and Crisis

—ᴍᴠ—

Western nations rely on energy and intelligence to compete with one another. To come abreast of them, China should plan to promote commerce and open mines; unless we change, the Westerners will be rich and we poor. We should excel in technology and the manufacture of machinery; unless we change, they will be skillful and we clumsy. Steamboats, trains, and the telegraph should be adopted; unless we change, the Westerners will be quick and we slow.

—Hsueh Fu-cheng,
prominent advocate of reform, 1879

"We are looking forward to the closer trading relationship," repeats an electronic baritone. This comment on China's entry into the World Trade Organization comes from a CD-ROM, *Gateway to Standard Spoken American English*, in Shanghai's Book Palace, a seven-story monument to Chinese bibliophilia. On weekends, a visitor has to pick his way through the crowded aisles, and the escalators are as full as conveyor belts in a fruit-processing plant, overflowing upward and downward with eager customers. The Book Palace and its neighbor, the Foreign Languages Bookstore, are a sketch of the paradoxes that are China today: a proud and nationalistic culture racing to embrace the West, a repressive society lurching into the free market, overseen by a political elite that desperately wants to prove there is no paradox here.

The appetite for English has produced its own architecture in these shops. There are tables piled high with pocket books on *Job Interview English*, *Visa Interview English*, *English for Domestic Help*, and *The American Way*, the last of which purports to explain American attitudes toward food, sports, shopping, and romance. Whole walls are lined with preparation materials for the Test of English as a Foreign Language, the Scholastic Aptitude Test, and the board exams for graduate school and programs in law, medicine, and business. English lessons on CD-ROM line the walls, the cover of each edition sporting a different speaker of Standard American English: Bill Gates grins crookedly from one cover, George W. Bush glowers unsteadily from another, and on a third United Nations secretary-general Kofi Annan beams beneficently.

Twenty years ago, primers on American culture concentrated on the evils of American capitalism: racism, the exploitation of workers, the decadence of the rich, and the corruption and alienation of consumer culture. Chinese textbooks still reflect some of that attitude. These guides to English, though, provide more benign lessons in American civic life and popular culture. The visa interview primers give exegesis of the Great Seal of the United States and chat lines on the virtues of bicameralism. The CD-ROMs feature upbeat discussions of interracial marriage, the poetry of Maya Angelou, and the Grammys.

This attitude toward America is the fruit of more than twenty years of change in China. When Deng Xiaoping took over leadership of the Communist Party in 1978, he set about restoring order after the disruptions of Mao Tse-Tung's Cultural Revolution, which had left millions of wounds in the life of the country. The Cultural Revolution began in 1966 with Mao's announcement that communism had stalled because party officials, professors, editors, and other social leaders were caught in bourgeois habits of thought. In order to enter communism, the nation had to purge itself. The immediate occasion for Mao's declaration was a struggle for power within the Communist Party, where the chairman faced a challenge from more moderate figures, but it soon became a decade-long episode of ideological mania and popular brutality. Universities were closed until 1973, when they began offering classes only to peasants and workers. Before the closings, students hounded, humiliated, and sometimes beat to death the professors whom they were now licensed to denounce as counter-revolutionaries. Teachers, professionals, and intellectuals were sent to the countryside, sometimes separated from their spouses and families, and consigned to farm labor. China was turned upside down.

Two years after Mao's death, Deng decided amid the wreckage that China's future lay with market reforms that would give its putatively socialist citizens opportunities to make money. He declared, "It is glorious to get rich," and then dissolved rural communes, giving peasant families long-term leases on their land; began turning China's inefficient factories into competitive enterprises; and opened up the cities to what soon became full-bore entrepreneurship. The United States, long the emblem of exploitative capitalism, now became a model of prosperity and efficiency which the Chinese hoped to emulate.

The most prized product of economic reform is Shanghai, which has become a hybrid of New York, with gleaming towers stretching for miles out of the city center, and Paris, with grand squares and boulevards that reflect its history as a center of French influence in the nineteenth century. The city bursts with clean, bright, high-tech malls that rival any in the world, and the pedestrians in its shopping districts are no less sculpted and chic than downtown Manhattanites. Most of the new buildings, city officials like to point out, have been built since 1990.

That is, they were erected after June 4, 1989, when Chinese soldiers shot unarmed student protestors in Beijing, after they had left a tumultuous pro-democracy demonstration in Tiananmen Square. Tiananmen has been a ceremonial center of Chinese political life since 1651 and was the site of many of Mao's pronouncements. The killings marked a turning point in Chinese reform. Throughout the 1980s some Chinese, particularly students and intellectuals, assumed that the American model was indivisible: a capitalist China would also become liberal and democratic. The sound of gunfire was eloquent: if it was glorious to get rich, it was nonetheless forbidden to become free. Although Deng remained in power until his death in 1997, the Tiananmen shootings were the second bookend of his regime, marking the outer limit of the openness he had declared a decade earlier. After the shootings, the Party began warning that American advocates for human rights and labor rights were enemies of China, whose real purpose was to keep the country poor and weak by shutting it out of the global economy.

There is a theory popular in the West that China's economic reforms will inevitably bring political change. President George W. Bush has urged, "Trade freely with China, and time is on our side." Trade, he says, will "help an entrepreneurial middle class and a freedom-loving class grow and burgeon." The view is widely echoed among free-traders, and not surprisingly: it promises all good things as part of an ineluctable progression. This theory rests on several hypotheses: that the government cannot give up control over the economy without surrendering control over other aspects of people's day-to-day lives; that people who control some of their own money and property will be able to stand up against attempted repression; and that those who benefit from new economic openness— inevitably called the middle class even when their lives bear little resemblance to what Americans mean by that term—will want not just personal autonomy, but open and democratic politics. In other words, people who learn to shop like Americans will also come to think about politics like Americans—not the lackadaisical citizens who register some of the lowest voter turnout rates in the world, but the civic patriots of the most heroic periods in American history.

China's government is trying to refute that theory, at least for the next several decades, by offering economic opportunity and personal freedom but no political liberty. Today it is possible, after threading through tables and shelves of books on management theory and the high-tech economy, to purchase a crash course in liberalism in a Chinese bookstore. There are English editions of John Stuart Mill's *On Liberty;* John Rawls' *Theory of Justice; The Federalist,* which first laid out the case for the American Constitution; Friedrich Hayek's anti-socialist classic *Law, Legislation, and Liberty;* and, for those concerned with the spiritual aspects of personal freedom, Henry David Thoreau's *Walden* and the essays of Ralph Waldo Emerson. A quick survey of works available in Chinese turns up the speeches and letters of Abraham Lincoln and Thomas Jefferson, Michel de Montaigne's reflections on the value of tolerance and the hazards of authority, and—not precisely a classic of liberalism, but a truly intimidating prospect in Chinese translation—James Joyce's *Ulysses.*

Yet a step over from the Book Palace's teeming aisles to the Internet café on the second floor reveals the only empty space in the building: a few Westerners checking e-mail, a Chinese attendant playing computer solitaire, and a dozen empty terminals. A part of the reason, perhaps, is that browsers have to list a name and identification number in order to use a terminal, and their activity is quite possibly recorded. Other Internet cafés, however, are full: one simply has to know where to go. Once on-line, getting information is a hit-or-miss affair. The *New York Times* is now available—a small revolution—but only because, in the course of an exclusive interview in August 2001, the editors asked President Jiang Zemin why their newspaper was forbidden in China. The site was un-blocked within days. The *Washington Post* and *Los Angeles Times* are still unavailable, as is the *Atlantic Monthly*. CNN.com is open, although other breaking news services are not. A Google search for information on a rumored airline mechanics' strike that threatens to delay my return to the United States leads me to a series of government firewalls and then eventually to the World Socialist Web Site, maintained by the Fourth International, which provides an opinionated but detailed account of President Bush's plan to avert the strike.

Seen with an optimist's eye, haphazard monitoring and cen-sorship are symptoms of authoritarianism's decline, as liberal economics and new technology erode the old edifice of repres-sion. However, it is imprudent to underestimate the Chinese Communist Party's capacity to hold on to power. The govern-ment realizes that governing at the point of a gun is the crud-est and least stable form of rule. A more effective repression directs people's own energies against freedom, giving them as much security, pleasure, and personal freedom as is compatible with the ultimate power of the rulers.

In today's China people with the resources to pursue it can usually acquire whatever information or entertainment they desire. The tone of public life, though, is set by the Chinese media, which is either state-owned or state-censored. If the government ever concludes that foreign media pose a real threat to its influence over the public mood, it will crack down on them. That is the point of today's intermittent censorship: it keeps the government's hand in the game in case repression needs to be stepped up.

Information is a microcosm of freedom at large. Those Chinese who have the liberty to think about it—who are not at the edge of survival, as many peasants and newly unemployed industrial workers are in a fast-changing economy—consider themselves more or less free. Besides spotty but adequate information and entertainment, they enjoy the friends, romantic partners, and private styles of life that they choose, with the prominent exception of the prohibition on having more than one child. In solitude and in conversations with friends, they enjoy freedom of conscience. Even members of Communist youth cadres speak about the Party with casual scorn, ridiculing the Marxist idiom it still adopts at moments of high import, and condemning it for the Tiananmen shootings—for which the government has issued no apology, let alone repudiation. But there is no place to express dissent in public. Unsanctioned opinions are unwelcome on the airwaves and the editorial pages. An Internet site where they appear too frequently or vociferously risks getting shut down. A political party or civic group that spread dissenting views would soon land its leaders in prison. The China Democratic Party tried to press for reform, and was repressed in 1997.

In other words, the government's tolerance ends at the border between public and private life. Individuals can think, speak, and even act pretty much as they like, but when they speak out or act together without the Party's blessing, they cross into lawlessness. Writers and scholars whose work threatens to become a focal point of dissent have been jailed or driven out of the country. The spiritual group Falun Gong, identified in the official press as "the evil addictive cult," is outlawed and hounded: despite having no politics of its own, it connects millions of people outside the control of the state. Independent ideas and organizations both cast shadows over the Party's monopoly on political power.

China is engaged in an experiment in the nature of modernity. The Chinese government's hypothesis is that a people can enjoy the freedom of the marketplace without the freedom of democracy. There are two parts to this idea. The first is that people who live in a market society will not necessarily demand democracy, but will be satisfied with prosperity and relative personal security. The second is that the marketplace can survive without democracy, that a free and efficient economy can coexist over time with an undemocratic state. For China's experiment to succeed, both of those ideas have to be true. If it succeeds, it will become the most significant challenge to liberal modernity.

The Wish for Kings

I am at lunch with a group of law students from Peking University, the best in China. We have just attended a two-hour session of their class on the American Constitution, specifically the concept of due process of law. Of my five Chinese companions, two are members of the Communist Party. One of the Party members has just landed a job offer from an accounting firm whose name I don't recognize, and which she identifies for me as "Big Five." The other is applying to American master's programs in law. Where, I ask? "Top twenty," comes the answer. She is the tallest, most poised, and the nearest to English fluency of the five, and was recruited by the Party because these qualities marked her as having good prospects. Like certain social clubs, today's Party tries to remain important by attaching itself to people who would likely succeed with or without it.

Thirteen years ago, these students might have been in Tiananmen Square. They are ambitious, critical, and cosmopolitan. They discuss the Party harshly. "I hate to hear the Party talk," says Yvonne, the top-twenty law applicant. "Everything it says is a big lie. Everyone knows it is a big lie, and the party knows, too. No one believes it." She is talking about Marxist-Leninist rhetoric, the pretense that China is pursuing "socialism with Chinese characteristics," rather than capitalism with autocratic politics. Stella, a short, sturdy Christian with a booming voice who has told me she wants to be a human-rights lawyer, goes further and suggests that the Party does not even deserve credit for the new prosperity: "It has only gotten out of the way, so that people can make money. If it were not still in the way, perhaps China would be even richer."

Yet they balk at proposing political change. As criticism of the Party's rhetoric grows, the accountant interjects: "It is easy to say that the government is bad, but what do we know? We are students. We do not have much experience. We cannot know the whole picture." A small, shy woman from a provincial town in the south adds, "It is better for the government to have power than for no one to have power. We have to look at the whole situation." Everyone nods, and now even Stella admits, "After Tiananmen, all progress stopped for three or four years." Her concession seems to bring the matter to rest, and Yvonne, speaking for the group, turns to me: "So, you see, we are less radical than the Tiananmen generation." She continues, "We Chinese are very different from Americans. We care most of all about stability and the common good. The community comes before the individual. Above all, we would like to be ruled by good kings."

This idea of good kings comes up everywhere in China, always tied to the assertion that Chinese civilization is Confucian, devoted to hierarchy, stability, and collective well-being. This idea usually involves two contrasts. First, the Confucian Chinese are unlike Americans, who are individualistic, self-involved, yet also capable of democracy. Second, and more mysteriously, the Chinese are unlike the Chinese of a decade earlier, the foolhardy Tiananmen dissenters. What goes unspoken is that they must also, therefore, be unlike the Chinese who launched the long civil war that culminated in the communist revolution, or who carried out the Cultural Revolution more than thirty years ago. For that matter, they must also be unlike themselves, the Chinese of today who are at once conducting vibrant entrepreneurship and violent gangster capitalism. (The weekend before this lunch conversation, twenty bombs went off in one Chinese province, including one that killed five people at a McDonald's. All were suspected to be the work of a businessman with a score to settle against a rival. The bombings were news, but not shocking. In the provinces, almost every week brings a new episode of labor unrest as workers protest corruption and firings at their factories.)

The dedication to stability and the wish for kings are artifacts of politics, like the bloody-minded imagination of Islamic and Hindu chauvinism. They are not a vise grip that history impresses on political life, but rather what politics has made of history. What history does impose is the recent memory of terrible disruptions: great movements of people across the landscape, massive loss of wealth and life, and the persistence of China's second-class status among the world's nations. The Confucian platitudes that a so-called revolutionary party has revived are like a charm murmured against the repetition of that history, and even against the instability latent in the pell-mell arrival of markets today. With every incantation the charm reaffirms the promise that China will continue, prosperous and stable, with no more nightmares.

I meet an aspirant to the throne of the good king at Tsinghua University, the chief rival to Peking University. Steven Dong is a professor of communications, a talk-show anchor on the state television network's English-language channel, and an ambitious adviser on a new project to launch a Chinese-government channel for the American market. Steven wants the channel to present what he calls "the real China." A former student at Cambridge University and elsewhere in England, he speaks for a consensus among savvy Party members that the present propaganda machine is clumsy and anachronistic.

I have to agree with that. The *China Daily*, the widely ignored official newspaper, is presently on a crusade against Falun Gong. On Tuesday it reported that a member of the "addictive cult" had killed his parents. On Thursday a front-page story headlined "Cult's Evil Condemned" announced that the China Anti-Cult Association had denounced Falun Gong, and helpfully explained, "The Falun Gong cult uses evil fallacies to control its followers' minds with the aim of doing severe harm to society and bringing tragedy to many individuals and their families, according to the [Anti-Cult Association's] statement." That last clause is typical of the paper's gesture toward objectivity, which is to compose its stories by quoting the statements of party officials and approved organizations. The next day, in case the point had gone unheeded, the lead editorial read: "No civilized society will tolerate such a cult as Falun Gong, which has proven to be anti-human and anti-society. The government's determination to thoroughly eradicate the cult is not only in line with [*sic*] people's wishes, but is also vital for safeguarding people's interests and maintaining social peace and stability. Such a firm stance displays the government's high sense of responsibility towards its people and society." And so on in that vein. Each day's front-page photo showed President Jiang locked in what appeared to be the same handshake with a foreign dignitary—Pakistan's president, Musharraf, the hugely unpopular but Beijing-anointed head of Hong Kong's municipal government, and the chief of Burma's brutal military junta. The last photo was accompanied by the headline "Myanmar Media Hail Jiang's Visit," giving the impression of an "After you, Gaston" routine between two authoritarian presses.

So I am curious about Steven's plans for the state media, and especially the upcoming expansion into the American market. He explains that the state's programmers take themselves too seriously. They insist on giving their programs matter-of-fact labels such as "Chinese Economics" and "Chinese Politics": "They don't understand packaging." Steven thinks China should follow the example of Mongolia. "We need a celebrity. Julia Roberts, the American actress, went to

Mongolia for a month. She lived with a Mongolian family, and it was all camera'd. When it was shown, she said Mongolia is a very beautiful, very interesting place. Now, Mongolia is really very boring, but because it was Julia Roberts, Westerners listened.

"So we should hire a celebrity, even though it will cost a lot of money, a celebrity who will speak for China. We need to introduce people slowly—not throw China at them, but wrap it in a very beautiful package, so that they will say, 'Oh, this must be beautiful, I want to look at it.' We will give them what they want—celebrities, entertainment. Then we will show them a little bit of the real China."

There is an old idea among Chinese modernizers that the country should import the techniques of the West but not its values, as though how a people does things had no relation to what it chooses to do. Usually, the topic is technology. Steven's idea of importing the techniques of public relations is an extension of that program. The aim is to seduce America as America has seduced the world, but with official Chinese content. "Packaging" means the same kind of seduction that America exercises on the world, but conducted through celebrity endorsements and soundtracks rather than the kind of life being offered. This program takes a rather low view of people's ability to judge their own desires, an attitude common to second-rate marketers and the propagandists of authoritarian regimes.

I want to see the Party's marketing avant-garde at work on the question that most puzzles me: Why should anyone believe that China is a peaceful, naturally authoritarian Confucian civilization, when it has been tearing itself apart and putting itself back together for more than a century? I mention the Cultural Revolution as an instance.

"But the Cultural Revolution was horrible," he responds with a small shudder.

But surely it doesn't sound like the work of a nation of Confucians?

"Ah. That's because Mao was a peasant, you see. The peasants and the common people don't think about politics, and they don't understand it. They think about themselves, their work and their families. Their politics is to build up grudges. They don't have any way to express these, unlike, say, in Britain, where people can complain in the public square or in Parliament. So every now and then they explode. That's what is happening in the countryside today."

So the Cultural Revolution was just another peasant rebellion—a small disruption in the natural order of power. But, I want to know, can you really avoid political crisis by forbidding people to learn self-government? Isn't Britain's free expression a good idea?

His response is not quite an answer. "It is a difference between Chinese people and Americans. If we have to choose between having democracy and having the most capable leaders, we will choose to have the better leaders."

In the Forbidden City, the ancient imperial palace complex opposite Tiananmen Square, is a great hall that was the ceremonial capital of China's elite bureaucracy, the Mandarins, who were selected by exams in classical learning and composition. Originally called the Hall of Practicing Moral Culture and later renamed the Hall of Preserving Harmony, it was where those who had passed the highest levels of exams were inducted into the paramount rank of *jin sha*. The names of the hall express the idea that a virtuous political elite is the keystone of a healthy society. More than fifty years after revolutionaries hung a massive poster of Mao the peasant on the gates of the Forbidden City, the Communist Party has returned to this self-image: Mandarins charged with guiding the country to a harmonious prosperity.

Previous Communist rulers claimed to love peasant revolts. Mao's tomb in Tiananmen Square is flanked by statues of peasants and workers charging forward into the future, some with sheaves of wheat held aloft, others with automatic rifles at their sides. This image is the present Party's nightmare rendered in stone. For today's leaders, the peasant rebellions that their predecessors glorified are the violent spasms of a politically incompetent population. The irony is that, by keeping its population politically incompetent—on the theory that it has always been incapable and so cannot be trusted now—the Party ensures that any unrest it faces will take the form of another peasant rebellion.

Steven is driving home his point: "Look at Tiananmen. So many people were shot there."

What do you mean, "were shot"? The Party's soldiers shot them.

"That was because the Party had to shoot them." I must look incredulous, because he is visibly pleased by the chance to surprise me with an explanation. "It is hard to explain to a foreigner. My father is a major general in the army. He was out of Beijing at the time of the shooting, but this is what he tells me. One soldier fired by mistake. Then the others had to fire, you see. Otherwise there would have been no way to explain what happened."

A lesson in Mandarin politics: one death is a scandal; many deaths are a policy.

Middle-Class Nationalism

Now, our inferiority is not something allotted us by Heaven, but is rather due to ourselves. If it were allotted us by Heaven, it would be a shame but not something we could do anything about. Since the inferiority is due to ourselves, it is a still greater shame, but something we can do something about. And if we feel ashamed, there is nothing better than self-strengthening. . . . We have only one thing to learn from the barbarians, and that is strong ships and effective guns.

—Feng Kuei-fen, reformer, 1861

The new Mandarin regime has two claims to legitimacy. One is the state's ability to provide security and prosperity. The other is nationalism, the belief that the state stands for the great but embattled Chinese nation.

Many Chinese see the United States as a worthy opponent in a great competition between two social orders, races, and civilizations. When I meet over dinner with a group of journalism students at Tsinghua University, the first thing they want to discuss is anti-Chinese bias in the United States. Their professors have recently presented them with stirring but almost certainly inaccurate statistics on American attitudes: 81 percent of Americans believe that Chinese Americans are more loyal to China than to the United States; only 11 percent of Americans would like to see a child marry a Chinese partner—"less than even for Hispanics or Blacks." All the students are prepared to discuss the case of Wen Ho Lee, the Chinese American scientist suspected of spying for China, whom they see as a victim of pervasive American racism. The ones whose internships permit them to view CNN in the studios of the official Chinese media—it is blocked elsewhere, except in tourist hotels—find it condescending and moralizing toward China.

Later the same evening, I guest-teach a class of about twenty, including the same students who ate with me and Steven Dong. After I finish a brief presentation, a young woman puts up her hand and announces, "I think globalization is valid only in economics. In culture, it is a fig leaf for invasion and exploitation." I ask her to elaborate: What does she mean by "invasion and exploitation"? Why are those cultural matters? She struggles, then replies, "You say we must learn Microsoft Windows, but in fact we have choices. We can use the abacus. We Chinese have used the abacus for thousands of years. Or we can use calculators." The students around her nod vigorously. I have been arguing that English, like Windows, has become a universal language, connecting people around the world, but that because it is also still a British and American language many students may feel that they learn English because of the West's cultural power rather than entirely out of free choice. I was thinking of the rows of CD-ROMs and phrase books in Shanghai bookstores. To be answered with the abacus is bewildering.

Now a man, a gangly engineering student, throws up his hand. "I am anti-globalization because globalization means greater exploitation. There is a man in Africa, and he gets money, and the first thing he does is to buy Coke. Then at the end of the month, he runs out of money to feed his family. The Coke company doesn't care. It only cares about making money." He also is getting adamant nods of agreement.

"Twenty years ago, China was helping African countries to build irrigation systems and many useful things. Today the United States and Japan give Africa money to build roads, and they sell their old car to the African man. He is very happy, and he spends all his money on parts to repair his car. And all the American company cares about is money."

These arguments are a globe-skipping hodgepodge of cultural atavism, moralizing, and Marxist economic theory. But this politics has local roots. The reality in the back of all these students' minds is that China has recently joined the World Trade Organization. It will now have to conform its economy and trade policies to the American model. Economics used to mark the difference between socialist China and the capitalist West: mobilized peasants and workers here, bloated capitalists and an exploited proletariat there. That was a myth, but now the myth is lost, and China is seeking another in nationalism. Nationalist sentiment compensates for the inflexible strictures of the new economic order. Pride fills empty places. It warms the areas that the market leaves cold and alchemizes resentment into self-righteousness. Above all, it gives a new public language, however violent and incomplete, to a country that long navigated by the words of Marx and Mao and now has no serious vocabulary for political conversation.

The new vocabulary risks running out of control. In 1999, when an American bomb hit the Chinese embassy in Belgrade during the campaign to save Kosovo from Serbian genocide, nearly everyone in China believed that the United States had struck a deliberate blow to humiliate the country. Thousands of Chinese stormed the American embassy in Beijing, hurling rocks and bottles, shattering windows, and prompting an evacuation. The attack was so severe that the ambassador and his staff expected a Tehran-style takeover and began shredding sensitive documents. Candid American diplomats say that the Chinese government encouraged the attack to the point of shuttling some of the protesters to the embassy. This was the last outburst to date in the regime's decade-long effort to foster anti-American nationalism. After its mob almost provoked an international crisis, the government tried to corral what it had unleashed. The American campaign in Afghanistan, which was fodder for anti-American sentiment around the world, was met in China with polite, factual news reports and little more. Muslim journalists in Beijing complained that they were not permitted to send reporters to Pakistan or Afghanistan, but were restricted to translating Western wire reports. Beijing wants to number among the great powers at the center of the post–September 11 order, not stand on its chaotic and resentful margins.

But nationalism, particularly the paranoid sort, is not like a broadcast signal that can be shut off from a command center. It is more like a virus, moving from host to host and mutating as it goes. Once Chinese got used to thinking of trade politics as an imperialist conspiracy, it was easy to expand that idea from labor and human-rights activists to the WTO. The biggest round of nods in the Tsinghua classroom goes to a young man who declares that "globalization is a political conspiracy." That is less a suggestion about facts than an assertion of mood. No one disputes that the WTO is the product of agreements among governments. To call it a conspiracy, an agreement undertaken in a spirit of deception and malice, shifts the tone to paranoia. When I ask whether the students support the WTO, fourteen say they do and six say they do not. But others mistrust what they support, and wonder whether they will not turn out to be its victims.

For now, much of the Chinese government's popular support rests on economic dynamism. For more than a decade the country's economy has been growing at a staggering official rate of 10 percent each year. At that pace, a child born today will turn twenty-one in a country eight times richer than the one in which she was born. But there is reason to doubt whether China can survive the next twenty years of growth without a serious economic crisis, which could turn into a political crisis. If that happens, the country's future will fall into the hands of a public that has been taught that it is incompetent for self-government, that it is the target of global conspiracies, and—a dangerous alloy—that it is the world's greatest civilization. These are ideal conditions for violent nationalism.

The Hunger for Virtue

In the present world our trouble is not that we lack good institutions but that we lack upright minds. If we seek to reform institutions, we must first reform men's minds.

—Ch'u Ch'eng-Po, imperial censor, 1895

Falun Gong may prove as important to China's future as nationalism. The attacks in the official press testify to the government's fear of this quasi-religious school of qigong, a traditional Chinese discipline of stretching and breathing akin to

tai ch'i. The elderly, infirm, and health-conscious have practiced qigong in China for many centuries. In its more modest
forms qigong is a therapeutic practice intended to sustain the
flow of energy through the body. Falun Gong is less circumspect. The school's teacher, Li Hongzhi, treats Falun Gong's
practice as part of the formula for salvation, along with ethical
behavior and, ultimately, God's grace. Li claims to have discovered that human history is a series of ascents and collapses, that
civilization has been destroyed eighty-eight times before now,
and that we are presently approaching what he calls "the final
havoc."

Since it grew apart from mainstream qigong practice in the
mid-1990s, Falun Gong has attracted between two million and
one hundred million devotees. Two million is an official government estimate, but since the government put the number at
forty million a year earlier, the lower figure is probably propaganda. Falun Gong's own figure of over one hundred million is
no more reliable than the government's numbers. Even at two
million, Falun Gong would be larger than any known civic
organization in China; at forty million it would rival the Communist Party. The movement has grown rapidly on the
strength of its simple and accessible exercise regimen, its use of
the Internet to spread its teachings, and an informal structure
that allows new practice centers to spring up wherever there
are adherents.

The government was chary of Falun Gong from the beginning. In 1996, it refused to recognize the group as a legitimate
"social organization." In 1998, Falun Gong's books were
banned for their unscientific and apocalyptic ideas. Then in
the spring of 1999, ten thousand Falun Gong practitioners,
mostly from townships outside Beijing, gathered in the heart
of the capital city's government complex to protest their treatment. This show of force alarmed the government. By summer, the Party had threatened to punish local officials who let

Falun Gong members travel to Beijing for demonstrations. Then on July 20, beginning just after midnight, the police arrested Falun Gong leaders around the country. For the next three days, the streets of thirty Chinese cities were full of protests. In Beijing and elsewhere, police arrested so many demonstrators that they had to hold detainees in sports stadiums. By the end of 1999, the state had revised its criminal law to make clear that Falun Gong organizers could be prosecuted as dangerous cultists, presumptively "enchanting and deceiving others by concocting and spreading superstitious fallacies, recruiting and controlling their members, and endangering the society." The government also launched a media campaign, recruiting army veterans, police officers, scholars, religious leaders (among them a Tibetan Living Buddha), and workers to denounce Falun Gong as a threat to society. In the following years, classes on the evils of Falun Gong were added to the Chinese elementary-school curriculum, and official newspapers reported that twelve million students had denounced Falun Gong in their composition assignments. The government set up "anti-cult task forces" in neighborhoods, universities, and state-owned businesses. Meanwhile, Falun Gong practitioners who kept protesting the new policies found themselves in "transformation centers," where beatings and brainwashing helped them to overcome their forbidden beliefs. According to the monitoring group Human Rights Watch, ten thousand practitioners were imprisoned at the end of 1999.

The government's denunciations had a consistent theme: Falun Gong would disrupt social order and derail China's economic development. The threat of social disruption is the Chinese government's favorite rhetorical bludgeon, but the worry was sincere, albeit motivated more by fear of losing power than concern about the common good. Even though Falun Gong has no political program, it combines two elements that alarm an authoritarian state: a charismatic leader who provides a center of moral, and potentially political, power outside the reach of the state; and dramatic, potentially unstable beliefs, in this case the expectation of apocalypse. A similar combination, derived from Protestant Christianity, inspired the self-declared prophet Hong Xiuquan to lead the Taiping Rebellion in 1851. His God Worshippers formed a rebel army that swept across half the country and installed him at the head of the Heavenly Kingdom of Great Peace in Nanjing. Not until 1864 did Beijing retake the half of China that had fallen to the rebels, and by that time millions were dead and a palace coup in the Forbidden City had installed a new regime more open to the West than its predecessor. If Hong's Christianity had been less bizarre (he claimed that God was his father and Jesus his older brother, and that he received regular divine communication), he might have attracted the support of the European powers and brought down the tottering Qing dynasty for good. China's great transformations would then have taken place under another imported idea than the communist myth that provided Mao's iconography.

Communist Party leaders fear that, like the Qing emperors who almost lost power to neophyte fanatics, they have an uncertain grip on authority. Falun Gong adherents appear to them in the garb of the Taiping rebels. Moreover, in one respect the Communist Party is in a more delicate situation than even the most decrepit imperial government. Imperial armies in hierarchical societies keep power unless they lose to other armies—which can of course be peasant armies as well as invaders. The Chinese government is trying, however cynically and inconsistently, to make itself a genuine popular government, with legitimacy founded on democratic sentiment if not on democratic elections. Its appeal to nationalism and its ambition to deliver prosperity rather than ideology acknowledge that even China lives in a democratic age, where most governments need to be tolerated by those they rule and organized discontent is dangerous to the powerful. In such a time, ten thousand peaceful demonstrators make for an alarming show of strength, even though the armies of three hundred thousand men that joined in battle during the Taiping Rebellion would have ridden through them with hardly a thought. Popular authoritarianism is a tricky enterprise.

Falun Gong is dangerous for another reason as well. It offers a form of moral community in a country where that value is besieged. The Party's elite young members are thoroughly cynical about their elders, and they find the official jargon of Marxism alien, scholastic, and hypocritical. There is little relationship in China between what leaders say and what they mean, or between public speech and the values of ordinary people. At the same time, between the brutality of the Cultural Revolution, the disruptions of sweeping economic transformation, and the specter of police repression, Chinese have learned to live with mistrust, betrayal, and shifting loyalties. Falun Gong's core ideas of virtue—truthfulness, benevolence, and forbearance, as the group's slogan has it—is a reproach to a whole ethic of cynical and self-serving activity that the government has taught its people to expect. From early Christians to early Protestants and the first Mormons, religious movements have styled themselves communities of the just trapped in a fallen world. Falun Gong exhibits the same spirit as the Western tradition of rebel believers that inspired the Taipings.

Many Falun Gong practitioners grew up during the Cultural Revolution. Their prospects were wrecked or greatly delayed in the decade of closed universities, mandatory farmwork, and ubiquitous violence. Younger Chinese describe many of them as haunted and embittered, a generation that was first sacrificed to the most extreme ideology, then set loose in an increasingly individualistic economy. Such experiences can produce hunger for a doctrine of simple goodwill.

The nationalists offer national revival and political strength. Falun Gong offers spiritual revival and moral strength. Both are in contrast to the opportunism and unprincipled use of power that the Chinese state favors. Both are, in their ways, emotionally and morally plausible as the Party cannot be, except insofar as it succeeds in wrapping itself in the nationalist banner. Both alternatives offer the sentiment of purity against the studied hypocrisy of a Party that gives with one hand while it takes with the other, seeking to make itself indispensable by subtly hamstringing the liberal reforms that would otherwise make it irrelevant.

The Hollow Center

What, then, is the way to effect our salvation and to achieve progress? The answer is that we must shatter at a blow the despotic and confused governmental system of some thousands of years; we must sweep away the corrupt and sycophantic learning of these thousands of years.

—Liang Ch'i-Ch'ao, reformer, 1905

China's economy and political system are locked together, and instability in one weakens the other. The basic facts are not in doubt. Corruption pervades the Communist Party. At the lowest level, petty inspectors live on bribes from businesspeople. Although a few of the top-tier bureaucracies have been cleaned up, especially for foreign investors, day-to-day operations still present regular opportunities for extortion. In the higher ranks of the Party, city and state bosses take millions or billions of dollars—not subtly, but in outright theft. Periodically executing a handful of these officials has become a set piece of the Party's anti-corruption efforts. Smaller kickbacks and favoritism in government contracts are widespread. President Jiang Zemin's son is head of China Netcom, the government's Internet service, and has put himself at the center of the Chinese high-tech economy. He is known for being able to come up with capital whenever he needs it, sources unspecified. For these privileges, the children of high Party officials are known collectively as "the princelings."

China's banks are engaged in brinksmanship with disaster. For years they have made loans to state-owned enterprises and politically connected private businesses, often with no expectation of repayment. In 2000 it emerged that 40 percent of outstanding loans from the country's four largest banks, all state-owned, were bad. Since those four banks alone have paper assets of $1.2 trillion, more than China's gross domestic product, their bad loans are an earthquake-in-waiting. Nicholas Lardy, a scholar of Chinese economics at the Brookings Institution, has estimated that those banks' total bad loans may run to more than $600 billion, 60 percent of gross domestic product. The government has begun a campaign to save the banks with direct infusions of capital and by issuing bonds to replace the debt, but if bad loans are as common as Lardy estimates, the cost of the bailout will be staggering. China is trying to grow its way out of trouble before the end of the next decade, when, under WTO rules, efficient foreign banks will begin to compete in a serious way for the deposits of Chinese customers, who now accept minuscule interest payments on their savings. Once China loses political control over its finance system, it risks an unmanageable crisis.

The next question is whether the growth will continue. The Columbia economist Jeffrey Sachs, among others, estimates that the Chinese government has exaggerated the country's growth rate, and that a figure of 8 percent annual growth is nearer the mark than the official 10 percent. That is in line with the experience of other East Asian countries, such as South Korea, Taiwan, and, until recently, Indonesia, which have concentrated on low-technology export manufacturing while moving tens of millions of people from peasant villages to industrial jobs. The growth numbers reflect the fact that, when someone moves from a medieval economy to an industrial one, she produces much more for each hour she works. Countries with large peasant populations and foreign markets for their industrial products grow fast as long as they are shifting workers from farms to factories. The real challenge begins when they have to keep improving the productivity of an industrial and postindustrial economy.

Whether Chinese companies can become more efficient depends on whether they can shake off their communist-era role as appendages of the government. Many state-owned enterprises, especially in China's industrial northeast, are still a kind of laborers' barracks, offering schooling, medical care, and housing along with employment—not necessarily what the companies are best able to do, and not always the soundest method of providing education and health care. State enterprises are often required to carry redundant employees for the sake of providing jobs.

Since the early 1990s, China has been restructuring its large companies to make them resemble Western corporations, with independent managers answering to shareholders. These reforms are a long way from being complete, and because the state tends to be the largest shareholder, they are often an artificial overlay on the old socialist economy beneath. The majority of the urban workforce is still employed by the state, and the figure may be as high as two-thirds, depending on who is counting in an economy where state and private enterprises can be difficult to distinguish. Old patterns of inefficiency have hung on, especially in traditional industries where the state remains dominant. In 1995, manufacturers of nine hundred major products were using less than 60 percent of their capacity: air conditioners, telephones, color televisions, tractors, and machine tools were being produced at about half the rate they could have been. In the late 1990s, close to half of state enterprises were losing money, with losses totaling about $10 billion a year. Nicholas Lardy, the Brookings Institution scholar, reckons that the situation is in fact much worse than this, because the companies continue to live on state loans that they will never repay. Since those companies employ so many Chinese, the symbiosis of the state banks and the state enterprises threatens the entire economy.

The government's plan is to keep getting richer, ease the economy into the efficiency of private enterprise, and root out corruption, all without giving up its monopoly on political power or its control over the media. The Party must maintain a united front: open dissension among high officials could mean disaster. Chinese politics is haunted by images of civil war; after all, the Cultural Revolution began as a Party power struggle. So, determined not to let power be divided, the Party is trying to create the rule of law in an authoritarian system wracked with corruption. Slowly but steadily, judges and prosecutors are being trained in Western-style procedures: not to take bribes, not to jail enemies or do favors for friends, not to apply—or ignore—laws with reckless whimsy. The judiciary, long populated by ill-educated Party hacks, is filling up with trained young lawyers who know something about American, European, and international law. The Party imports eminent American law professors to cajole its regulators out of their habits of extortion. And, of course, there are the periodic executions of corrupt local officials.

In democracies, reform generally happens when the media report abuses and a rival political party takes advantage of public disgust or outrage to win power. Authoritarian attempts to restructure political and economic systems seldom succeed without inducing a political crisis. Japan moved from a feudal to an industrial social and economic order in the Meiji Restoration of the late nineteenth century, but that was no sure thing. Despite a homogeneous population, a tradition of respect for authority, and a great reverence for the newly elevated Meiji emperor, the Japanese underwent serious unrest as the Meijis ousted the samurai warlords who formed the backbone of Japanese feudalism. China is trying to do much the same thing with disputatious minorities in Tibet and the Muslim northwest, a recent history of revolutionary disruption, and a ruling party whose own members often despise it.

If open conflict comes—if a peasant rebellion finds a leader and an ideology, if the next version of Falun Gong is more political than the present one, or if a financial crisis rocks the new monied classes—the Party's policies ensure that China will be ill prepared for it. There are no free-standing civic organizations or political leaders, and few independent voices in public life. Civil society, which frightens the government, is also just about the only way a country can survive a political crisis without descending into chaos. As China attempts to thread the needle of reform, it raises the stakes at each stage, increasing the likelihood of ruinous failure.

All opinions about the future of the Middle Kingdom reduce to two views: China will make it, or it won't. These are not forecasts as much as bets. Chinese officials, international investors, and the United States government have concluded, with varying degrees of enthusiasm, that there is no viable future apart from the Party's. In this view, the Communist grip on power will perhaps loosen in twenty, thirty, or fifty years, when the fear of disorder has passed. Some businesspeople, journalists, and independent observers think it more likely that something will snap—rural unrest, a crisis in the banks or the industrial sector, a new charismatic movement to replace Falun Gong, or a split in the Party. If that happens, the country may spiral into the rule of local warlords and rival armies that consumed it in the years before the communist takeover in 1949. Intelligent people in each camp admit that the other may have it right. After all the statistics and forecasts, the optimists' view comes down to this: the Party is too powerful, too determined, and too smart to fail. The pessimists' response is that the economic, political, and social storm that China is entering is too enormous for the country to survive without crisis.

China has overcome a legacy of poverty, bloodshed, and humiliation by the West, but at the cost of chaining itself to the past. The myths of the good king, the orderly Confucian community, and the eclipse and revival of national greatness are founded on fear: of chaos, failure, and bad rulers. The regime exhorts, controls, and corrupts because it does not trust the people to make their own future. That trust is the critical gamble of modern liberty, the linchpin without which the other parts fall into disarray.

The Chinese government is betting that a growing market and happy consumers will be enough to make the country a great power. American free-marketers hope that the same economic forces will turn China into a modern democracy. It may be that both beliefs are the hardly recognizable legacy of Marxism's tendency to elevate economics above all else. A people's economic life takes place in the political house it builds for itself—framed with laws and filled out by sentiments and habits: civic life, open speech, trust in government, the belief that the whole affair is partly one's own. Without a politics that can force reform and survive crisis, markets alone will not enable a nation to navigate between liberty and violence.

The Indonesian Storm

Jakarta is a city of glass and steel from fifteen feet above street level to the peak of the highest skyscraper. This elevated metropolis is home to branches of Citibank, the Hong Kong and Shanghai Bank of Commerce, Planet Hollywood, General Electric, Ferrari, Maserati, BMW, mall after mall, and a cacophony of banks: Lippo Bank, Bank IFI, Bank Mashill, Metro Bank, DBS Bank, Bank Mandiri, Bank Niaga Niaga, Bank Syariah Mandiri, Bangkok Bank, Bank Indonesia, Bank

BTN. Some of the structures are imposing and ambitious, aping the Empire State Building or clawing at the sky with daring architectural contortions.

Below the fifteen-foot line, where most of the people are, Jakarta is a city of dirt and broken concrete, more like India than it is like the hypermodern metropolis of the skyscrapers. There are sidewalk fruit stands, curbside loungers, and tiny shops in low-slung row buildings. Off the thoroughfares, the crowds of pedestrians, motorbikes, cars, and human pack animals hauling huge loads move in slow currents. Despite its many mosques, Jakarta is Indian also in its names: Ramayana Insurance, Laxmi Tailors, Sri Krishna Enterprises, the Dharma Building. The ubiquitous residue of a Hindu-Buddhist Southeast Asian civilization persists at street level, while many of the mosques press up into the sky with glimmering materials that rival the splendor of the finance centers.

The financial hurricane that leveled Indonesia in 1997 and 1998 brewed in the bank towers. Through the middle of the decade, Indonesia was a boom country—or, more precisely, Jakarta was a boomtown, and the surrounding area of West Java grew rich. Indonesia's archipelago contains more than thirteen thousand islands scattered over three thousand miles of the equator, encompassing many languages; various proportions and varieties of Islam, Christianity, animism, and Hinduism; and physical appearance ranging from the Malays of Java to the people of West Guinea, who resemble aboriginal Australians. Many of the islands are rich in timber, gold, and other resources. Some were effectively looted, with the revenue from mining and logging going to Java while the military kept restive local populations under control. In the meantime, foreign money poured into Indonesia, much of it in dollars, to finance local enterprises. In 1995, foreign banks lent $210 billion to Indonesian businesses. In 1997, the figure was up to $274 billion—as if every American had lent an Indonesian a thousand dollars. That amounted to about a quarter of the country's gross domestic product in 1997. The money built a lot of malls, towers, and mosques.

At the end of 1997 a panic hit. Neighboring Thailand's currency, the baht, had collapsed against the dollar, signaling that investors doubted the health of the region's economy. Indonesia's currency, the rupiah, soon followed. Foreign investors began to call their money home. Banks and other lenders demanded heavy installments on loans that borrowers expected to repay over many years. Like a sudden ebb tide, foreign money roared out of Indonesia. Trying to secure themselves against growing losses, international financiers sank Indonesia deeper into crisis. When the value of the rupiah collapsed, Indonesians had to collect several times as much local currency as before to exchange for the dollars that foreign lenders demanded.

The International Monetary Fund soon intervened. Set up as a global lender of last resort, the IMF has become deeply embroiled in the economic reform of poorer countries. Typically the IMF offers a package of loans to see a country through its crisis, and in return the government commits itself to reforms designed to bring the economy under control and prevent trouble from returning. The IMF offered Indonesia a harsh program. Sixteen troubled banks were closed immediately to prevent further outflow of capital. The IMF ordered other banks to build up their money reserves, so they would not find themselves pushed into insolvency. The government had to cut spending enough to go from a modest deficit to what the first IMF plan forecast as a small surplus. Finally, interest rates went up, meaning anyone who wanted to borrow money had to pay more for it. The aim was to stop cash from circulating and bring the spiral of panic to a halt.

The problem was that the plan didn't fit Indonesia. The model was devised during the IMF's involvement in Latin America in the 1980s, where it first directed national reforms.

Latin American governments had spent money they didn't have, financed by generous and sometimes reckless loans from North American banks—many of which were eager to unload a glut of dollars deposited by Middle Easterners profiting from a petroleum boom. But prices fell for major Latin American exports such as coffee, and repayment became difficult, then impossible. National governments printed huge sums of their own money to pay off loans, but the piles of currency just reduced its value, and inflation rose to staggering levels. The IMF intervened to stop the spiral by stanching the flow of increasingly worthless money.

In Indonesia before the crisis, as in much of Southeast Asia, inflation was less than 10 percent per year—higher than in most rich countries but manageable—and the government showed a budget surplus in all but one of the first seven years of the 1990s. Moreover, Indonesians were saving and investing their money at high rates. All of this suggests that the economy's growth was more than a bubble fueled by speculative foreign investment. There were concerns that the government had less foreign cash on hand than it might have had, and that short-term debt to foreigners was growing quickly, but as long as growth and investment continued, those were not serious warning signs. International investors, the World Bank, and other monitors considered the country's economy more or less sound until investors panicked.

When the IMF program came, a country that had been abruptly bled of its cash was denied quick transfusions. There was hardly any money to be had for payments on debts to foreigners, for payrolls, sometimes even to pay for existing orders that had only to be shipped. Across Indonesia, weak and solid companies alike lurched to a halt or fell apart. Unemployment climbed fast, and many urban workers returned to their family villages, looking for farm work or, at least, food. They found the countryside devastated by the worst drought in a decade.

In Jakarta and elsewhere, there were large, angry protests against the austerity measures, where the newly unemployed held aloft hand-lettered posters reading "IMF = I'm Fired."

The IMF loosened its restrictions soon afterward, but the damage was not easily reversed. In 1998 the rupiah kept falling, to 25 percent of its mid-1996 value. After years of growth, the economy shrank between 15 and 20 percent. Unemployment rose to 20 percent. Crime rates increased. Rioters targeted the shops, cars, and sometimes the homes of Indonesia's ethnic Chinese, who are wealthy and prominent in most of the country's industries and were thought to have a special relationship with the longtime president, Suharto. More than five hundred people died, stirring memories of the waves of violence that swept the country in the early 1960s. That earlier unrest, abetted by government security forces and private vendettas, may have killed as many as a million people, many of them either Chinese or affiliates of the Indonesian Communist Party.

As public discontent intensified, President Suharto's security forces fired on a group of protesting students. The incident crystallized popular anger at the aging and ailing Suharto. Under enormous pressure, the president handed over power to his longtime protégé, B. J. Habibie. Habibie, in turn, began to loosen the country's censorship laws, relax repression of political dissidents, and prepare for the first genuinely free elections since before Suharto took over the government in 1965.

In 1999, a new parliament was elected. Power fell to Megawati Sukarnoputri, daughter of Sukarno, the leader whom Suharto ousted in 1965. Her government expanded Habibie's political reforms and devolved considerable power to Indonesia's regions, where resentment of the central government had been growing for decades. Newly powerful regional governments took their place alongside Jakarta in a haphazard arrangement that lacked clear lines of control and responsibility. Meanwhile violence broke out in the Moluccas Islands, well to the east of Java, where hundreds of Muslims and Christians died in fighting along religious lines. Fighting continues there and in the Aceh district of Sumatra. Some regional governments have become resistant to reforms from the center. Efforts to sell nationally owned companies have failed because regional governments claim to own company assets in their territories. Megawati's government is widely seen as too weak to impose order by force. Although the economy has crept out of its devastation, Jakarta, where the deals of the Suharto era were consummated, still has the feel of a broken, shocked place.

The Hidden Hand

It is well into Ramadan when I visit the National Mosque in central Jakarta for Thursday evening prayers. The parking lot is full of Mercedes, SUVs, and row after row of the tiny scooters that many people ride around the city. The early December evening is hot and damp, and inside the mosque everyone is sweating slightly. Rather than invade the prayer rooms, I take up my station outside with two teenage girls in headscarves who are heading the mosque youth group's Ramadan charity drive. They are more indulgent than enthusiastic about my presence, so I mainly listen while they chatter about their boyfriends. Occasionally a boy comes by to flirt, including one wearing a T-shirt that displays the glowering face of Osama bin Laden. Sidewalk vendors have been selling bin Laden's image throughout Jakarta. When I catch his eye and ask about the shirt, the boy's whole body turns apologetic. He shrinks, throws one hand over his heart, and says, "It is only his passion I like. It is his confidence." "Confidence"—the word that young men here use whenever the subject of Osama arises.

When the worshippers emerge, I strike up a conversation with a large bearded man who has a friendly, inviting manner. His English is good, although he apologizes for it, explaining that it is less refined than his Japanese. He lived in Japan for seven years, working as a sound engineer, before returning to Jakarta. He is very worried about the war in Afghanistan. He thinks the United States is an arrogant power, that it has set itself up as an empire, that it is given to violence. Islam, in contrast, is a religion of peace. Even if Osama is guilty, Muslims cannot accept the American war against the nation and people of Afghanistan.

This is the default position among most Muslims outside the United States, at least in conversation with Westerners. But then he takes a different turn. "Americans are a great people, though. Really, there is no conflict between Muslims and Americans. The conflict that we both have is with the Jews. I have been reading about the Illuminati . . ." Something in my expression must warn him that he has too much of my attention, because he drops the theme. "But perhaps you are Jewish," he mutters before shaking my hand and hurrying out of the mosque.

The Illuminati figure in one of the oldest of the modern conspiracy theories, in which the world is run by a small band of shadowy financiers, usually Jewish. The Illuminati are said to be bankers who control financial markets and engineer crises that advance their designs on global power. Their plan for world domination is credited to one Adam Weishaupt, a Jesuit-trained Catholic who converted to the worship of Satan in exchange for promises of power. Weishaupt completed his blueprint for world domination on May 1, 1776, which is why May Day remains a holiday in communist countries—communists being, along with fascists and Zionists, major elements in the Illuminati's conspiracy. Those who believe in the conspiracy hold that agents of the Illuminati started the American and French Revolutions and the Napoleonic Wars to wreck the great powers of Europe. They used the resulting chaos to grab control of Europe's financial markets, which they have since extended to Wall Street, Tokyo, and the other financial capitals.

The Illuminati next directed Karl Marx to devise communism, and German and Italian nationalists to generate the seeds of fascism, so that the Illuminati could orchestrate a struggle between these ideologies. That struggle helped the Illuminati to foment two world wars with the aim of discrediting national governments and clearing the way to a single, global regime under the direction of the international bankers. The Illuminati's chief institution in the United States is the Council on Foreign Relations, but their webs of influence run through elite universities, the upper echelons of government, and the banks and investment houses.

Conspiracy appeals to people who feel powerless and used by history. It portrays a world that is opaque to most individuals, but intelligible to the elect who know its secrets. Secrets confer a form of power on those who know them, even while explaining their powerlessness. The search for the hidden hand is as natural as the impulse to see a god behind the tornado or lightning bolt. Moreover, Indonesia's recent history coincides unsettlingly with the legend of the Illuminati. The financial meltdown that struck this country did not pause to explain itself. It wiped out wealth as mysteriously as the boom had brought it. One thing that everyone in Indonesia knows—after all, it is verifiable fact—is that international bankers had something to do with the wreckage of their country.

The sound engineer in the National Mosque probably does not know that John Williamson, the economist who coined the term "Washington Consensus" to describe the cluster of reforms the IMF developed in Latin America and implemented in Indonesia, had this to say about economic crises: "If it indeed proves difficult to identify cases of the sort of extensive policy reform needed to make the transition to an open, competitive economy that were not a response to a fundamental crisis, then one will have to ask whether it could conceivably make sense to think of deliberately provoking a crisis so as to remove the political logjam to reform." In other words, we should consider wrecking people's economies in hopes of encouraging them to improve their politics. Williamson's attitude is far from the ambitions that the Illuminati are supposed to cultivate: he is out to make economies work better, not to conquer the world. However, if his remarks were more widely known here, the difference would not seem so clear to many Indonesians, who have already intuited that their economy is subject to violent and almost casual revision at the hands of great powers. Those powers, moreover, are shadowy: neither the large investment banks nor the IMF is designed to be open and accountable. Lines of responsibility are tortuous, and they run to obscure sources. The combination of what Indonesians know about their national disaster and, equally important, what they cannot know is well suited to the cultivation of dark theories.

It would be wrong, though, to put all the responsibility for Indonesia's crisis on the shoulders of foreigners, and particularly the IMF. Since the country became independent after World War II, Indonesians have learned to expect that powerful institutions are reliably corrupt and that most public pronouncements are half-truths or lies. During Suharto's thirty-two years of rule this lesson came through his repression of dissidents, his manipulation of massive amounts of public money through so-called charitable foundations linked to his family, and above all his willingness to treat the national economy as a personal holding company. He, his offspring, and his political allies were the chief beneficiaries. Five of his children developed what the *Wall Street Journal* described as "business empires," which included some of the banks that funneled money into and out of the country during the boom, an expensive and heavily subsidized effort to manufacture an Indonesian "national car," and electric power operations involving so many complex kickbacks that resource-rich Indonesia today has some of the most expensive electricity in the world. His successor, B. J. Habibie, long oversaw an international free trade zone where he installed his brother-in-law as the head of several businesses, while one of Habibie's sons spent more than $2 billion of public money trying to develop an Indonesian commercial airplane. The Habibie empires were linked to the Suharto holdings by joint ventures, and both depended on government contracts or the president's power to extract favorable terms from foreign investors. When more subtle means failed to revive his family's free trade zone, Habibie persuaded Suharto to require all cargo planes flying to Jakarta to stop over at the airport in the Habibie complex before continuing to their destination.

This sort of device suggested to some Western commentators that crisis was inevitable in such a corrupt and inefficient economy. Their term for Indonesia's system was "crony capitalism." The idea attracted adamant criticism, partly because it risked letting the international financiers and the IMF off the hook, and partly because it seemed to suggest that Asian culture is incompatible with free economies and widely shared prosperity. Experienced Jakarta hands, however, insist that crony capitalism was real: pervasive corruption was an everyday fact under Suharto, a fact that does not excuse the foreigners who made the crisis deeper, harder, and more abrupt than it otherwise would have been.

Just as important as inefficiency was the moral lesson that Indonesia's economy taught. Indonesians learned that capitalism is what Adam Smith might have called a courtly economy, run by the powerful for themselves and their favorites. Its fruits are distributed by patronage as much as by merit or diligence. For those who are born well, such capitalism guarantees comfort, prosperity, and the admiration of social inferiors. For the lowly and unlucky, the way up is to tap into an entourage or a scam such as Indonesia's "national car." Dignity is inherited or taken by graft, rather than achieved by one's own effort.

There is no surer formula for disaffection from economic and political life than believing that it is someone else's game, and a closed game at that. On the global scale, this belief generates conspiracy theories. At the domestic level, it can foster long frustration, culminating in riots.

Economic reform is always also a political experiment. It tests whether a country can undergo a sweeping change in the structure of privilege, opportunity, and often demographics, within a generation or so, without political revolt. The economic hurricane that swept Indonesia in 1997 and 1998 wrecked its government, inspired a spasm of incoherent reform, and left the country so politically disabled that it cannot now restore itself to economic or political health. The popular insurrection in Argentina at the end of 2001 took place despite, and partly because of, a self-conscious effort to tie that country's economy irrevocably to global markets by removing policy discretion from the national government. And the real tests are yet to come. Seven hundred million rural Chinese, six hundred million rural Indians, and many tens of millions of industrial workers in both countries are within a few decades of obsolescence. The Indians can vote. The Chinese cannot, but they have a long tradition of rebellion. That prospect is so terrible that their government uses it to extort support from the United States and its own educated classes, saying in effect: "We may be authoritarian and paranoid, but at least we aren't a peasant revolt."

Whether these upheavals will have terrible political results depends on whether the people of rapidly changing countries experience change as something undertaken or as something undergone. If reform is a collective gamble on a future they could not otherwise have, then its inevitable costs will be less likely to bring revolt. If reform is understood as an imposition, its prospects are much poorer. Inconvenience, even suffering, has different meanings, depending on whether one has shouldered it or had it thrust upon one—especially by an alien power. As Burke reminded the House of Commons, the "empire of opinion" is "the strongest part of human nature, and more of the happiness and unhappiness of mankind resides in opinion than in all other external circumstances whatever." Global commerce cannot escape submitting itself to that disordered tribunal.

CHAPTER 11

The Commercial Spirit

—⚊—

We have been looking at the free market as a tectonic force that shifts populations and shakes governments. Markets can sow discontent, anger, and fear. They arrive with the inscrutable, irresistible, and seemingly arbitrary force of the Fates of Greek myth, indifferently disrupting human lives. Worse, sometimes they are both cruelly impersonal and also personal in the worst way: full of the private fiefdoms of powerful people.

But markets also weave people together in peaceful and equitable ways. Adam Smith believed that markets could give ordinary people dignity by honoring independence and competence instead of the privilege of hereditary nobles. Smith's French predecessor, Montesquieu, founded a tradition of thought called "*doux commerce*," sweet commerce, on the idea that commercial life makes people gentler and more tolerant than other social orders. Alexis de Tocqueville developed the idea in his study of American democracy, where he suggested that humanitarian sentiments are a hallmark of modern commercial life.

These ideas are alive in the concrete present.

Bombay is India's financial and cultural capital, the New York of the subcontinent, squeezed onto a small, overbuilt peninsula surrounded on three sides by the Arabian Sea. Bombay is also the headquarters of one of India's most virulent purveyors of ethnic anger, the Shiv Sena, a nationalist party founded in 1966. The name means "warriors of Shivaji," after a seventeenth-century warrior who led the Maharashtrians, the Hindu people of Bombay and the surrounding region, against their Muslim overlords. The Shiv Sena began as the self-appointed defenders of local Maharashtrians, who were increasingly squeezed from above by Muslim and Gujarati merchants and landowners, and from below by villagers who came from South India in search of work. They exacted revenge through intermittent terror against immigrants and their businesses. Their armies were bands of young men who collected protection money from shopkeepers, broke windows, and administered beatings.

They also organized shadow governments in the Maharashtrian slums, providing charity, punishing criminals, and resolving disputes among Maharashtrians. Their leader, a political cartoonist and gifted demagogue named Bal Thackeray, became an icon second only to the warrior Shivaji himself. Delighting in attention, he liked to declare his admiration for Hitler and offer himself as a "benevolent dictator" to replace India's "sham democracy." Posters of his crooked, sour, yet mischievous face, adorned with huge spectacles, are a common sight in Maharashtrian Bombay.

In the 1990s, the Sena adjusted their ambitions. A wave of Hindu nationalism had arisen across the subcontinent. Since before independence in 1947, nationalists had argued that India should recognize its Hindu nature—more than 80 percent of the country is Hindu, with the remainder comprising about a hundred million Muslims and an assortment of Christians, Sikhs, Jains, and others—and unite around that tradition. The nationalists objected to the pluralist liberalism of India's first president, Jawaharlal Nehru, who permitted Muslims to maintain separate civil courts administering Islamic law, swear on the Koran in court, and otherwise maintain elements of a parallel life within the country. In the 1990s, growing regional and caste-based parties amplified the nationalists' fear that the country would fragment if it did not unite around a common idea, while popular disgust with corruption in the ruling Congress Party created an electoral opening. Sighting an opportunity, the Sena declared themselves pan-Hindu nationalists. They turned some of the non-Maharashtrian Hindus they had previously menaced into supporters and cultivated connections with longer-established Hindu parties.

In 1992 a mob of Hindu fundamentalists ignited Indian passions nationwide by destroying the Babri Mosque, built on the site in northern India where the Hindu god-king Ram is said to have been born. Bal Thackeray responded with a series of inflammatory anti-Muslim addresses, which were followed by religious riots in which thousands of people died, most of them Muslims. In a few months, revenge bombings damaged important sites around Bombay, including the stock exchange and the Shiv Sena headquarters. Two years later, the Sena took a batch of seats in Maharashtra state elections under the slogan "Be proud to say you are Hindu," and formed a coalition government with India's largest and most diverse Hindu nationalist party, the Bharatiya Janata. With great flourish, they renamed the city by its Marathi designation, Mumbai. Although Thackeray took no office, he was widely believed to direct the actions of the Sena legislators. Other than changing the name of the city and blocking criminal charges against Thackeray for inciting Hindus to the 1992 riots, the nationalist government did little to distinguish itself from its mainstream predecessors.

I am about to meet with Sunbash Desai, one of Bal Thackeray's oldest companions, the publisher of the Sena newspaper, *Samna*, and the self-described ideologist of the party. The appointment is to take place in the newspaper's editorial offices, in a Maharashtrian neighborhood forty-five minutes north of Bombay's cosmopolitan downtown. The narrow, uneven streets are lined with tiny stone houses, with low tin roofs and curtains serving as doors. One of every few house-fronts doubles as a store, offering a few racks of shirts, scarves, or bolts of cloth. Small vegetable carts line the sidewalks. The streets are a chaos of pedestrians and traffic. Nitin, the Maharashtrian journalist who has brought me here, keeps his hand at my elbow to pull me aside as cars sweep past.

The Sena office is a suspicious place. We are challenged as soon as we enter, and Nitin looks anxious as he explains in rapid Marathi that we have an appointment with Mr. Desai. While he threads a path through belligerent young editors, I survey the office. Bal Thackeray's face is ubiquitous, resembling someone's cranky uncle rendered eight times larger than life. The poster of Thackeray's son, who is being groomed to replace his father, is more arresting: he is portrayed as Shivaji, armored astride a white stallion that stands on a red sea. His upraised scimitar glints in the sun. His plump, bespectacled features, with a heavy mustache and clumsy part in his thick black hair, make him an unprepossessing warrior.

Desai has a polite and disciplined manner. He tells us that the Sena is evolving to defend the interests of the Indian people against globalization's depredations. By "globalization," he means trade liberalization—which, like most people who are critical of trade, he is quick to identify with imperialism. India has a history of conquest by foreigners out for profit, and the World Trade Organization and multinational companies fall easily into a rhetorical line of descent from the East India Company. "Of course, they do not wish to conquer the land of India. Today no one wishes to conquer land. But they wish to dominate us." The Sena does not oppose greater integration with the world, Desai says, but they will stand against domination. The first duty of a government is to protect its people, and the security of "the local sons of the soil"—a phrase the Sena popularized to describe the local

Maharastrians, and which Desai now applies to all of Hindu India—must be paramount.

"Look at our youngsters. From morning to night, they have foreign goods. Their toothpaste and shampoo are Colgate and Palmolive, their tea and crackers are Lipton and Britannia. The shoes are Nike, the trousers are Levis, the pen is Montblanc. They drink Pepsi or Coke. All of these products can be made locally, but they are not. This is the effect of globalization." Desai neglects to mention that when Thackeray first traveled outside India, in his fifties, he went to Disneyland and pronounced it fabulous. He also does not disclose that most of the goods that threaten Indian manufacturers come from China, Cambodia, and Vietnam, where imported technology and weak or nonexistent unions help multinational companies to outdo their Indian competitors. The fast-moving poor countries are outpacing the sluggish poor country, with the rich nations serving as middlemen.

What India needs, according to Desai, is gradual globalization—time to build up its domestic industry, and especially its agriculture, before opening itself to full-on competition with the richer countries. On the one hand, this is what India has in theory been doing since 1947, during which time it has fallen further behind the developed nations. On the other hand, the newly wealthy East Asian states followed a version of the process that Desai is describing, and China has arguably been doing the same thing with some success. At least half the point of such step-by-step liberalization is to ease the force with which people are uprooted from familiar economic patterns— people such as India's more than five hundred million villagers and tens of millions of industrial workers, who might not survive a rush of imports from the farms and orchards of the West and the factories of East Asia. If the Sena program picks up support, it will come from those villagers, and from the urban poor who leave rural areas in search of city work.

This is the party of anti-Muslim riots and Hindu chauvinism, but except for the reference to "sons of the soil," I can extract no bigotry from Desai. When I ask him about Hindutva, the concept of Hindu civilization that nationalists put at the heart of Indian nationhood, he will only say that "Hindutva is much more than religion. It is about forms of life, forms of community. People can practice their own religions in their homes." This is the cautious note that nationalists everywhere sound when they wish to avoid controversy. The Islamicist Muslim Brotherhood holds that Egypt is so deeply Islamic that even its Coptic Christians are culturally Muslim. In India, according to Desai, even the Muslims are Hindu. America, one sometimes hears, is a Christian nation. The public culture should reflect the leading religion, not because it represents one group's domination over another, but because it is a common legacy. This official position may seem menacing enough to members of minority religions, but its smooth argument conceals the overt violence in which the Sena have historically dealt.

After we leave, I ask Nitin whether Desai is sincere in his tolerance of minorities and his concern for the losers from Indian liberalization. The tone of Nitin's response betrays the clear-eyed bitterness of a disappointed admirer: "He is a politician. He may have a position, but that is about it." Nitin's two sentences capture the unalloyed cynicism toward politics that Indians have learned in more than a half-century of independence. A politician's work is to gather votes, amass power, and distribute resources to those he favors. Like a gangster or a sports star, he will attract an entourage, especially young men without other prospects, who acquire status and power by attaching themselves to him. What some people call corruption is not a perversion of politics. It is simply the business of politics. When you listen to a politician, you ask not what he believes, but what he is trying to get from you. "They ran as a party with a difference, and many people believed in them. Now all the local people are despairing of politics. There is no party with a difference. Every party will be the same."

Nitin is small and solid, with a broad, handsome face. He moves with the deliberate grace of an athlete. Raj, the owner of the cafeteria where we stop for an afternoon snack, is larger and heavier, with acne scars, a bit of frizz in his black hair, and softer eyes than Nitin's. Raj joins the two of us at a small table and orders us dosas and sweets. What does he think of the Sena? He reflects a moment before responding. "Do you mean as a human being or as a shopkeeper? As a human being, I feel that they protect my community. In the riots between Hindus and Muslims, I felt that we were safe because of the Sena.

"But as a shopkeeper, I think they are a mob. Any day they might stone my shop to get their money." And which side of his personality is winning? "Ten years ago, even five years ago, I would have said the human being. But I am getting older, I have more family and more money. I think that now the shop-keeper is winning."

Raj has just summed up some four hundred years of thought about the relationship between commerce and the passions. Montesquieu wrote, "It is almost a general rule that everywhere there are gentle mores, there is commerce, and everywhere there is commerce, there are gentle mores." Raj's formulation, though, is somewhat more arresting than those of his European predecessors: "As a human being . . . as a shopkeeper." Raj's use of "human being" to refer to his religious loyalty is strange to a Western ear more accustomed to hear "human" attached to such universal ideas as "human rights" and "human dignity." Raj's use of the word is close to the grain of experience, however, especially in countries such as India, where life is embedded in religious and ethnic communities and politicians unashamedly play to those loyalties. In their emotionally candid, "human" moments, many people think first of the tribe. The unnatural, cultivated prudence of the shopkeeper draws them the other way, toward openness and tolerance.

Raj is familiar with the higher-flown meaning of "human being": a member of the universal tribe of humanity. He even finds it admirable; he simply does not accept it for himself. When I ask him and Nitin whom they find to admire in Indian public life, Nitin says that he considers Mohandas Gandhi the only great man ever to figure in his country's politics. Raj demurs. "Of course I admire the Mahatma, but I have also been a great admirer of the party that killed him"—Hindu nationalists whose descendants belong to the same broad current as the Shiv Sena. "I see him as the mother of the country"—the mother, not the father. "He treated all people fairly. That was his greatness. But for me, fairness would have meant favoring my community."

Fairness would have meant favoring my community. It is a moment of uncommon candor. India presents a challenge to anyone who hopes for the spread of liberal values—meaning, roughly, tolerance, openness, the belief that other people's rights are as important as one's own, and a determination to prevent governments from violating these principles. In the West, liberalism is thought of as a political and economic doctrine. Any such doctrine, though, succeeds or fails to the degree that it is rooted in people's lives. The only thing necessary to defeat its appeal is to look it in the face and shrug, as Raj has just done. The founders of independent India hoped that politics would educate the country's new citizens in liberal practices and sentiments. It has done some of that, but it has also schooled people in cynicism and given them new vehicles for old but freshly aggressive religious loyalties.

Sometimes commerce can prove a better educator in liberal values than politics. It sets a lower standard. It does not generate noble sentiments, but draws on the familiar motives of ordinary life: prudence, a concern for security and comfort, and care for one's family and property. A shopkeeper need not be drawn toward high ideas of justice to be pulled away from too passionate a loyalty to his community, or too intense a devotion to his faith. Self-interest properly understood, although not an inspiring sentiment, can go some way toward achieving that. When the alternative is being a human being in the sense of the Shiv Sena's followers, the shopkeeper is the better man.

The Brahmin as Entrepreneur

N. R. Narayana Murthy's placidity manages to suggest great tension concealed beneath his friendly but often expressionless face, heavy glasses, and somewhat asymmetrical features. It would be sufficient explanation for the tension that he is India's answer to Bill Gates. Infosys, the software company he founded in 1981, is India's second-largest high-technology enterprise, with a market capitalization of $4.3 billion and a NASDAQ listing. In the past decade the company has grown between 20 and 70 percent annually, tilting toward the larger number. In 2000, a poll of India's business elite found Infosys hands-down the most admired company in the country. It is both a pioneer and an icon in an industry whose explosion in the 1990s marked India's first real boom in its half-century of independence. Mention Murthy's name anywhere in India and you will get a nod of recognition.

Since the company's total value is considerably less than the Microsoft founder's personal fortune, it might appear that Murthy is a less important figure than Bill Gates. The difference is that India has not produced a Bill Gates, or a Narayana Murthy, before now. Its Rockefellers, the Tatas and a few other manufacturing families, made their money through wartime contracts with the British government and multiplied it after independence when the national government gave them leadership of the industrial economy. The hand of the state, the "license raj," was so heavy that when Murthy founded Infosys he had to wait six months for permission to import computers, and a week each time he needed authorization to leave the country and meet with a foreign client.

Entrepreneurship was rare because of bureaucratic impediments, but it also went against the grain of the culture that produced Murthy. He is a Brahmin, from the literate caste that traditionally furnished India's priests and scribes and has more recently produced many scholars, journalists, and technicians. He also comes from southern India, a region of high literacy, a slow-moving social life, and widespread observance of Hindu and Brahmin personal codes, such as vegetarianism and the prohibition on alcohol. India's north and south are also divided by language and even by language group: northern languages, including Hindi, come from Sanskrit roots, while the southern tongues belong to the Dravidian family. Murthy's father, a mathematics teacher with a high sense of personal probity, did nothing to incline his son toward the northern-dominated, vulgar, and corrupt world of Indian business. So after Murthy finished his engineering degree at the elite Indian Institute of Technology, went to France to help design the cargo-handling system at Paris' Charles de Gaulle Airport, and spent a few years working at the prestigious Indian Institute of Management, he seemed prepared for a comfortable life. His decision to found a company with a few hundred dollars in family savings was, to say the least, unpredictable.

Murthy's unorthodox choice was possible only because of the great change that the global economy had begun in Indian life. Communications technology and relatively open borders enabled Murthy and his programmers to export their work in the blink of an eye to New York, London, or Silicon Valley. The traditional refinements of the Brahmins—abstract analysis, manipulating symbols—were suddenly basic commodities, and easier to trade internationally than any others. Some Indians joke that programming is the perfect Brahmin industry because it turns symbolic manipulation into money, as the priests have always done by collecting fees for their Sanskrit prayers, astrological forecasts, and ability to read and write. Infosys has turned what was once a local monopoly on knowledge into an integral part of the global trade in knowledge. Murthy's company is part of a general revolution in Indian economic life: of the twenty-five largest industrial houses ten years ago, only three are still among the top twenty-five today. Economic reform, driven by the imperatives of the world economy, has eclipsed the license raj. The question now is what will replace the economic power of the great families that kept Indian economic life stable, then stagnant, for four decades.

Murthy's answer is social and moral as well as economic. India's most successful businessmen move in an atmosphere of cronyism, bribery, nepotism, and spectacular consumption. Indian companies are typically treated as family possessions. Murthy has set himself against all this. He famously lives in a modest home in Bangalore, capital of India's high-technology industry. He makes a point of announcing that his children, to whom he is said to be devoted, will have no better chance of employment at Infosys than the ordinary applicant. Infosys regularly makes its finances public, contrary to the custom of Indian business. Murthy is the only leader of Indian industry to call on the government to tax his company and others that export services, like programming, to foreign clients.

Infosys was also the first Indian company to offer stock options to all levels of employees. When the stock was at its highest at the end of the 1990s, Infosys employed more than a hundred millionaires. Even now that the boom has cooled, Murthy's personal driver and many other ordinary employees are worth more than half a million dollars apiece. Murthy has begun giving away large chunks of his personal fortune to fund scholarships and chairs at India's cash-strapped universities, and Infosys has entered an initiative to install computers in tens of thousands of elementary schools.

Murthy's social commitment comes from taking seriously the objections to India's capitalist class. He thinks of his own life and his company as living defenses of the free market against credible and important criticisms. He appreciates that defending capitalists against charges of selfishness and vulgarity requires changing the face of Indian capitalism. "This is a feudal society," he tells me early one morning in Bangalore, "founded on convincing the great mass of people that they belonged in the orbit of the damned. It is our job to show that this is not so. We have to demonstrate that opportunity is real for ordinary youngsters." The great industrial houses, with their government contracts and high-living rulers, look to most Indians like the same "feudal" landscape they have always inhabited, he explains. The wealth they produce doesn't change a young Indian's idea of what he can hope to do with himself. The only capitalism worth defending is the kind that changes the landscape of power and opportunity.

Murthy displays the jagged unease of a man who says in one sentence, "Economic power is the only thing that matters in this world," and in the next that he will run Infosys only as long as it is an exemplar of business ethics and generosity. He is, as a man of his culture and caste, something of an outsider in the world he has conquered. Yet he conquered it partly to show that he didn't have to play by its rules. He lives between worlds, trying to bring each of them closer to his own eccentric trajectory.

He also lives between India and the West. Success for him means showing that Indian companies can be as good as any in the world, but showing this requires purging certain aspects of being Indian: nepotism, entitlement, the slovenliness of businessmen who expect to serve protected markets. He says to me, and has said elsewhere: "When you enter the Infosys campus"—which is modeled on Microsoft's Redmond complex—"you will see clean roads, large fields, and clean offices. When you see all of this, you will think that you have left India. You will imagine that you have entered the United States, or"—he pauses—"or even Switzerland. This is to show our foreign clients that we are serious, that we are world-class." When I ask whether it ever troubles him that appearing world-class means mimicking Silicon Valley down to the level of casual Fridays, and that seeming "too Indian" carries a specter of inadequacy, he answers on an anti-idealist note: "The weak always have to play by the rules the strong have made. If we play well, maybe in two or three generations we can make our own rules." Until then, one must take care not to appear too Indian.

Murthy is a mass of repudiations: of his caste tradition and the business culture he left it to join, of Indian particularism and impersonal capitalism. But, after all, the modern world is built on repudiation, the betrayal of the dense family networks and precise social roles that once structured most of human life. It runs together the sacred and profane, putting priests and untouchables in adjacent programming cubicles in Bangalore. Paradox is the natural consequence.

Talking with Narayana Murthy brings to mind a curious feature of English: a three-way link between custom, betrayal, and commerce. The Latin *tradere* means hand over, surrender, or pass down, and so "tradition" is what is passed on from one generation to the next. But the word took on another meaning among early Christians: a *traditor* was one who handed over a fellow believer to the authorities for punishment, a traitor. The word is a reminder that once something—a secret, a belief, a convention—is placed in someone else's hands, it is beyond the control of the person who gave it. That is the moment of betrayal. Anything, good or bad, might become of what has been handed over.*

*I am indebted to Jack Balkin for this etymological point.

It is no wonder that a commercial society, one founded on trade, is inconstant, with traditions forever crossing the world, falling into new hands, and returning in a different shape. Does vindicating India's capitalist potential mean repudiating the present Indian reality in the name of principles that come half from Silicon Valley, perhaps a tenth from European leftism, and the rest from the austere attitudes of a Brahmin childhood? It seems strange only for a moment.

The best thing about the complex survival of the past into India's present is the uneasy fit that Narayana Murthy has developed between tradition and betrayal. A civilization that comes into modernity through a million small self-renunciations may be less shaken than one that sweeps off the past with a single, violent gesture. India's kind of change may make less attractive the embittered conclusion of nationalists and fundamentalists that liberal modernity betrays everything precious. The moral potential of commerce—trade, *tradere*—is not just that it gives shopkeepers something to think about other than religious identity, but also that it makes partial self-repudiation feel less like an act of self-betrayal.

It is a mistake to think of "global capitalism" as if it were one thing, an inexorable logic that, depending on one's point of view, either imposes inequality and exploitation wherever it goes or liberates every upward-striving individual it touches. Free markets do both these things, but the proportion between benefit and harm is set by politics, culture, and individual commitment. Life in a commercial society, like life anywhere else, brings out familiar motives: greed and honor, recklessness and prudence, arrogance and openness, hopefulness and resentment. The critical question is how these are brought into concert: in a way that produces anti-Chinese riots in Jakarta, or one that squelches anti-Muslim bigotry in Bombay; with the shadow and intrigue that produced the Suharto clan and now foster anti-Semitic conspiracy theories, or the openness and candid moral concern that have made the awkward Narayana

Murthy one of India's most admired men? There is no neat formula for achieving one or the other, and the balance between them is always a question of degree. The proportion between dignity and humiliation, pragmatic optimism and despair, is often enough to decide a country's future. The same may now be true of the future of the world.

IV

THE ORATORY OF COMMERCE

Everyone is practicing oratory on others throughout the whole of life.

—Adam Smith, *Lectures on Jurisprudence*

CHAPTER 12

Benetton Politics

—⚭—

In the protests that shut down the World Trade Organization's 1999 meetings in Seattle, one young man in Nikes became an icon of political confusion. A photographer captured his image as he smashed a window of Seattle's Niketown, striking a blow against worker exploitation, corporate political power, and the collapse of culture into a giant shopping mall. All the while wearing his Nikes: his nice, clean, fairly expensive Nikes, stitched together in some factory in the third world, purchased no doubt at a shopping mall. What else would you wear to a protest?

The vandal with the impolitic footwear was widely taken as proof that the protesters were too naïve to connect their slogans with their own lives. His indiscretion suggested that even if most people would like a fairer world, they see no contradiction in also wanting fashionable shoes. He seemed to show that the protesters were just out for the thrill of smashing something, and had no point to make.

The photograph captured an irony about the politics of globalization: wherever protesters go, the corporations they oppose are already there—and, to judge by their slogans and advertising images, they are more radical than the protesters. Nike's Web site portrays the company as a force for human liberation. It offers its wearers "No rules . . . no refs . . . no plan . . . just play." It invites women to become "Nike goddesses," descendants of the Greek deity of victory: "We want to take this spiritual idea and redefine it for today's woman." It doesn't just sell products—that would be crass and obvious, which is why Nike's Web site promises "No miracle creams" while flashing a facetious miracle-cream ad that inquires, "Want an instant tight ass?" Nike doesn't make empty promises. It offers the combination of discipline and inspiration that free you to be a better you: the image of the Nike goddess along with "a slap on the butt" to speed you to Olympus. If the buyer is still worried about child labor after all this, the Nike site also advertises a chance to "Raise Havoc for a World Fit for Kids"—exactly what some of the protesters thought they were doing, except that "Raise Havoc" turns out to be a Nike-sponsored workout class that gives some of its proceeds to a mentoring program.

Nike understands that in the wealthiest civilization ever, people don't just want more things. They want better selves: fuller lives, sharper feelings, and more satisfying relationships. Consumers want to do good and be good. If that means breaking rules, defying inane ad campaigns, understanding that material wealth doesn't bring spiritual satisfaction, and raising a little havoc to make the world fairer, Nike wants to help. It wants to be your sassy, mischievous, co-conspiring friend, there at the right time with a slap on the butt. You need to smash something to complete your goddesshood, Nike has smashing footwear for you. What else are friends for? What else *would* you wear to a protest?

The Oratory of Commerce

The protesters who have disrupted gatherings of the rich and powerful around the world in the past few years oppose what they called corporate domination, cultural homogeneity, and exploitation. They mean that large companies have been able to dominate national politics and create international trade agreements that assist their unrestricted operation. As the protesters see it, corporations are free to break unions, pay a pittance to third world workers, and slash, burn, and pollute with impunity. At the same time the companies push attractive but unhealthful products such as Coca-Cola into traditional societies, making every place from India to Zambia look more like an impoverished version of suburban Seattle. In the protesters' view, private wealth has overrun both public life and cultural diversity, to the loss of everyone except corporate executives and stockholders.

In response, defenders of free-market globalization argue that economic change is setting people free everywhere. Those who can start their own businesses, hold their own property, and work for any entrepreneur rather than just for, say, the local landlord or the government have more freedom than others who lack these choices. Traditional societies slot their members into hard-and-fast roles and, often, concentrate wealth and power in a small class. Non-capitalist societies such as the old Soviet Union put economic life under the control of unelected bureaucrats. By opening economic choice and opportunity to everyone, capitalism enables people to shape their own lives in more ways than any other system, even if it means that some end up sleeping under bridges. In this view the Seattle protesters and other critics of globalization are the inadvertent enemies of freedom, unwitting allies of repression and poverty. The real problems are despotic traditions and authoritarian repression. Because neither side makes much sense to the other, the Seattle protests and others that followed have consisted mainly of armies clashing in darkness. The boy in Nikes and the reaction to him exemplified the mutual incomprehension.

The Niketown episode also captures a deep unity between the competing sides. The protesters' allegedly anti-capitalist slogans take much of their content from the language of commerce. The anti-capitalist humanitarianism that drives the protesters has some of its sharpest and most pervasive expressions in advertising, the free-market lubricant that the protesters blame for global homogeneity.

Take the Italian clothing company Benetton, which has expressed every stage of anti-corporate and humanitarian discontent in the past decade. In 1984, in a period of Euro-American conservatism under Ronald Reagan, Margaret Thatcher, and Helmut Kohl, Benetton launched an ad campaign titled "All the Colors of the World." The early ads showed children of all races, draped over each other in playful affection, in Benetton clothes. The images were appealing but, as advertisements go, fairly conventional. Still, they captured part of the experience of a generation that, for the first time in American and modern European history, was growing up amid widespread racial integration. For those young people, sharing classrooms and playgrounds with black, white, East Asian, and Indian kids was natural. But they also knew that it was something new and unusual, that it was more of an event for their parents than for them, and that race mattered at the same time that it didn't matter. The ads put right up front some of the energy and tension of a changing culture, and soon multiracial groups of high-school friends were draping themselves over each other for photos and mouthing "United Colors of Benetton."

The company grew more bold. The campaign had begun as a self-conscious effort to sell clothes with ideas and impulses, not just pictures of clothes. As the theme succeeded, the clothes dropped out. Driven by the photographer Oliviero Toscani, Benetton ads moved away from the product altogether. A mid-eighties campaign that centered on images of the globe in the hands of fashionable young people began with multihued Benetton fashion plates but soon proceeded to a photo of a young Arab and an Orthodox Jew, both in traditional costume, their hands linked by a small globe. By the 1990s, a Benetton ad was an aesthetically precise study in racial contrast, marked as commercial photography only by the logo tucked into one corner. A dark African baby and a blond European face each other, naked, on potties, their legs interlinked, and a chocolate-brown forefinger rises up to touch light-pink lips. A crew team pulls with all its energy, long arms straining, hair wet with water and sweat, faces contorted with effort and pleasure; two are white, one Asian, one black. A tiny black infant's hand rests in a white palm. Many ads featured no clothing at all, and if they did the clothing was not from Benetton. The concept was the product: Benetton is diversity.

The ads still took their energy from an uneasy combination of sentiments about race. On the one hand, almost all viewers accepted the official notion that racism was a thing of the past, and that tolerance and even open enthusiasm were the new currencies of interracial exchange. On the other hand, race was still an event. These images of the new American creed had none of the comfortable domesticity of, say, Norman Rockwell's portrayals of upright American ways. Those dark bodies thrown up against white ones were full of erotic potential. They were alive with an undercurrent of boundaries being crossed, rules being broken, and conservatives growing alarmed. These were not Robert Mapplethorpe's light-drunk, black-on-white homoerotic photographs, the ones that made him a cause célèbre and nearly brought down the National Endowment for the Arts; but the effect was not entirely different. When the Italian city of Milan prohibited Benetton from displaying its naked infants on the world's largest billboard in Piazza Duomo, the company knew it had succeeded. Benetton still boasts that it managed to attract outright censorship in an age of almost perfect tolerance.

Partly to keep up the tension, Benetton pressed its boundary crossing further. Two bakers, one black and one white, embrace as the flour on their faces and arms lightens them both in a photonegative play on the blackface of America's old minstrel shows. A black miner laughs as he runs his finger along the cheek of a blond comrade whose face is dark as a minstrel's with coal dust. An albino African woman stands slightly apart from a throng of black Africans, who eye her with suspicion, pity, and fascination. A "family of the future," naked except for the pea-green blanket that covers all three members, includes a Nordic mother, a black African father, and an East Asian infant. Moving from race to sex, a beautiful blond woman stands sidelong to the camera, her slim arms crossed to conceal her breasts: just below her taut woman's stomach, opposite her generous gluteal curve, hangs a set of male genitalia. Toscani wrote about this photograph: "at times people . . . find themselves with both feminine and masculine genders. That's how the beginning of unity occurs, the unification of genders after that of races. That's where the relationship with the United Colors of Benetton has its origins."

At the same time, Benetton began to pick up a new theme: the suffering body. A series of ads centered on AIDS, with closeups of naked body parts—a backside, an arm, an abdomen running down into a dark patch of pubic hair—stamped, in the blue ink of a death-camp tattoo, "HIV Positive." In a more celebratory mood but still on the theme of AIDS, Benetton linked five colors of translucent condoms to replicate an Olympic flag. Expanding the treatment of suffering, another photo showed tiny Indian children, hardly more than toddlers, carrying bricks through blazing sunlight. In another picture, a set of military fatigues lies empty, the white undershirt stained the rusty brown of dried blood. In an image with special poignancy for Italians, Albanian refugees fleeing their wrecked homeland leap into choppy surf from a dangerously overloaded ship to swim ashore to Italy's Adriatic coast. Elsewhere, an African soldier stands with an automatic rifle strapped across his back, gripping as if in triumph a sun-bleached human thighbone.

Over almost twenty years the Benetton campaign has presented a visual symphony of human solidarity. It is a very particular sort of solidarity. What unites people in this image is not, as many religions have proposed, their common souls; nor is it, as philosophers have argued, their ability to reason and deliberate. It is their bodies: their capacity for erotic pleasure, for appetite, for sickness, for suffering, and even for violent death. People are one because we can all be tortured and broken; we can all die of AIDS or rot away to bare thighbones; and we can all touch, we can all kiss, we all find ways to make love.

All particular qualities dissolve into this commonality. With flour and blackface smeared over faces, we have the power to erase the myth of race altogether. The family of the future is not interracial: it is postracial, so far past race that it doesn't matter that—for now—Korean babies don't come from Danish mothers and Ghanan fathers. As for culture, Jewishness and Arabness are just different clothes hung on the same human bodies, which themselves cling to the same common globe. Genitalia are no closer to the core of things than skin color is: a woman becomes a woman by how she carries herself, by the tilt of her head and the angle of her hips, and by the pleasure she seeks and the ways that she finds it. In Benetton's images, gender is what the body desires, not the shape it assumes.

There is vestigial Christianity in these images. The suffering body of Jesus is central to the Christian imagination, and especially to the bloody iconography of Catholic Italy. When Milan's Catholic leaders condemned Benetton, they might have sensed a special kind of sacrilege. Benetton, like the Church, takes the image of the suffering body as a way toward deeper unity among humans. Some of the power of Benetton's race mixing comes from the uneasy relationship between official anti-racism and squeamishness about the blending of black and white, but Benetton's humanitarian images also draw force from Christianity's visual language.

At its core, though, Benetton's is a pagan ethic. It is a fundamental distinction between Christian and pagan worldviews—meaning by "pagan" the classical Greeks and Romans and the pre-Christian peoples of Northern Europe—that Christianity believes in sin. Sin means that some part of our nature always tends toward evil—destruction, cruelty, and self-degradation. For that reason, behaving naturally or following one's bliss can never be an ethical code, because people are half angels and half beasts, and the bliss of beasts is abomination for angels and destruction for women and men.

Without the idea of sin, it is possible that nature itself might guide human lives. In this spirit, Benetton's Toscani comments on an ad showing a coal-black stallion mounting a white mare: "Benetton's white and black horses show us nature's spontaneity, in our artificial world where nothing is authentic. Because of maliciousness sometimes the human mind sees ugliness in beauty and censors not only the expressions of freedom but is also against the Will of Creation. The Benetton horses take us back to innocence and truth, because they are authentic and beautiful. This forces us to think about what we so often forget: what is natural is never vulgar." So Benetton's image of human solidarity appeals to a "natural" upwelling of sentiment: pity for the suffering body, desire for the graceful body, sympathy for what we can see as human in a person separated from us by continents and civilizations. In this view, nature is deeper than culture, deeper than race, and deeper than gender; it expresses itself through sexual desire that overruns all social boundaries. Morality is the sentiment that responds spontaneously to beauty, erotic impulse and pain.

Benetton has anticipated, joined in, and exemplified the leading humanitarian themes of globalized politics. Its child workers prefigured the fight over sweatshops. Its AIDS victims were salvos in the American fight over political morality that made insensitivity to AIDS unacceptable. Its race-mixing photos and African bodies express the spirit of global moral concern that carried the AIDS fight across the Atlantic and transplanted the activism of ACT UP to South Africa. Its refugees and the thighbone of a genocide victim are reference points for the moral imagination of human-rights activists.

Benetton has captured something about the contemporary moral imagination. We conduct much of our cultural argument through images and the feelings that we attach to them. The sweatshop debate turned not on objective findings about economic growth and employment, but on images of pain and exploitation on the one hand, of economic opportunity and growing prosperity on the other. The fight over AIDS in Africa has less to do with the economics of pharmaceutical companies and the purposes of intellectual property law than with the fact of sick and dying people whose images appeared every day through newspapers, television, and computer screens. The repertoire of advertising—the indelible image, the flash of desire or revulsion, the instant of association between a feeling or idea and a product—is also the vocabulary of culture and politics.

This is also a time of authenticity, when being true to oneself is the touchstone of morality. Authenticity is an especially appealing standard in global humanitarian politics because of the distances—geographic and cultural—that this politics traverses. One can hardly know precisely who is doing what to whom in Indonesia, Sierra Leone, or Bangladesh, let alone the connection between those events and decisions made here in the United States. For most people, the candid answer to the question of whether wearing Nikes helps or harms the third world is that it hurts to think about it. Concentrating on authentic moral sentiment instead ensures that whether you wear your Nikes when you march on Niketown doesn't matter much. The point is the spirit in which you march.

The Benetton ethic only pretends to erase the differences between people. To state the obvious, race and culture run deeper than clothing or a dusting of flour. AIDS and factory work, to name just two instances, have different meanings in different places, especially when some of those places are very poor and struggling with other diseases and other forms of hard labor. Dissolving all of these differences into the shared sensuality of the human body, as Benetton politics does, achieves a false satisfaction. It extends the sentiments of the first world consumer or humanitarian, without closing the distance between her and the person about whom she is made to feel concerned. This first-worlder is left confident that she can tell right from wrong without knowing much about the place where right and wrong are being applied. There is less need to ask someone what she wants when you can see her soul written on her body.

These limitations, though, do not make Benetton sentiments illusory or corrupt. In an advertising-drenched culture, even though every public argument may resemble an ad, commercial values take unexpected, even radical and anti-commercial, turns. Marketers may propagate values, or pick them out of the cultural ether and adapt them for their purposes, but they cannot control their mutation and energy. The global humanitarian sentiment that young Americans and Europeans have been cultivating is a potent, if imperfect, thing, and its story is far from over.

Adam Smith's Lace Waistcoat

Is it strange that the free market should bend the imagination to call its own workings into question? It would not have seemed strange to Adam Smith. When Smith set out to explain why markets exist at all, he did not rely on the desire for efficiency, or even the wish for comfort, pleasure, or gain. In his *Wealth of Nations* he posited a "propensity to truck and barter" that has become famous—and infamous, because to some uncharitable readers it has suggested that the Scotsman believed all people everywhere were born as canny and penny-pinching as his stereotypical countrymen. Elsewhere in his writing, though, Smith proposed that the "propensity" had its roots in a deeper feature of human nature: "the natural inclination everyone has to persuade." We want to bring others into line with our own desires, to see our sense of the world reflected in them, and so in whatever we do "everyone is practicing oratory on others throughout the whole of life."

Life is shot through with moral and aesthetic argument—which sometimes takes the form of marketing. We may not think of this as an eighteenth-century Scottish view, but there it is. Smith's neglected insight that the desire to persuade is essentially human would come as no surprise to students of branding. For them as for Smith, economic life is about human passions: hunger for status, lust for beauty, the desire for grace, and the wish to be right. Little has changed but the technology.

The concept of a brand is that some of a company's value comes not from the usefulness of its products, but from all the other qualities that buyers associate with it. Nike is youth, vitality, and sexy energy. By purchasing the brand, customers participate in those qualities—with a slight danger that their edgy vitality may overflow in the vicinity of Niketown. Nokia is elegant and so up-to-the minute as to be almost futuristic. Ralph Lauren's Polo brand is languorously aristocratic—at ease, diffident, and in command. Wearing or wielding one of these brands imparts some of the same qualities to the buyer, in others' eyes and in her own.

For decades, interest in branding was restricted to marketing strategists in companies that made consumer goods such as cookies, jeans, and pickup trucks. Now even industrial giants such as Boeing use branding programs to plot their movement into new markets. There is a new consulting specialty in megabranding: helping companies to predict which new products will be able to carry the cachet of the old brand: for Boeing, say, cell phones or even watches might benefit from association with the avant-garde of hard-bodied military technology; a line of scented soaps is probably inadvisable. The point is to keep the same winning personality while expanding it into new areas where it will be welcome.

The content of branding has gotten richer. At one time, a bank—to the extent it advertised at all—would have stayed with the themes of personal finance: stability, reliability, and maybe convenience. Now Citigroup, the giant financial services company, presents itself as a lifestyle choice. "Live richly," its advertisements advise. The ads are populated by such characters as a dreadlocked young white guy, his face contorted with laughter, miles from the old image of an important bank customer, let alone a banker. Citigroup also mocks the very concern with wealth that is a bank's purpose, advising its consumers not to confuse lucre with happiness and asking in one ad, "Why do we spend our youth chasing money and then, when we have it, spend our money chasing youth?" The point is to appeal to the spirit of anti-materialist materialism. Perhaps excessive concern with money is not only crass, but a formula for a stunted life. Perhaps the most important things in life lie elsewhere: in intimate relationships, intense experiences, and spirituality. The most important things are not free, however. In the spirit of MasterCard's "Priceless" campaign, which scrupulously lists the expenses leading up to a perfect kiss or an idyllic moment of bicycling in southern France, money is the irreplaceable road from here to perfection, but one does better not paying the road too much attention.

Not every brand cultivates as delicate a paradox as Citigroup's anti-materialist materialism, but many are less about product quality than about quality of life. Nike, and Polo are all about being a certain kind of person. So are Volkswagen Beetles and Harley-Davidson motorcycles. And once everyone is playing the game, it is hard to avoid gaining or losing points oneself, even inadvertently. Branding decisions attach to us all like burrs in a meadow, in our shoes, jackets, cars, furniture, entertainment habits, and neighborhoods. The ultimate advertising strategy would be to make the daily lives of attractive people into extemporaneous and unending advertisements for a product. In fact, some companies have hired stylish young women and men to praise their products in public, without announcing that they are paid advertisers. A growing number of people have the disconcerting sense of dwelling not just among walking billboards—the Nike T-shirt is very old hat— but amid a living ad campaign.

The anti-brand sentiment that pervades the youthful, North Atlantic reaches of globalization politics is a response to advertising's saturation of daily life. One expression of this spirit is to adopt brands ironically: wearing an old Joe Camel logo or an "I'm a Pepper" T-shirt from an early 1980s Dr Pepper campaign. Another is to seek out bits of fashion that come from outside the world of mainstream brands: baseball caps advertising tiny bars in the rural Midwest or Appalachia, the castaway shirts of gas-station attendants with first names stitched in cursive, or the indigenous clothing of people from Thailand or Peru. Each of these is a way out of the giant mall of a branded world—and, paradoxically, a way of being hipper than the hippest brand could be, and so winning at the brands' game.

The other response is more explicitly political. It is almost axiomatic among young dissenters that brands are bad: they make the world flat and homogeneous, turning every little town into the same strip mall. They replace spontaneous and sincere relationships with status symbols and ridiculous catchphrases. They channel rebellious energies into rebellious consumer posturing—shopping at Urban Outfitters instead of Gap, buying American Spirit cigarettes, and banking with Citigroup to show disregard for mere money. And they conceal exploitation, maintaining a lovely dream world for rich consumers whose products are manufactured in sweatshops abroad. That litany of sins is enough to damn any institution— and is also pretty much the same list of complaints that has been nailed to capitalism's door every few decades since the seventeenth or, depending how one is counting, the thirteenth century. Because the brands are the most visible emblem of capitalism nowadays, they catch the brunt of anti-capitalist discontent. Being a symbol is a risky affair.

Young activists have turned the instability of symbols to their advantage. Because they rise and fall with popular sentiment, brands are more vulnerable than other assets. Nike's margin over its competitors is largely in the brand, and much the same is true for many companies that specialize in the visible symbols of personality and status: clothes, footwear, cars, and so on. That is why, if Nike's name were suddenly associated with exploitation, inhumane factories, and virtual slavery among third world workers, the company could be devastated. Whether the associations are fair hardly matters: is it true or false that Nike exudes vitality, youth, and freedom? The currency of branding is perception, and it is subject to sudden and dramatic fluctuations in value. A branding campaign is a kind of moral and aesthetic promise, which can be broken by actions that have nothing to do with the quality of the product but contradict the message of the brand.

So as consumer life becomes more and more about values beyond convenience and function, the brands and their critics are caught in a curious embrace. The companies that press humane, nonmaterialistic lifestyles increase their profits, but they also make themselves vulnerable by aligning themselves with the same values that their critics invoke to criticize the world economy. The companies give credence to the very people who want to bring them down, or at least to change them fundamentally. In the question of who embodies humane values, the battle between money and conviction is a strange arms race.

At the same time, the critics find themselves doing what they profess to hate: marketing. Their campaigns to turn the power of the brands back on themselves require better images, better slogans, and a savvier sense of what moves people. As the companies dress themselves up as hippies and anarchists, the hippies and anarchists learn the skills of advertising consultants. This is the Alice in Wonderland world in which globalization politics takes place.

The Eternal Argument

There is a conventional view, shared by free-market brand defenders and left-wing critics alike, that branding is an innovation of high-speed, high-tech capitalism. From Rainforest Action Network activists to the *Economist*, one can hear how, in the old days, companies such as General Motors and Hoover rested on their products' quality, and advertising just served to let people know where they might find a good car.

This is one version of an endless story: at one time the world made sense, but then something—the decline of the old gods, the fall of Rome, the rise of merchants and money-lenders, the industrial revolution, or advertising—turned human nature upside down and social life inside out. But why, then, did Adam Smith propose that we are all always practicing oratory on each other? Why did he believe that commerce is persuasion, and that rather than using persuasion to get what we want, we persuade because persuasion itself is what we want? Because he thought that what people want most is the admiration of their fellows. We want them to recognize us as graceful, dignified, and good. We want their eyes and their hearts to follow us. Persuasion brings others' feelings into line with ours, producing a harmony that is the triumph of what Smith called our oratory.

In any social order, charisma works as a currency alongside money. Smith asserted that when we see the wealthy, the powerful, or the beautiful, our feelings go out spontaneously to them. Without intending or perhaps even knowing it, we imagine ourselves sharing in their fame, adulation, and seemingly effortless excellence. "The man of rank and distinction," Smith wrote, "is observed by all the world." At the opposite end of things, "the poor man goes out and comes in unheeded, and when in the midst of a crowd, is in the same obscurity as if shut up in his own hovel." Those who pass him in the street do not see him, and if they do they draw back as though affronted by the reminder of human wretchedness. Poverty means more than lacking money: it encompasses the lack of status as well, and the ultimate poverty is to be outside the esteem of other people—to be socially invisible.

This is why only half of Adam Smith's endorsement of capitalism came from his belief that it would be more efficient than the semi-feudal hierarchy it replaced. The other half came from the conviction that it would bring a new currency of esteem, and with it a better kind of man. In a traditional, courtly society, power and influence were mainly inherited. Great men were assured of their positions from birth, which gave them the grace of perfect self-confidence and impeccable training. But this also bred bad character: men with nothing to work for fell into frivolity. Even worse, the only way for those not born to greatness to achieve it was to make themselves sycophants to the powerful, laughing at bad jokes and following fashion slavishly in hope of winning a superior's affection. In any time and place, people will seek to be admirable: but in the world of kings and courts, the appetite for admiration made everyone involved despicable—to Smith's eye at any rate.

In a market society, though, everything was up for the taking. Commoners in the marketplace didn't have to choke on their own tongues as they delivered flattery to a social superior: they could instead apply "real and solid professional abilities, joined to prudent, just, firm, and temperate conduct." A man with those qualities might be respected for the wealth he earned, but the wealth was an emblem of character and skill.

Entrepreneurs, craftsmen, and shopkeepers had a chance of being respected for traits that were genuinely respectable, and therefore were also grounds for self-respect. The representative man of the market society was not just more productive but also more admirable than the man of the lordly courts. He might look crass to the aristocrat, but that was because he didn't need aristocrats: he answered to different rules and cultivated different virtues. The "great man" of the new order would be simpler, more capable, and freer.

When Smith penned his sentences on the great and the invisible, he might have been thinking of a fellow Scot, Sir John Luss, who a century earlier had been fined the astonishing sum of five hundred marks (then £350) for wearing a waistcoat lined with lace. Luss's fine was more than most Scots, even those of reasonable means, could have paid. His fine put other fops on notice that they could be ruined if they didn't correct their behavior. Perhaps Luss was fortunate that the prosecutor opened only his pocketbook. In Tudor England, the unfortunate Thomas Bradshaw, a tailor, was led through the streets with his hose slashed to pieces until officials judged that he had had enough humiliation and dropped him at home. In 1577 in Southampton, England, a local court prosecuted Walter Earle for wearing velvet in his hose, and his wife for a taffeta hat lined with velvet. Court records show that the unnamed wife of the Earles' neighbor, John Delyll, was prosecuted for sporting a petticoat lined with velvet. Courts met infrequently then, and it was most unusual for the prosperous to be dragged before one for peaceable behavior. But the Earles and Mrs. Delyll must have known that they were taking a chance with their velvet and taffeta.

These impertinently dressed Britons were prosecuted under statutes called sumptuary laws, which were in place across Renaissance Europe. Modern dress codes generally enforce uniformity in a school or workplace. Sumptuary laws expressed and reinforced social differentiation. In England, for instance, they forbade purple silks to anyone below the rank of an earl, gold and silver embroidery to anyone less elevated than a knight, and velvet doublets and satin cloaks to everyone below knights' eldest sons. Elsewhere gold, diamonds, colorful scarves, and particularly new and dramatic fashions were prohibited to commoners and even to lesser nobles. Because fashion, visibility, and status went together, safeguarding one meant regulating all three.

Today we are experiencing only the latest instance of the perpetual interweaving of economic life, social status, values, and identity. The difference is that the wish to be good, graceful, and beautiful—and recognized as such—now roams freely across classes and continents. Brand logic is a freed-up and accelerated extension of what, in Scotland before the American Revolution, it already seemed that life had always been.

The paradoxes of branding politics are eminently human ones, recognizable across centuries. An economy is not just a set of rules for efficiently turning soil into food and silicon chips, steel into guns and cell phones, children into carpenters and entertainment lawyers, and money into more money. Rather, commerce is about how people want to be seen and who they want to be. In a world where commerce is everywhere, those desires have a new pervasiveness and intensity. But the dense and complicated interweaving of images, status, commerce, and moral and political values is nothing new.

CHAPTER 13

The Balaclava Union

—⟋⟍—

On January 1, 1994, the day that the North American Free Trade Agreement (NAFTA) took effect, several hundred masked guerrillas entered eight towns on the border of the Lacondon Jungle, in the southern Mexican state of Chiapas. Wearing black balaclavas and carrying light weapons, they created an effect that was as much theatrical as military. With the advantage of surprise, they rapidly occupied the towns. The rebels identified themselves as Zapatistas, named for the Mexican revolutionary Emiliano Zapata. When the Mexican army regrouped and sent in reinforcements, the guerrillas fought for four days and then retreated into the jungle of the Lacondon. About 150 people died in the fighting, most of them guerrillas.

That should have been the end of the story. Small and ineffective guerrillas fill the margins of Latin American history like comic characters in a Shakespearean play, darting onstage to utter something inapt, then disappearing while history takes its course. Some stew in the mountains for a time, then drift back into the cities to slip into civilian life. Che Guevara, the guerrilla prince of the last generation, died in the Bolivian jungle in a laboratory-pure test of the theory that charisma and righteousness can conquer superior force.

The Zapatistas' leader, a former university instructor and urban radical who called himself Subcomandante Marcos, was a new kind of tactician. He knew that on military grounds he and his comrades could do no more than annoy the Mexican government. Their weapons were announcements of purpose as ritualized as a knight's throwing down the glove in a medieval joust. Had the Zapatistas entered sustained combat they would have stood no chance. Marcos' weapons belonged to the theater of a global age. He assembled an army of sympathizers worldwide, who encircled Chiapas with electronic eyes.

As the insurrection broke out, communiqués began to appear over the Internet, signed by the subcomandante and laying out the Zapatistas' purposes. The documents explained that the Zapatistas were revolutionaries, but also democratic—in fact, cripplingly democratic. When not on the battlefield they worked by consensus, even if a holdout cost them days of repetitive deliberation. In place of the runaway power that had discredited other revolutions, they offered power so strictly constrained that one marveled it could hobble around at all. These were revolutionaries for someone who liked the emotional frisson of revolution, but who had learned from the twentieth century not to trust revolutionary government or revolutionary justice.

The Zapatistas presented themselves as an indigenous peoples' group, representatives of the local Maya population. They wanted government policies to make space for their culture and language, and to direct resources to their poor region. As indigenes, they carried the last, best stamp of authenticity for liberal humanitarians in the North. They traced their struggle back to Columbus' arrival in 1492.

The Zapatistas also thought globally. They had chosen the day of their insurrection to highlight their opposition to NAFTA, which Marcos denounced from a balcony in the tourist town of San Cristóbal de las Casas as a "death sentence" on Mexico's Indians. NAFTA promised to end the livelihoods of small corn producers across Mexico, particularly in Chiapas, by sending subsidized American corn across the border. In his manifestos Subcomandante Marcos struck out at neoliberalism as an oppressive regime that benefited the already rich and powerful at the expense of the poor and weak. He identified liberalized trade as the latest act in a five-hundred-year chain of oppression and exploitation. NAFTA's opponents, who were already seeking confirmation that the trade agreement was not a panacea for Mexico, could not have received a more heartening message, or a more striking messenger.

Marcos' strategy worked. Within days, a virtual community had formed around the Zapatistas. Marcos insisted that anyone, anywhere could be a Zapatista: just put on the balaclava, literally or in your mind, and join the struggle. You didn't have to know a thing about Chiapas. The Zapatista image stirred an appetite for solidarity in a segment of the North American population—a very wired, moderately wealthy segment. And everything about Marcos' movement was custom-stitched for the evening news, from the guerrilla aesthetics to the NAFTA hook. The initial burst of international attention ensured that the people who needed to know about the Zapatistas found out. After that, the Internet and a small army of reporters did the rest.

When the uprising began, the Mexican novelist Carlos Fuentes called it a reminder that, as Mexico moved toward union with North America, parts of the nation were still mired in the feudal existence of Central America. The idea that the Zapatistas were an atavism, though, was too simple. Although the Zapatistas took free trade and economic liberalization as their leading complaints, their revolutionary theater would probably have been futile without NAFTA. Nineteen ninety-four was an election year, and President Carlos Salinas, whose Institutional Revolutionary Party (PRI in its Spanish acronym) had governed the country for seventy years, was staking his legacy on economic integration with the North. Unlike European economic integration, which brought huge aid and development packages for poor countries such as Spain and Greece,

NAFTA simply opened the borders of radically different economies. A quarter of Mexicans worked on farms and plantations, and many of those would lose their jobs. Already more than 20 percent of the population was looking for work or scraping by in black markets. The Mexican government classified almost forty million of its people as "poor" or living in "extreme poverty." The sell-off of state monopolies had created new private wealth, giving Mexico as many billionaires as Britain. Trade liberalization promised to spread the gap between rich and poor even wider.

The guerrillas crystallized popular discontent. At the end of the year, a national poll showed that almost 60 percent of Mexicans had a favorable view of the Zapatistas, and four-fifths thought their demands were justified. Marcos became one of the most popular political figures in Mexico, with the cachet of being a revolutionary bandit king rather than a deal-making legislator. In light of all this, some of the foreign investors whom NAFTA had attracted began reflecting that a country with despotic politicians, vast inequality, remnants of a feudal social order, and stirrings of mass unrest might not be such a promising destination, after all. When the *Economist* announced in mid-January that investors were having second thoughts, it sent a chill through the halls of Mexico City.

Moreover, Salinas' hands seemed tied. If he wiped out the Zapatistas, the act would announce to the world that Mexico was a violent and potentially unstable regime. Investors might agree, and whatever their opinion of violence, they feared instability. The upcoming poll was a problem, too. The PRI had flagrantly stolen the presidential election in 1988, shutting down vote-counting for a day when an opposition candidate moved ahead, then reopening it with the announcement that the government's candidate had taken the lead. That was the last open theft the regime would get away with. The world knew what had happened, and if it occurred again investors would doubt the regime even more. Spokespersons for the Mexican diaspora in the United States had denounced the fraud and urged the American government to punish Mexico by withholding aid and trade. The last thing Salinas needed was Mexican Americans working against the PRI.

So a standoff developed. The Zapatistas remained popular, but with the government in PRI hands and the army surrounding the Lacondon, they had nowhere to go. The guerrillas' electronic publicity campaign, though, was enough to keep the government more or less at bay. Ernesto Zedillo won the presidential election for the PRI, and the guerrillas hunkered down further. Early in 1995, a year after the uprising, the army pressed a campaign of attrition against the rebels, reclaiming small towns that the Zapatistas had occupied and pushing the guerrillas deeper into the jungle. Peace talks continued for a time, but broke down after the government ignored commitments on indigenous rights that it had accepted in an agreement known as the San Andrés Accords. It seemed that the most the government could do was to make the Zapatistas uncomfortable in hopes that they would abandon their efforts.

Then someone pushed the offensive too far. Three days before Christmas in 1997, men in black uniforms, some of them with automatic weapons, massacred forty-six Indians in Acteal, a village known to be sympathetic to the Zapatistas. The murdered men and women were praying when the attack began. Almost everyone believed the killers were somehow affiliated with the PRI, although more likely with the state party or a local landholder than with the national leadership in Mexico City. The massacre was a flashpoint in a pattern of violence: an anti-Zapatista association calling itself Peace and Justice had sprung up with support from the PRI, conservative Catholic priests, and wealthy landowners, and had intimidated peasants and burned churches thought to be sympathetic to the government's political opponents—not only the Zapatistas, but also the PRD, the left-wing opposition party. Landowners hired their own security forces to prevent peasant takeovers of their property. Human-rights groups reported that some 250 other people had been killed in Chiapas in the four years since the uprising, a hundred of them in the year before the murders in Acteal. More than ten thousand others had left their homes to escape the piecemeal violence.

The massacre brought a fresh wave of international attention that confirmed what the government had suspected: wiping out the Zapatistas would be a disaster. The global Zapatista tribe poured into Chiapas: journalists, academics, clerics, human-rights observers, and unaffiliated enthusiasts who attracted the dismissive sobriquet of "revolutionary tourists." United Nations secretary-general Kofi Annan landed in Chiapas. One hundred thirty-four Italians who called themselves Gia Basta—the Italian version of the Zapatista slogan, *Ya basta*, "Enough already"—arrived and milled about until the government pressed them out. Meanwhile, back in Italy, fifty thousand people marched in Rome to show support for the Zapatistas.

President Zedillo understood that his government must not be seen to be on the side of the killers. The rebels and their supporters had the moral upper hand after securing the support of a mobile and articulate international community. He took the unusual step of launching a federal investigation that led to the arrests of fifty people, including the mayor of the municipality that included Acteal. He made a show of firing his interior minister. The standoff resumed.

The elections in 2000 were the fairest and most open in Mexico's history, and they brought to power the first non-PRI president since the leaders of the Mexican Revolution settled into power early in the century. Vicente Fox won on media skill and personality rather than on party connections. That made him a populist, but he was different from the old-style populists who appealed to peasants and the urban poor over the heads of party leaders—such as Cuauhtémoc Cárdenas, the candidate whose probable victory the PRI stole in 1988. Fox was a big, brash former Coca-Cola executive, a man of the global business class. He had a businessman's taste for innovative programs and a manager's sensitivity to the danger of bad publicity. He decided to make dealing with the Zapatistas a touchstone of his first year in office. He pulled the army out of Zapatista areas and, over the objections of his mostly conservative National Action Party (PAN), introduced legislation to codify many of the Zapatistas' demands: greater political autonomy for indigenous communities, separate courts for Indians, and communal rights to natural resources on traditional Indian land. The last provision was especially threatening to the same Chiapas landowners who had been driving the Maya from their property and paying gunmen to keep them from returning.

Marcos responded with what he called the Zapatour, a show of support for a strong version of Fox's proposal. A procession of Zapatistas and supporters began a march to Mexico City, protected by Mexican police operating under orders from Fox. Again the Zapatista tribe was out in force. Northern sympathizers joined the march, among them José Saramago, the Portuguese winner of the Nobel Prize for literature, and Danielle Mitterrand, the widow of the former French president. The two-week journey culminated with an entrance into Mexico City, where vendors offered Zapatista hats, badges, scarves, dolls with black ski masks, and T-shirts with Marcos' face on the front and the Zapatour's dates on the back. President Fox was there to welcome the marchers, whose empire of sentiment seemed to have become a commercial empire of revolutionary bric-a-brac as well.

The talks on indigenous rights legislation broke down. The Mexican Congress passed a bill, but not before conservatives from Fox's own party weakened its critical provision. Conservative commentators objected that the bill's plan for community land ownership and political autonomy would lock Indian communities into primitive economic arrangements and preserve the power of local political bosses. Chiapas should follow the NAFTA model, they said, integrating with the rest of the country and the continent rather than drawing back into its traditional arrangements. For the legislators who scuttled Fox's bill, pragmatic motives were more salient: large landholders among their supporters recoiled from the idea of the government's backing Indian land claims. The Zapatistas left the capital without a victory.

Had they already won a larger victory by transforming Mexican politics? They did inspire imitators. For instance, the Popular Revolutionary Army, a guerrilla group from the state of Guerrero that dated back to the 1970s, tried to change its image. After years of violence targeted at police and the military, the group tried its hand at the quixotic media relations that the Zapatistas had perfected. Following decades of reclusion and a year in which they had killed more than two dozen people, the guerrillas began granting interviews, sending reporters whimsical gifts such as teddy bears, and ironically lamenting the dearth of poets in their ranks. They had supporters in the villages where they operated, but no international community sprung up around the Guerrero guerrillas' Comandante Antonio. The northern reporters who did take notice commented wryly on the Popular Revolutionary Army's attempt to be as cool as its infinitely cooler older brother, Subcomandante Marcos.

There is an inherent limit to the politics of spectacle and sentiment. The world's attention can indeed rush into some remote place—or as great a capital as Beijing, as it did during the Tiananmen Square demonstrations in 1989. Global sentiment can protect locals from violence or even help them to achieve their political goals. But the world sees only what catches its eye, and winning attention takes a combination of entrepreneurship and lottery-winner luck. When one wins, others do not. There could be only one Subcomandante Marcos, because the northern media had time and space for only one.

The great paradox is how much the Zapatistas were creatures of NAFTA—not just the trade agreement that they opposed, but the interweaving of the Mexican and American economies, media cultures, and populations. The vitriolic NAFTA debate in the United States ensured that when the Zapatistas rose up on the treaty's first day, they would catch the attention of the North. Carlos Salinas and Ernesto Zedillo held back their troops because of that attention, which carried the possibility not just of moral disapproval but also of investor panic. Vicente Fox's victory came on waves of popular agitation for greater democracy, and from the governing party's awareness that northern eyes might not tolerate another blatant electoral theft. Only in the age of NAFTA would having helped to run Coca-Cola be a political asset in Mexico.

The Zapatistas' radicalism wound up focusing as much on culture as on economics, ultimately endorsing a colorful variety of multiculturalism familiar in North American political culture. Latin American elites are intensely conscious of race. Small differences in skin hue can make a big difference in social standing, and Indian features put one at the bottom of Mexico's hierarchy. Indian villages with their poverty, ancient languages, and half-pagan rites were long a source of embarrassment to the elites of Mexico City. How could a country become modern and cosmopolitan with such strange, dark, anachronistic people in its midst?

That smug racism is obsolete. The new global elite embraces diversity. President Fox must have learned something about that at Coca-Cola. Coke's official Web site announces that, far from homogenizing the world, the company is "very much a local operation, meeting the demands of local tastes and cultures with more than 230 brands in 200 countries." It also offers specific Web sites for different countries. Colombia's is filled with brawny soccer players, China's with miniskirted and computer-savvy young women, and the United States' with plenty of multiracial buddy scenes. A savvy country proves that it is up-to-date by embracing—with self-conscious tolerance, to be sure—what is most particular and unusual in it.

In the eight years since the initial uprising, some of the Zapatistas' predictions about NAFTA have come true. As many as a million Mexicans have left their small corn fields, driven out of business by the big, efficient, and subsidized producers to the north. Forecasts for future displacement run to ten million and higher, although no one can say how deep and quick the change will be. Many head north to the maquiladora factories of the border or the cities of the United States. Vicente Fox's international agenda centers on winning new recognition for these transient workers as an integral part of the North American economy—inscribing a human face on the economic logic that NAFTA put in motion, and integrating Mexico more fully and irrevocably into American life.

The Zapatistas' campaign for small farmers was always the reactionary side of their crusade, and it has faded as its futility becomes evident. The former peasants are going north on every bus that leaves the southern hill country. Some of those migrants, or their children, will think back nostalgically on the villages they left behind. When they do, they will have moved closer to the Zapatistas' international constituency: modern people who delight in being reminded that the world still contains many cultures, many kinds of clothing, and many strange gods. This sentiment is perfectly compatible with living in today's cosmopolitan world; it may even sell some Coca-Cola before President Fox is done in Mexico.

CHAPTER 14

Rebranding Capitalism

—ᴍᴍ—

"Absolutely," Patrick Reinsborough shouts, his speeded-up cool-kid voice spurting and slouching. "We're trying to put a new brand on global capitalism." He is talking to me from a cell phone in Idaho. I lose him twice, get him back both times, and then lose him for good. Shortly before he cuts out for the final time, he explains: "We're saying this is a suicide economy. We're saying that there's a crisis, and the rules have to change."

Reinsborough is the lead organizer for the Rainforest Action Network, an environmental group that has put itself at the radical forefront of globalization politics. RAN, as its members and friends call it, got its start in the 1980s as a shoestring campaign. Mike Roselle, a veteran of the hardline environmental group EarthFirst!, traveled the country harassing Burger Kings with a giant papier-mâché cow. He fed his cow rain-forest trees, and she defecated Whoppers. The message was simple and clear: Burger King = unappetizing destruction. Wherever he went, he recruited appreciative audience members. The performance had both the crafty vulgarity of a sixties-era protest and intimations of the brand consciousness of the nineties. RAN soon retired the cow, but kept the brand consciousness. Its activists were guerrilla marketers, turning brand logic against the branders.

Roselle believed that environmentalism had grown disconnected from its roots in protest. The confrontational politics of the 1960s had inspired the first Earth Day, in 1970, on college campuses around the country. The protest culture joined with traditional conservationism, buoying the efforts of legislators who had long wanted to strengthen environmental regulations. Congress passed a series of new laws in the 1970s, and environmentalism became a sort of secular religion, particularly among students and liberal professionals.

In the next decade, the major environmental groups found it easy to settle into Washington, D.C., and concentrate on protecting the laws they had won while pressing forward a few new ones. They attracted many lawyers and some scions of the same elite northeastern families that had pioneered American conservationism. Their broader membership consisted mostly of donors, not activists, and their work revolved around lobbying, lawsuits, and cajoling the major newspapers and television networks. When Roselle took his cow on the road, he wanted environmentalism to be a festival again.

The college students and other young people who signed on brought their own ideas about politics. The old model of activism was to pressure state and national governments for changes in the law. The new activists considered that approach outdated. Beka Economopoulos, a RAN organizer who works out of a storefront in the Williamsburg section of Brooklyn, puts it this way: "The nation-state is obsolete. The de facto locus of power is Wall Street." So they decided to take the fight to Wall Street.

It didn't really matter whether the nation-state was obsolete in general. A few clever kids needed tools that didn't rely on numbers or money. They lit on marketing, which is wilder and less predictable than law. A single person with a good eye can sometimes make more difference than a million people or ten million dollars. The most successful marketing tends to pick up popular attitudes that are pervasive but not fully articulated, strongly felt but not yet painfully obvious. It shows people's

own desires back to them, made more beautiful and gracious—
or wittier and more sardonic.

The RAN organizers bet that many Americans felt
inchoate discontent and wanted a way to express it. People
sensed—so the organizers thought—that a lot of environmental destruction was afoot and didn't like it, but they had
trouble saying just who was responsible. On some level, they
knew that they were as much the cause of the destruction as
anyone, but they didn't *feel* like destroyers of the natural world.
They were inclined to blame large corporations, but which
ones? Oil, banking, and chemical companies were already
advertising their ecological concern so aggressively that a
reader of their brochures might have mistaken them for
environmental groups. The somewhat disoriented discontent
needed a target.

RAN gave it an unexpected one: Home Depot. The
Atlanta-based company is the world's largest timber retailer,
with over $30 billion in annual sales. It operates throughout
North America and in parts of South America. In the late
nineties the company's sources of timber included old-growth
forests in British Columbia, Brazil, and Southeast Asia. RAN
and other environmental groups had tried to pressure logging
companies into withdrawing from those forests but had run
into a familiar problem: resource-extraction companies, such
as loggers, miners, and drillers, are invisible. Their products
are the buried substrate of an economy that pretends to run
on information. They work far from population centers, in
remote forests and arid plains. They set their operations one
ridgeline back from the nearest major road. In southern West
Virginia, which was recently being torn apart by mountaintop-
removal mining, only a few private dirt roads can provide a
view of a strip mine. In the Pacific Northwest, ribbons of
untouched forest line the highways, concealing clear-cuts a
quarter mile away.

The extraction companies are also unbranded. Their product sells because there is no other way to get wood siding or floorboard, or, in the case of coal, no cheaper way to fire a power plant. Few people have heard of the giants in these industries, such as Arch Coal. They have nothing to gain from visibility, and very possibly something to lose. Home Depot sold directly to individuals, and that made it vulnerable. In the fall of 1998, RAN and other environmental groups took out newspaper ads criticizing the company for selling picture frames, doors, faucet knobs, interior trim, and other wood products made from old-growth timber. Local environmentalists in more than seventy cities picketed Home Depot stores. Protesters scaled a two-hundred-foot crane outside the company's Atlanta headquarters and stayed at the top for more than thirteen hours. In a stunt designed for cameras, Greenpeace installed a ten-thousand-square-foot Home Depot logo in the middle of a British Columbia clear-cut. Activists showed up at the company shareholders' meeting in enough force to make the attendees uncomfortable.

The campaign lasted almost a year. RAN kept up the appearance of momentum by convincing more than twenty companies, including Nike and Lockheed Martin, to "limit or eliminate" their use of old-growth wood products. For most, it was an easy exchange for a stamp of green approval. Environmentalist techies hacked the Home Depot public-address system to announce Rainforest Tours, in which white-coated activists led interested customers through the aisles, explaining the timbering practices of the company's suppliers. Store managers found their own loudspeakers politely inviting customers to take a break from shopping and join the tours. RAN also set up toll-free numbers that directed calls to the company's public-relations offices. Hundreds of environmentalists could jam the lines and keep Home Depot staff members busy fielding their complaints. Word about upcoming actions went out over the Internet to far-flung cells of activists, most of whom had never met each other, many of whom had never met a RAN organizer.

Home Depot complained that the campaign targeted it unfairly. Its policies were no worse than any other company's: if anything, they were better. *Fortune* magazine had called Home Depot one of America's most admirable corporations, praising its environmental and social policies. None of that mattered to the activists. Home Depot's fame helped RAN to tag it with new associations: clear-cuts, extinction, erosion, and corporate irresponsibility. Almost without knowing why, a few of the 75 percent of Americans who claim to avoid some products because of environmental concerns might begin turning into the Lowe's parking lot instead of Home Depot's.

Home Depot executives understood this, and seem to have begun planning a change in company policy almost as soon as RAN's campaign started. In the fall of 1999, the company announced that it would stop selling products from old-growth forests. There was no way to make the changeover instantly. Retailers don't keep track of where their timber comes from, and timber companies don't document their environmental transgressions. But already institutions were springing up to do the work. A Mexico-based consortium of environmental and scientific groups, the Forestry Stewardship Council, had developed environmental and social standards that it used to certify timbering practices as sustainable. Home Depot announced that it would slowly phase in a policy of buying only sustainably harvested timber, which at that time included only about 1 percent of the world's timber reserves. The World Resources Institute, a scientific research organization, began preparing a global map of forests, keyed to their ecological value and the danger they faced from excessive logging, which promised to help responsible companies target their buying. In the interim, Home Depot would phase out cedar, redwood, and a Southeast Asian tree called lauan, unless the wood met environmental certification standards. It also promised to absorb any short-term cost increases from the adjustment, rather than pass them on to customers.

The ultimate aim of the campaign was to change industry practices. A few months later, Lowe's agreed to phase out old-growth and other ecologically delicate timber. RAN organizers say that, after the Home Depot victory, they could get a meeting with executives of any other home-products company just by placing a phone call. The confrontational campaign eased the way for civility.

In one view, the Home Depot campaign was opportunistic bullying by a group that didn't have the numbers or the resources to change the law and so picked on a vulnerable company instead. From another perspective, the RAN campaign worked only because it played on a widespread feeling that companies shouldn't cause environmental destruction when they can avoid it. Home Depot spokespeople never said—and couldn't have said—that the RAN campaigners were wrong, either about what the company was doing or about what it should be doing. They could only object that the protesters were asking for too much of the right thing, too fast. In this view, RAN started with something close to a moral consensus about how timbering ought to be done and made it politically effective. Seen this way, a branding campaign gives voice and force to values that are already widespread, but diffuse and politically weak.

This view of branding campaigns finds some support in an observation that political scientists have made about the law-making process. The hardest kind of law to pass is one that disadvantages a few big, powerful, and well-organized interests but benefits hundreds of millions of people in small and sometimes unnoticeable ways. Timber companies care more about logging laws than anyone else, and they will fight to defeat new regulations. Few of the many people who would rather not have faraway old-growth forests logged are likely to spend time lobbying about the issue, or even to write a letter to a congressional representative. They do care, but they care about lots of other things, too, and those have a way of becoming more urgent in day-to-day life.

This means that—whether or not the nation-state is obsolete—people who want to change timbering practices have to find pressure points where a little bit of effort can make a big difference. The American political system is famously designed to prevent anything from getting done without a lot of struggle and argument. A little effort is likely to get lost in the Capitol. By contrast, the American market is attuned to small differences in people's desires. Branding campaigns tap into that sensitivity. In cases like this, a branding campaign can help democracy work better.

But democracy is not the only political value. American government is designed to slow down politics precisely so that spasms of fear or anger do not express themselves in law. By circumventing lawmaking, branding campaigns make those spasms more effective. The decisions that result will tend not to reflect accurate knowledge or careful judgment. The success of consumer boycotts in keeping genetically modified foods out of Europe is a perfect example. Whatever the merits of genetic modification turn out to be, the European battles have been hysterical and accusatory, and there is no reason to expect good policy to emerge from them. Any way of making public decisions, though, has both advantages and dangers. A majority appears to like RAN's position on timbering, and its campaign has done what legislation has not: begun to change what happens in old-growth forests. Moreover, there is something attractive about winning with the opponent's tools. RAN picked up the marketing techniques that it found on the littered floor of the American carnival of image and desire, and put them to a new use.

The decision to go with marketing came out of RAN's read on the political landscape, but it also reflected the attitudes of the young activists. Beka Economopoulos is explaining this to me in the Green Parrot, a Williamsburg restaurant with many vegetarian entrées and flyers by the door advertising yoga classes. She is tanned nut-brown, with her dark hair pulled back from her forehead. She is four years out of Northwestern University, and although she has a few gray strands in her ponytail, by her face she could be seventeen. Her brown eyes frame a slightly pugged nose, and her symmetrical smile displays a tiny gap between her front teeth. She talks at a steady, efficient pace, mixing youthful epithets with phrases that could come out of a management consulting session. The intended effect is clear: smart as a McKinsey associate, bad as a Brooklyn punk girl with hippie origins.

"Going after politicians is *political*," she explains. "That's attractive to some people, but it turns a lot of people off." Traditional politics is ineffective and boring. It attracts nerds and power seekers. When Economopoulos says that the center of power has moved to Wall Street, she also means that the center of activists' political imagination has moved there. If the ideal protest was once a march on the Capitol, now it is a takeover of a corporate headquarters, or jamming the communications of an international investment bank.

This is partly because the things that bother RAN's constituents don't strike them as having much to do with politics. "A lot of young people feel a more concrete discontent with merger mania. They know it sucks when their local bookstore gets closed down. They hate sprawl." A version of this litany comes up again and again among activists on the radical edge of globalism politics. The new style of youthful discontent is directed at a homogenizing and destructive economy, and discontent begins at home: in bland suburbs, proliferating Starbucks and Barnes and Nobles, and the belief that all of this is linked to environmental degradation and human exploitation far away. The discontented see a dark aspect in the relentless multiplication of clean, well-lighted places across North

America. They suspect that all the ways of economic and political power are corrupt, and that the corruption is spreading. RAN builds its support on this attitude.

The activists respond with what some of them see as a new morality. Economopoulos says, "We're the first generation to value diversity as a primary commitment. That applies ecologically, it applies culturally, and it applies to business." There is some irony in anti-corporate activists defining themselves by way of an idea that Coca-Cola and Benetton have done much to popularize. When Economopoulos tells me that "my family comes from France and Greece. I don't want to go there and find it's just like Jersey City," she is echoing her archenemy in the war of ideas, *New York Times* writer and globalization defender Thomas Friedman, who, in *The Lexus and the Olive Tree*, laments the thought that someday a travel guide to Bali may read simply: "Too late. Go somewhere else." Although RAN activists talk about cultural diversity as an analogy to the biodiversity of healthy ecosystems, it is difficult not to hear the tourist's concern that the world should remain visually interesting, with many kinds of faces, clothes, and cityscapes.

The other pillar of the Rainforest Action Network ethos is a view of economics. RAN activists like to say that "unlimited growth is impossible in a finite ecological system," that is, the earth. Patrick Reinsborough announces that "cancer is not a metaphor for our economy, it's a diagnosis." This idea leads the activists to doubt the legitimacy of today's basic economic tenets: growth and its fruit, profit. RAN organizer Ilyse Hogue asks, "Where does the rate of return that we expect from our money come from? Is the money in my savings account earning interest because it's coming out of the quality of the world that my nieces and nephews will live in? If that's true, then I don't want it. I'll consider myself richer if I know that the world in two generations will still have the same good things that it has now."

The Home Depot victory brought RAN to a crossroads. Changing the practices of one corporate giant, then working out from there to shift the entire industry, was a model grassroots victory. It was a great moment for the traditional environmentalist tendency in the movement, which tries to save as much land as possible from sudden and destructive change. It was not enough for the aspect of RAN that believes we live in a suicide economy.

In globalization politics, the model activist is both a pragmatic nerd and an apocalyptic prophet. RAN's organizers pore over company earnings reports, learn the main points of international finance, and follow the comings and goings of corporate boards. Many of them can argue the outline of a scientific dispute, and all can quote numbers and dates to substantiate their opinions. They are children of the age of information and expertise. But their belief that they live in a corrupt world gives them a consciousness of sin. Like certain Christians, they are deeply implicated in the present world but refuse to identify entirely with it. For many of them, the principles of ecology occupy the same moral position as a vengeful God: they exist to rebuke human hubris and smite the enemies of the righteous.

RAN wanted its next campaign to express both its practical and its apocalyptic spirit. It needed a target as big as global capitalism, a company that summed up everything RAN was fighting against, but that might actually give in and change its behavior. Happily, at about the same time that the Home Depot campaign was beginning, such a company had appeared. It was born of a merger between Citibank, a huge consumer bank, and the Travelers Group, an equally large investment bank and insurance company. The new entity was called Citigroup, and it immediately became the largest financial services company in the world. (It was surpassed shortly afterward by the merger of two German banks.)

Citi, as both its marketers and its antagonists call it, was born in minor infamy. The Depression-era Glass-Steagall Act forbade companies to engage in both consumer banking—such as personal accounts, mortgages, credit cards, and student loans—and the high-stakes maneuvers of investment banking. Following the 1929 crash of a highly speculative stock market and the failure of banks around the country, Congress wrapped the financial world into a protective but constraining web of regulation. Keeping the personal accounts of farmers and shopkeepers separate from the battles of financiers was a central principle of the new order. Citi defied the law outright, betting that Congress would revise the rules before the Federal Trade Commission objected to the merger. The law changed a year later.

Critics like to present the new law as a straightforward case of money buying legislation, and when the world's largest agglomeration of money gets its way, that analysis cannot be all wrong. But the power of money at high levels is often less about bribery than about gravitation: money attracts people and ideas, and those who keep company with the lords of capital learn to think like them. At the peak of the booms in high technology and the stock market, common sense seemed to have shifted its ground, with all presumptions now in favor of the untrammeled market. Customers would be able to get investment advice where they cashed their checks, a merged company could eliminate managers and clerical workers whose work was duplicated between the two old corporations, and the savings would make everything faster and cheaper. The change was easy to present as a triumph of efficiency over bureaucratic barriers.

In the same period, private capital was becoming the most important factor in global economic development. Before 1990, 80 percent of the money that went into developing countries came from the governments of rich nations, and only

20 percent from private investors. After 1991, government contributions slackened and private investment grew rapidly. Recently, as much as 80 percent of the money flowing into developing countries came from private investors—an inversion of percentages in a little more than a decade. The amount of money moving around the world in global currency markets increased eightfold between 1986 and 1998, to $1.5 trillion every day—almost a hundred times greater than the value of actual trade in goods and services. These exchanges formed part of global financial nervous system, capable of imparting speed and precision or, as in the Southeast Asian and Russian crises, inducing a seizure.

In the same period, personal investment became increasingly populist. For years after the crash that set off the Depression, stocks and risky private bonds had mainly been the preserves of the wealthy. In the late 1990s, though, shares in pensions and mutual funds made about half of American households investors in the stock market. As people's financial lives got caught up in private capital, the stock market became headline news, with updates flashing across television screens every few seconds. Talk of portfolios entered ordinary conversation, and some hopeful souls resigned from their earlier lives to become professional day traders.

These are some of the elements that RAN activists have in mind when they say on the one hand that the nation-state is obsolete, and on the other that the world is being crushed into homogeneity under the steady pressure of expanding capitalism. The same forces that passed billions of dollars around the world in an electronic second also colonized the American imagination. With an empire that spanned personal credit cards and multibillion-dollar development projects, Citi embodied the forces that the more apocalyptic activists believed had taken over the world.

But empires have their own weaknesses. The growth of private capital and individual investing gave activists a new route to decision makers. In 2000, the Chinese government hired the investment bank Goldman Sachs to arrange the American sale of depositary receipts—basically shares in a company not traded on American stock markets—in PetroChina, the government's oil company. PetroChina was active in Tibet and Sudan, which earned it the animus of both American human-rights activists and Christian conservatives who objected to the repression of Sudan's Christian population. Labor unions hated China as a repressive regime with low wages and poor working conditions. This coalition convinced a number of investment funds, including the public-employee pension plans of California and New York, to declare that they would not buy the PetroChina shares. The sale had been expected to raise $5 billion for the company, but in the end it attracted only $3 billion. Perhaps not all of the difference came from the boycott, but the campaign was effective enough to put investment banks on notice: politically unpopular clients might have financial costs.

RAN wanted to supplement the new toolbox of investment-as-activism with its own specialty in activism-as-marketing. In Citigroup, the same company that arranged financing for factories, oil rigs, and palm-oil plantations suddenly had to present itself to college students and other consumers as the best place to get credit cards, checking accounts, and personal loans. That took it into RAN's territory.

The Citi campaign, like RAN's other recent efforts, lives on-line. Many Web pages are devoted to Citi-financed oil pipelines and palm plantations, and suggestions on how to make the lives of Citi employees less convenient with e-mail, phone calls, demonstrations, and takeovers of bank branches. On one "global day of action," organizers expected pickets to show up around Citi branches in fifty or so countries. The next day, they got e-mail from self-appointed activists in five additional countries who had staged their own protests, inspired by RAN's Web site but otherwise on their own. Ilyse Hogue recalls with amused delight: "Fifty-five Swiss activists took over a Citi branch in Geneva for more than twenty-four hours. We didn't hear about it until they had left."

Such coordination-by-inspiration makes globalization politics resemble early Christianity, or Protestantism in the chaotic years after the Reformation. A gripping set of ideas and images takes wing into the world, and where it lands people make what they can of it. No authority can resolve differences that spring up as ideas adapt to local passions and exigencies. This spirit suits a campaign intended to unsettle a global institution at as many points and in as many ways as possible. If RAN ever begins negotiating with Citi as it did with Home Depot, however, it may relearn an old lesson about the dangers of unharnessed enthusiasm: inspired schismatics are hard to call off, particularly in a movement that lacks a nominal head or charismatic figure.

For now, RAN is a long way from that problem. Nonetheless, it does have a concrete agenda that its organizers hope to hash out with Citi executives someday. They want Citi to stop financing timbering in old-growth forests, get out of fossil-fuel projects, and begin incorporating environmental damage into the cost-and-benefit calculations that determine whether a project is worth undertaking. Ultimately the activists want Citi to stop reacting to the vicissitudes of the market and instead become a pioneer in remaking the economy.

That is a lot to ask of a company whose specialty is making and moving money. However, the idea that corporations are vehicles for public aims is not new. RAN's activists are pressing for a revival of the nineteenth-century idea of a corporation, in sharp repudiation of the twentieth-century conception. Originally, state legislatures issued charters permitting a company to operate only if, in theory, they were convinced that it would benefit the polity. Corporate charters were subject to periodic review, and could be revoked if a corporation were acting against the public interest—or the interests of powerful legislators. Today in American and, increasingly, global law, corporations are treated as legal individuals with a full complement of rights.

Today's model of the corporation suits a time when markets are the lords of common sense. Most economists would say that any corporation that turns a profit is by definition serving the public interest, since it must be providing a good or service that people want. Letting legislatures pick and choose among corporations just gives power to prejudice and favoritism. The egalitarian, democratic thing is to allow any entrepreneur the chance to found a corporation and every consumer the choice of whether to patronize it.

RAN's riposte is that corporations are effectively the stewards of enormous tracts of the planet's resources. They often outrun the laws that governments make for them, and their decisions eventually affect everyone's future. Those who are powerful enough to shape others' lives in basic ways—especially others who are politically weak or not yet born—should be constrained by more than their self-interest. Ecological responsibility belongs in the ground rules of the market, because a socially or environmentally irresponsible market will eventually ruin the source of everyone's wealth.

This idea takes some support from conventional economics, where the theory of externalities holds that markets are imperfect when they allow people to act in ways that hurt others while giving those who are injured no recompense. Pollution and environmental degradation are classic externalities: companies get the profits of their activities, and everyone else has to deal with the carbon-filled air and eroded soil that result. If Citi were required to take those harms into account up front, it would sponsor less environmental degradation. This is a perfectly mainstream economic idea, but there are at least two problems with it. The first is technical: Is there a reliable way to measure environmental destruction and conservation in dollars and cents? The second is political: Does anyone have enough power to require giants such as Citi to take those measurements?

RAN's vivid and relentlessly contemporary campaigns have brought it around to an old, obvious, and irredeemably dull idea: regulation. The only way that economic giants will serve the common good is if the rules they play by tilt toward fair wages, good working conditions, and environmental responsibility. This, not laissez-faire libertarianism, is what replaced the old idea of legislatively chartered corporations. Regulation is one of government's main purposes, and global environmental problems may be regulation's biggest challenge in the next century. Regrettably, the regulator is not a heroic figure in today's political imagination. Regulation stands for everything that is slow, tedious and oppressive in tone, gray in color, and—in Beka Economopoulos' word—obsolete.

Pursuing the ends of regulation by means of marketing campaigns makes them vivid in what activists call the "carnival of resistance," but by declaring traditional politics obsolete the carnival-goers pull away from lasting reform even as they demand it. By addressing themselves directly to corporations, they ensure that their campaigns will be entertaining, and they gain a better chance of short-term victory than they could have in traditional politics. At the same time, they discount the only institution that really might revise global capitalism: government.

That is not a fatal paradox. It may even be an appropriate one. Ralph Waldo Emerson observed in 1844 that those who want to change the world should not usually begin by passing better laws: "Republics abound in young civilians who believe that the laws make the city . . . that commerce, education and religion may be voted in and out; and that any measure, though it were absurd, may be imposed on a people if only you can get sufficient voices to make it a law. But the wise know that foolish legislation is a rope of sand which perishes in the twisting; that the State must follow and not lead the character and progress of the citizen." Emerson might judge that, by addressing popular attitudes first, the young rowdies of the Rainforest Action Network have avoided at least one mistake of the politically naïve.

The new activists' politics is an odd hybrid. It is founded on ecological sentiments that are as close to religion as to conventional politics. It is also infused with another of today's secular religions: the elevation of the market as the arbiter of all disputes. These paradoxes are bred in the bone of globalization politics, and of modern political and cultural life. Whether they will prove fruitful or fatal for RAN and like-minded activists is an open question. Certainly they are not going away.

V

LIVING IN
HISTORY

—⁂—

Nothing can be sole or whole that has not been rent.

—William Butler Yeats,
"Crazy Jane Talks with the Bishop"

CHAPTER 15

What Is the Future For?

In the nineteenth century, when London was a city of disease-wracked slums, Henry Mayhew was the great student of its street populations. His *London Labor and the London Poor* documented the lives of the Street Irish, Street Jews, Garret-masters, Coal-heavers, Lumpers, Street Musicians, and the Destroyers of Vermin, among other colorful and destitute tribes. In four volumes of opinionated reporting and vivid line drawings Mayhew judged that wealth and order could never come to the blighted city. Population was growing across Britain and Ireland, while factories and farm machinery drove agricultural laborers from the land without creating new jobs for them. Mayhew concluded that the influx of desperate people "appears to me to be the main cause of the increase of the London street people, and one for which I candidly confess I see no remedy."

In time, though, the deprived and dissolute slum dwellers became today's Londoners. Their rich city draws immigrants from the new metropolises of poor countries, where people live today in the conditions Mayhew described. Looking at the slums of Bombay or Cairo today, it can be as hard to imagine that prosperity could ever come there as it was for Mayhew in London; but that is a failure of imagination, and also of historical learning. Despite all the sober pessimism of the past, today's wealth and order are hard facts. Nothing essential distinguishes the Street Irish from today's Calcuttans.

Yet we do not have a picture of the future that does this fact justice. Ideas of the future pattern hope and organize effort. They make possible commitments that do not yield immediate rewards. Today's dominant visions of the future are few and narrow. One is apocalyptic: through environmental destruction or modern warfare, we are stalked by self-destruction. Another is complacent: we can expect more of the same, perhaps with less suffering around the edges; indeed, there is little we can do to stop it. Apocalypse threatens despite anyone's best efforts, and more-of-the-same promises to unfold on its own power, regardless of the genial approval of pundits or the indignant opposition of anti-globalization protesters. Neither picture has much space for hopeful politics.

Modern politics is basically the business of structuring power. Liberalism, not in the broad sense of temperament but in the narrower meaning of political rules, protects individuals from the power of the state and from large clusters of private power, such as corporations. Democracy makes the state—and, through the state, private power—answerable to popular pressure. Together, liberalism and democracy envision a world where people live with as little humiliation, deprivation, and arbitrary interference as possible—in short, a world where personal dignity is available, if not guaranteed.

This book has been concerned with many kinds of power: network power, the power of seduction and resentment, the power of branding and rebranding. Power matters, though, when it finds an object: when it injures, constrains, protects, or strengthens a person. Directing power to protect and strengthen people is the proper ambition of liberal and democratic politics.

Economics, too, is about power and dignity as well as wealth. The point of Adam Smith's endorsement of the free market, as I've said, was partly that markets produced prosperity, but just as much that they promoted a new form of dignity. Each worker or tradesman stood on his own two feet, free of hereditary obligations and social hierarchy. Smith believed that market transactions held all concerned to standards of competence and basic civility, and that these conditions produced more dignity than feudal grandeur and hierarchy. The social superior could no longer do certain things to his subordinate: humiliate him, beat him, separate him from his family—all the abuses that a master can inflict on a slave, a serf, or a courtier. Threatened with these abuses, the free bargainer could take his business elsewhere. The American dream is a picture of immunity from humiliation: a house on a piece of land, a secure job, no one to grovel before, no one with arbitrary power over you. This is why, for immigrants with memories of widespread indignity, the American idea means much more than a bundle of consumer goods.

In practice the free market has never lived up to this ideal, in America or elsewhere. The criticism of capitalism arises from the repeated rediscovery of the indignities of market life: Karl Marx's image of the alienated laborer and John Ruskin's lost ideal of the craftsman, Henry David Thoreau's mockery of smallholders obsessed with their property and Upton Sinclair's account of exploitation and injury in slaughterhouses. Adam Smith envisioned market relations as bargaining among equals, and unequal power has undermined his vision again and again: when employers can fire one worker and choose from among ten others, when there is no unemployment insurance, when the company can move to Mexico—when, in short, one bargainer needs the other more than the other needs him.

A hopeful politics would look toward a future in which economic conditions and human decisions combined to favor dignity. That would mean not permitting political repression and corruption to pollute prosperity, as has happened in China; nor economic chaos to hamstring democratic reform, as in Indonesia; nor poverty to compromise democracy, as it has in India's first fifty-five years of independence. It would require circumstances more generous than humanity has ever enjoyed, and also political wisdom.

What are the reasons for hopefulness today? There are many starting places, but I will begin with demography for several reasons: from Thomas Malthus and Henry Mayhew forward, it has inspired despairing pictures of a perpetually poor and overcrowded world; it still pushes to the fore in pessimistic images of the slums of poor countries, as seemingly condemned to crowded poverty as Mayhew's London; and demographers have recently produced a few pieces of tentative good news.

In 2001 and 2002, scholars of population growth moved toward a new consensus. Instead of rising through the century to eleven or twelve billion, the world's population would probably peak by 2070, perhaps at nine billion, and then stabilize or begin to decline. The chief reason is that women in most of the world, partly excepting the Middle East and sub-Saharan Africa, are choosing to have fewer children. Education, employment, birth control, and the move from villages to cities are all leading even very poor women to make decisions more like those of women in the rich countries. Women born in rich countries today have fewer than two children apiece—the level of zero population growth. The population of Europe would be shrinking without immigrants, and almost all the population growth in the United States is due to immigration. When women in poor countries make similar decisions, world population growth will end.

Population growth is not, in itself, the main cause of poverty or environmental degradation. If India still had the several hundred million people who inhabited the country at independence, rather than the one billion who live there now, those hundreds of millions would be less crowded but probably just about as poor as today's population. Technology, education, and equal opportunity (for instance, letting women be doctors or opening the professions to the lower castes) matter much more than raw numbers. Environmentally, a village stripping the local slopes for firewood can do more harm than a more affluent town with relatively clean electricity. For these reasons, critics deride those who worry about population growth as confused, overwrought, and misanthropic—all of which are sometimes true.

But a stable, and then shrinking, population can affect power and politics. When there are fewer people relative to the total needs of the economy, each person becomes more valuable. That is why many historians believe that, after the Black Death killed between a quarter and half of the population of Europe, the survivors earned better wages and had more opportunities than their ancestors. It wasn't just that they divided up the goods of the deceased, although there must have been some of that; workers were able to drive a harder bargain for all the farm labor, wagon making, and other tasks that still needed to be done. Better pay meant more chances to save money, buy land, pay for a child's training, or otherwise add one's bit to the pervasive restlessness that culminated in modern life.

Population trends also affect social spending. Of course, shrinking populations will strain retirement programs as fewer working adults support more retirees. The optimist's side of that coin is that social investments, such as education and childhood nutrition, are easier to make when there are only as many children as adults, rather than, say, three children for every two adults. Other things being equal, stable populations should mean a better situation for each successive generation of children. The usual fallacy about smaller populations meaning more prosperity actually holds for children, because each generation is raised on its parents' wealth, which is a fixed amount as far as the children are concerned. Better educated and healthier young people who can bargain more aggressively with those who want to employ them or lend them money have a chance at a greater share of the world's resources.

I am making no promises for demographics. Extrapolating the future from present trends and expectations is a most risky business. The scrap heap of history is piled high with predictions of perpetual peace on the one hand, overpopulation and imminent ecological disaster on the other. I am not trying to predict the future, because the future is not meant for prediction, but for imagination and decision making. The purpose of pausing over Henry Mayhew's London and our present population trends is to remember how dramatically the world can change, and in how many ways it can defeat the expectations of the moment.

We can now imagine an end to the ever-ready supply of cheap labor from the villages of China, the Philippines, and Vietnam that enables factory owners to press down wages and beat back organizing efforts not only in Bavaria and Alabama, but in middle-income countries such as Thailand. The motto of international companies in recent decades has ironically echoed Che Guevara's call for perpetual revolution: "two, three, many Vietnams!" In a hundred years, if economic progress continues and population growth stabilizes, it is imaginable that there will be no more Vietnams: no more countries where people are willing to work on nearly any terms the owners and bosses offer. There would still be great inequality, but the balance of power would have shifted in favor of workers. People would enjoy more control over their lives, more security, and wider opportunity. For the first time, the world would begin to approach Adam Smith's vision of universal dignity.

The folly of trying to predict the future is that we cannot wait complacently for a better world to arrive. Human decisions make the difference all the way down. To stay with the example of demographics for a moment, if world population stabilizes, it will be because billions of women are hopeful enough to have fewer children and invest more in each one. That hopefulness will reflect political decisions to give women education, job opportunities, and a place in public life. Population growth is not slowing in the places with the worst prospects, particularly for women: the Islamic Middle East and sub-Saharan Africa. Population growth there expresses pessimism about the future. (The falling fertility rates of the former Soviet Union and parts of Eastern Europe are a special case. Those are relatively wealthy societies afflicted by economic and political breakdown, social disorder, and a perception that many individual futures are more insecure now than they were under authoritarian governments.)

Many threats could turn our decisions away from a dignified future. The next hundred years are—like the previous century—a critical period. First, there is the social and political turmoil of the developing world. This book is a minor document of a major trend: everywhere aspirations are outrunning reality, as people want and sometimes demand what they cannot yet have. Tocqueville noted in his analysis of the French Revolution that uprisings happen not among the hopelessly downtrodden—most people have been peaceably downtrodden since the advent of agriculture made slavery and serfdom profitable for masters—but when people's hopes are stirred, then disappointed. One of today's special paradoxes is that hope can be stirred by images from far away—American prosperity on the television screen, or even in the windows of import shops—and dashed locally, by a bad government or a failed economy. Anger can express itself either locally or globally, in riots and rebellions or in anti-Western agitation and terror. Desire and ambition flow more freely today than ever before, and their violent consequences can take more forms than in the past.

Environmental disaster could also divert progress. There is a near-consensus among scientists that global climate change threatens droughts, floods, and ferocious storms. If tens of millions of refugees flee Bangladesh and other low-lying countries, or droughts devastate China, social unrest may follow. Tropical deforestation, the depletion of fisheries, and massive pollution in countries such as China and India also pose threats whose consequences we cannot foresee. About war, one can say only that it always threatens: anything from a land war in Central Asia to a massive terror attack in the United States could press the rich countries into fortress posture or divide the world into mutually hostile blocs.

This sketch of what is at stake in the next century gives definite tasks to the rich countries. These are the things we would do if we appreciated that the coming centuries' balance of liberty and violence, and of prosperity and deprivation, may turn on the decisions of the next few decades, and that our decisions are among the most important. There is no reason to expect that we will undertake all these actions anytime soon, but there are a few hopeful signs, and sometimes change comes fast.

We should be generous and fair-minded in our influence on global economic change. Today the risks and burdens of development lie disproportionately on already poor countries. The United States and Europe press for our banks, manufacturers, and restaurants to be allowed into India, China, and South America, but persist in protecting local agriculture and favored industries with import tariffs and subsidies. The flow of investment and speculative capital into Southeast Asia in the 1990s benefited both local people and northern investors for a time; but when the crisis of 1997 and 1998 hit, the rich countries acted through the International Monetary Fund to bail out the investors and speculators while the economies of countries such as Indonesia and Thailand collapsed. Reformers should press for a more principled approach to economic integration, in which the wealthy shoulder responsibility for risky investments, international institutions show more solicitude for stability in poor countries, and rich countries' expedient protectionism is called out as hypocrisy.

Foreign aid has a bad reputation nowadays, because donor governments often put political ends over humanitarian needs, and recipient governments squander even good-faith assistance. Philanthropist George Soros and others have outlined ways to make aid more effective: coordinating donations through independent bodies governed by accomplished and independent individuals; directing funds at non-governmental programs with records of success; and subsidizing basic reform and social investment, especially comprehensive education, health care, environmental protection, and the rule of law. Foreign aid should become a coordinated effort to improve conditions in poor and middle-income countries.

A humane path of development would include investment in "global public goods," which benefit everyone but are neglected because they do not give any investor an easy profit. Environmental protection is one of these. Another is research into the diseases that especially affect poor countries, notably malaria and AIDS. The efforts to create global funds for AIDS research and prevention and a malaria vaccine are major steps in the right direction. Maintaining such funds should become a basic expectation of decency in this century.

So far, there is less progress in international environmental protection than in disease control. In both areas, societies with money will have to put up some of it if they want to see improvement. At home in the United States, the past decade has seen an explosion in land-trust arrangements, in which conservation groups pay landowners to guarantee that they and their heirs will keep property forested, farmed, or otherwise free of development. In this as in much else, we owe the rest of the world the same consideration that we accord each other. Indonesian rain forest is a bargain. African governments with fragile wildlife populations are desperate for money. We should be willing to pay for what we see fit to demand.

We should also distinguish our broad hope that the world will gain in freedom and prosperity from any particular formula for reaching those goals. In Latin America, the recent political turn against doctrinaire free-market reforms is a reminder that in a democratic time even the most sophisticated program stands or falls by its effect—and, just as important, its perceived effect—on ordinary people. If the natural aspirations to freedom and prosperity do better when nations find their own, perhaps unorthodox, ways of pursuing them, what should concern us is only that they do find a way. If the one that any nation hits upon does not meet our standard of maximum efficiency, it still may turn out to be the most effective path for that people, with its particular appetites, tolerances, and demands. There are many variations on the theme of living freely, and so far no one knows for sure which ones can flourish in modernity.

Rather than dictating the terms of others' reforms, we should provide a compelling example of one liberal response to modernity. The more the rich countries remain free and egalitarian in the coming decades, the more that will be the shape of the future. Their best qualities are under some strain now from massive immigration. Europe in particular needs young workers as its population ages and its active workforce shrinks; immigrants fill these jobs. Poverty and mobility ensure that even more migrants will come to Europe and America in search of work. The United States now has its largest share of immigrants since the beginning of the last century, and much greater linguistic, religious, and ethnic diversity than ever in the past. European immigration rates are approaching and surpassing American levels for the first time.

Dealing well with these changes would require both Europeans and Americans to give up some political self-indulgence. Europeans' customary ethnocentrism, from the German expectation of living among Germans to the aggressive French pronouncements of cultural nationalism, is not compatible with living in a time of great migrations. The sooner Europeans stop expecting public culture to be defined by deep and elaborate common inheritances, the less discontented they will be. That is a sacrifice, but one that the time, not the immigrants, is asking.

As for Americans, we cannot afford the devil-take-the-hindmost policies that have defined economic life here since the early 1980s. American tolerance of falling wages for lower-income workers is a major reason that many Latino immigrants are not entering the middle class but staying in poor neighborhoods and, often, watching their children join the American underclass. It is also a reason that the white and black workers who compete with the new immigrants may prove susceptible to anti-immigrant resentment in hard times. One decent principle for immigration policy is that a country should take as many people as it can assimilate into its civic and economic life, allowing that immigrants will necessarily change the country's religious and cultural habits. Civic and economic assimilation, along with openness to cultural and religious change, are obligations a country owes both to its immigrants and to itself. European obsession with cultural integrity and American indifference to economic inequality both represent failures to live up to this principle.

If either the United States or Europe comes more closely to resemble, say, Latin America, with social, economic, and racial status dividing the servants from the served, then the global promise of dignified prosperity will be seriously compromised. Adam Smith and the more visionary American founders hoped for a world without servants, and emphatically without servant classes, even as they dealt with a world of peasants and slaves. Giving up their hope would be a betrayal of the best in the liberal and social democratic traditions of the North Atlantic, and, since those together represent the most humane prospects of a capitalist world, it would also be a betrayal of the future.

The Bargain of Modernity

Of course no prosperous future would settle the restlessness that has always stirred women and men. There are other motives than getting regular bread, and they are arguably higher: understanding mortality, coming to terms with imperfectability, surviving the tendency toward ennui and despair that seems endemic to self-conscious life; and appreciating beauty, cultivating reverence, and trying to live well among other people. By all evidence, these are perennial difficulties. No system of political economy could solve them, and the occasional attempts to do so have been disasters. By the same token, the fact that prosperity cannot resolve these difficulties is not an objection to prosperity.

Alexis de Tocqueville offered a caution to critics of American democracy when he asked: "What do you expect from society and its government? We must be clear about that." To be sure, many of the refinements of aristocracy would disappear in the hurly-burly of democratic capitalism. That was to be regretted. But to condemn democracy for not being something other than itself was a sign of confusion. Tocqueville continued:

> But if you think it profitable to turn man's intellectual and moral activity toward the necessities of physical life and use them to produce well-being, if you think that reason is more use to men than genius, if your object is not to create heroic virtues but rather tranquil habits, if you would rather contemplate vices than crimes and prefer fewer transgressions at the cost of fewer splendid deeds, if in place of a brilliant society you are content to live in one that is prosperous, and finally if in your view the main object of government is not to achieve the greatest strength or glory for the nation but to provide for every individual

therein the utmost well-being, protecting him as far as possible from all afflictions, then it is good to make conditions equal and to establish a democratic government.

This is the bargain of modernity. It means not purporting to order public life by the highest certainties, but instead building common life on the low but stable ground of ordinary motivations. Modernity exiles the higher aspirations from politics, and assigns them to spiritual, ethical, and aesthetic pursuits that now belong to the private life of families and communities. Those who wish to recreate ancient religious civilizations or reattain the heroism of their warrior ancestors are trying to get out of the bargain. They judge modern freedom and prosperity for not achieving ends that they were never meant to achieve. These judgments are not just wrong, they are perniciously confused.

A prosperous world would not make people noble, bring them (much) closer to immortality, or produce splendid and beautiful acts. Not necessarily, anyway. In fact, it would probably generate a great deal of junk and nonsense: bad television, cheap toys and wash-and-rip clothes, and strip-mall architecture. But it would also provide the control over daily life, the security against starvation, beatings, and being worked to exhaustion, that help people to turn their attention to ultimate questions. Those questions are probably irresolvable in human terms, which is why religions look outside the world for their answers; but the capacity to dwell on those questions is a sign of a high civilization. Aristotle believed that the life of contemplation was the highest possible, and that Greek citizens could achieve it only with the support of slaves. To have the same freedom without exploitation would be one of history's great achievements, and if many people squandered it, that would be better than if they had never had the chance.

Nor would a prosperous world be safe. People would still be moved by violent nationalism, religious zealotry, historical resentment, the fear of powerlessness and the pleasure of power. The violent passions will never go away, any more than the penchant for foolishness and self-indulgence. But if violence has fewer occasions, and foolishness more, that would be exactly the change in proportion that Tocqueville endorsed. So long as greater foolishness also means greater dignity and security for ordinary people, that is the bargain of modernity. We should bend our politics toward it.

CHAPTER 16

Living in History

—⚉—

Having a destination in mind, one must also know the terrain
one will have to cross to reach it. In politics, the terrain is
human nature, and its maps are drawn from history and introspection.

The twenty-nine volumes of the 1910 *Encyclopaedia Britannica* were intended as such a map. Its editors aimed "to give
reasoned discussions on all the great questions of practical or
speculative interest." They set out to say what there was to
know, and what a person of good sense should think about it.
The *Encyclopaedia* was an era's effort to give an account of itself:
its achievements, its convictions, and its purposes. Four years
after the eleventh edition appeared, that era tore itself apart in
the First World War. Seven years later, the Bolshevik Revolution tried to overturn the world the *Encyclopaedia* described.
The following decades brought the Nazis, Italian and Japanese
fascism, and the collapse of the European empires.

On the brink of all this, the liberal West peered into the
future and saw its own face repeated into eternity. In his
thirteen-page article, "Peace," Sir Thomas Barclay, Officer of
the Legion of Honour and Member of Parliament for Black-
burn, began by contrasting his time with all earlier history.
Peace had long been "a purely negative condition," just the
period between wars. But in the modern era,

peace among nations has now become, or is fast becoming a positive subject of international regulation, while war is coming, among progressive peoples, to be regarded merely as an accidental disturbance of that harmony and concord among mankind which nations require for the fostering of their domestic welfare.

Barclay's optimism rested on four cornerstones. Statecraft had grown more sophisticated, so leaders could avert war. Private advocates of peace, who were many in that high-minded time—as they are now—pressed for cordial relations among nations. The world's borders were at long last rational, having achieved "the grouping of mankind in accordance with the final territorial and racial limitations of their apparent destiny." The most important reason was that democratic societies with large citizen armies would no longer hunger for war. Barclay's example was Germany. German soldiers were also German citizens, trained to reason as well as to fight. Both the soldiers and their families at home could be trusted to make peace "a family, and hence a national, ideal." Four years later at the Battle of Langemarck, 145,000 young Germans rushed to their deaths in a series of transparently futile attacks, singing the *Deutschlandlied.* The next thirty years of history were more in the spirit of that charge than that of the *Encyclopaedia.*

Barclay spoke for the Establishment of an empire at the peak of its strength. What, other than strength's complacency, made that empire blind to danger? The eleventh edition suggests an answer. These volumes are built around the idea that violence and irrationality have been conquered by reason. The *Encyclopaedia*'s article on "Civilization" follows the ages of history—the Lower Period of Savagery, the Middle Period of Barbarism—to our time, the Upper Period of Civilization. Throughout history, the *Encyclopaedia* explains, technology, personal liberty, and social equality have driven civilization forward from stage to stage.

These civilizing forces, however, have not changed international relations, where hostility and force still dominate. The present age is the first in which civilized values may overcome the sources of war. Economic and technological progress is dissolving borders. Nations rely ever more on each other for raw materials and manufactured goods, and

> this implies an ever-increasing intercommunication and interdependence between the nations. This spirit is obviously fostered by the new means of transportation by locomotive and steamship, and by the electric communication that enables the Londoner, for example, to transact business in New York or in Tokio with scarcely an hour's delay; and that puts every one in touch at to-day's breakfast table with the happenings of the entire world. Thanks to the new mechanisms, national isolation is no longer possible; globe-trotting has become a habit with thousands of individuals of many nations; and Orient and Occident, representing civilizations that for thousands of years were almost absolutely severed and mutually oblivious of each other, have been brought again into close touch for mutual education and betterment.

This is a picture of what we today call globalization. The *Encyclopaedia* forecasts that globalization will bring the time of Cosmopolitanism, the final age of humanity, when war will become as unimaginable as cannibalism. Soon

> mankind will again represent a single family, as it did in the day when our primeval ancestors first entered on the pathway of progress; but it will be a family whose habitat has been extended from the narrow glade of some tropical forest to the utmost habitable confines of the globe.

The origin of the age of peace is not just technology: it is reason. In the view of the *Encyclopaedia*, man is a rational, prudent character who has long been possessed by the demons of superstition, nationalism, and bloodlust. History is a tale of cumulative exorcism, and the patient is now almost healed. The encyclopaedist

> is privileged to forecast, as the sure heritage of the future, a civilization freed from the last ghost of superstition—an Age of Reason in which mankind shall at last find refuge from the hosts of occult and invisible powers, the fearsome galaxies of deities and demons, which have haunted him . . .

Reason is what remains of humanity when all perversions and detritus are stripped away, and it brings peaceful cosmopolitanism. In 1910, reason, history, and human nature seemed to have come together to usher in the new age.

It is easy to mock such passages. Forecasts of universal peace seem fatuous after almost a century of war. But mistakes can teach as much as successes, especially noble mistakes. The eleventh edition of the *Encyclopaedia Britannica* describes one of history's more decently motivated errors. Taken on their own terms, these volumes stand for universal peace, democracy, and human rights, for overcoming the bloody nightmare of the past and making a good life possible for every citizen in a universal community. Readers today may wonder whether those goals are attainable, but we are unlikely to offer higher ones.

The effect of reading the eleventh edition is not comic but tragic. Every passage displays a world lurching toward destruction, yet unaware of any danger. Its rationalist optimism lives, like the protagonist of the archetypal Greek tragedies, in a world whose elemental forces are kept secret from him. He believes he is directing his life, until he discovers that greater powers have carried him their own way, far from his designs, to a terrible end. The *Encyclopaedia* describes an age that does not understand its own achievements and limitations, and for that reason is vulnerable to awful failure.

Germany embraced barbarism in the name of a superstition called racial science and a passionate nationalism that advancing civilization was supposed to have made impossible. The Bolsheviks' savagery was advertised as the way toward cosmopolitan peace, or communism. Britain's own empire—the *Encyclopaedia* is dedicated to His Majesty George the Fifth, King of Great Britain and Ireland, and of the British Dominions Beyond the Sea, Emperor of India—disappeared, and many of its former subjects and rulers decided that it had stood for warlike chauvinism rather than universal civilization.

That is not to say that "progress" and "civilization" are meaningless words, that there is no such thing as barbarism or savagery, or that reason is a conceit. The error of the *Encyclopaedia*'s liberal optimists was not that they believed in those things, but how they believed in them. They were convinced that civilization and barbarism sprang from different parts of human nature, civilization from reason and its humane dictates, barbarism from superstition and violent passions. Once superstition was overcome, universal civilization should emerge from reason like a carpet of young, green wheat in a weedless field. Such beliefs did not prepare the liberals of the time to make sense of the world that soon overcame them. Afterward, many dismayed observers took liberal goals to be as discredited as the method of the optimistic rationalists.

Reason About Unreason: History and the Passions

We find a different view of history and human nature in one of the most important pieces of American political thought: the tenth *Federalist* paper. Like much American thinking about politics, it is not the product of a theorist's leisurely rumination. It came from the pen of James Madison, perhaps the most intellectually gifted of the American founders, in the midst of a hard-fought political battle. It has the marks of haste, but also the precision and clarity that indicate a fine mind at work on an urgent problem.

The Federalist is a series of eighty-five short essays written for the newspapers of New York State during the fight over ratification of the American Constitution. The newly independent states adopted the Constitution in 1789, after loose-knit arrangement under the Articles of Confederation proved unworkable. The proposed constitution represented a decisive step away from a league of free states and toward a single, indivisible nation. The states had their own traditions and institutions, and many voters were reluctant to put supreme power in the hands of a national government. Opponents warned that the constitution would lead to tyranny and corruption, the vices of big, distant government.

The *Federalist*'s three authors—Madison, Alexander Hamilton, and the ailing John Jay—argued that the national government described in the constitution would not destroy liberty, but make it more secure. At the heart of *Federalist* no. 10 is the idea that political communities will always be divided against themselves. There will always be some who are willing to override the common interest and the rights of other citizens to achieve their particular aims—the spirit the authors called "faction." The national government of the proposed constitution would work against faction, the authors promised. By selecting legislators from large bodies of voters—a handful to a state, rather than one for each county as in some states— it would filter out the extremist, the local crank or militant, and tend to elevate people devoted to the national interest. Not every public official would be a high-minded patriot, but because the new government would draw from a vast and diverse country, its members would also be diverse, and the factious elements would tend to cancel each other. There might be a stray monarchist here, a radical populist there, here a servant of the timber industry and there a legislator bought and held by regional merchants, but none of them would be able to impose their will on the country.

This attractively pragmatic idea has contributed to the impression that American government is a kind of mechanical device: factions come in here, the machine of representation disciplines them by means of the famous checks and balances, and as long as the parts are running correctly, the machine extrudes something approximating the public interest. That view is not wrong, but it is incomplete. *Federalist* no. 10 also contains an idea about the relationship between politics and human nature that sits silently at the base of the American political tradition. Madison believed there was no way to eliminate faction because being divided is the permanent situation of human beings.

As Madison put it, "there are two methods of removing the causes of faction: the one, by destroying the liberty which is essential to its existence; the other, by giving to every citizen the same opinions, the same passions, and the same interests." Madison judged the first cure—tyrannical government—worse than the disease. The second pretended to be enlightened political theory: a government should find a true political doctrine and assimilate all to it. But the "theoretic politicians" attracted to this idea would soon end up as tyrants themselves. When politicians assume that all their people are identical, they shortly find out otherwise, and either change course or lay citizens on a procrustean bed to make them alike by mutilating them.

At the same time, Madison rebuked admirers of small, republican communities, who envisioned political harmony within a band of the virtuous and like-minded. There would be factions in such places, too, he wrote, and without the machine of representative government they would fall on each other like wolves: such polities "have in general been as short in their lives, as they have been violent in their deaths." In all, there was no way of eliminating factions without losing liberty.

The only way to preserve liberty was to begin in doubt that it could be preserved at all, confident only that there were no easy formulas for its preservation. Madison's careful pessimism sets him apart from the authors of the *Encyclopaedia Britannica*'s eleventh edition, with their confidence that historical progress would bring the world into unity. That reckless optimism is alien to the spirit of *Federalist* no. 10. If division is the permanent condition of humanity, no Age of Reason or Cosmopolitanism will end our division unless it changes human nature.

Why is humankind permanently divided? Madison gives three reasons for humanity's factious estate: interests, opinions, and passions. The first, meaning economic interests, was as commonplace in Madison's time as it is today. The second, opinions, sprang from interests and also from sheer, wandering speculation—the unstable vessel of human reason. (Madison is shifty on whether opinion is more than a hybrid of interests and passions.) But faction had another taproot, an independent and disruptive force in politics and history: the passions. People were moved by the charisma of contending leaders and thinkers, which divided them into parties and movements. They were moved also by ambition, the hunger for power and prestige, and by a zeal for conflicting views about religion and politics that kept "opinion" irrational no matter how reasonably one tried to argue with it. Humanity was the species that perpetually came together and fell apart in violent and dangerous ways. "So strong is this propensity of mankind to fall into mutual animosities," wrote Madison, "that where no substantial occasion presents itself, the most frivolous and fanciful distinctions have been sufficient to kindle their unfriendly passions, and excite their most violent conflicts." In politics as in love, the heart has reasons that reason knows not of.

As a student of the passions, Madison belonged to a living tradition in his time. Edmund Burke insisted that "History consists, for the greater part, of the miseries brought upon the world by pride, ambition, avarice, revenge, lust, sedition, hypocrisy, ungoverned zeal, and all the train of disorderly appetites which shake the public with the same." Burke believed that revolutionary upheaval appealed not to reason but to the passions: it stirred aesthetic excitement and provided the moral gratification of imagining oneself on the side of infinite and perfect justice. These feelings pulled people out of their ordinary lives, with all the grudging accommodations and mundane habits of decency that enable people to live together. Once wrenched from that everyday moral world, rulers were susceptible to another, baser passion: tyranny, the sheer satisfaction of exercising unbounded power over others. Modern politics promised to make people more than human, and ended up making them less than human by stripping away their common life of mutual regard and affection, and replacing it with sheer power. Other students of the passions, such as Adam Smith and Alexis de Tocqueville, were less bleak, but they saw the world as moved by many of the same motives.

Politics was rife with unreason, but that did not make it an irrational activity. Instead, acting rationally in politics meant understanding the play of the passions, being alert to the dangers they posed, and acting in a way that averted their worst possibilities. One had to understand human irrationality in order to be fully rational. In creatures moved by the passions, there is no hard-and-fast division between reason and irrationality. Our motives combine the weave of aspiration and principle with the sinew of appetite and need. The passions can produce peace or violence, order or disruption, sterile pride or productive ambition, liberty or tyranny, all from the same brew. Anyone who wishes to understand a political, social, or economic order must have some idea of how it shapes the passions, which ones it excites and which it quiets. Anyone who pretends to banish unreason, or to be untouched by it, disables himself from promoting liberty and averting violence—the proper aims of politics. To undertake as hopeful a project as American democracy, the constitutional framers needed to appreciate—and believe—all the reasons for pessimism about politics.

Because he saw the world in this light, Madison would not be surprised to survey today's world and find it populated by Islamic extremism, Hindu chauvinism, Chinese nationalism, Christian fundamentalism, and many more and less decent forms of patriotism. He would expect that even nominally economic disputes, such as the fight over "globalization," would be shot through with convictions of religious intensity, for and against capitalism, American culture, and trade. These dramas emerge, he would say, not only because people are rich and poor, or Muslim, Christian, and agnostic. We live in these dramas because we are human beings, animated and distorted by the heart's reasons.

Today the end of the Cold War, the renewal of human rights as a universal language of justice, and the rise of democracy as the world's chief basis of political legitimacy have restored the aims of liberalism to the status they enjoyed in 1910. Yet in important ways we are as naïve as our ideological ancestors, and perhaps also as vulnerable as they were. We think of economic life—the liberal economy we have set out to extend globally—as the product of universal principles of reason. We can hardly imagine that anyone would not choose to enter into this scheme, and once a people has entered it, we decline to believe that they might leave it again. Where our aims—our mostly commendable aims—meet opposition, we are inclined to attribute the failure to atavism, a residue of barbarism still abroad in the world. Like the governors of the British Empire, we do not pause to consider that we bearers of civilization might display some barbarism ourselves.

The eleventh edition of the *Encyclopaedia Britannica* and the theory of the passions represent different ideas of today's most important question: how people become and remain liberal, fit for modern liberty. For one, the answer is, By overcoming history. For the other, the answer must be, By living in history. The *Encyclopaedia*, composed in the studies of Oxford and Cambridge, proposes that the forces of progress will liberate us from the old sources of violence, unreason, and destruction. With that optimism, its authors lost sight of those dark forces, which then took them unawares and almost destroyed them. The American manifestos, scratched out by lamplight during political battle, insist that we never escape the worst human motives, and that complacent optimism is therefore our most dangerous tendency. In this view, liberalism rests on the recognition that violence is always lurking somewhere near the surface of our common lives.

I believe that this view is right, and that because liberalism is the best spirit of civilization yet tried in modernity, recognizing the mixed, unstable nature of human beings is a requirement for civilization. Being modern, liberal, or whatever else we are does not free us from the interplay of barbarism and decency, good and evil, reason and unreason. The worst dangers and best possibilities of the modern world are written in the same language as all of history, everywhere shared and everywhere holding the same lovely and horrid potentials. Civilization and barbarism are real, but they have common origins in human nature, and both are always possible, everywhere.

Living in History

The dominant forces in today's world—capitalism, democracy, nationalism, and America's prominence—produce both liberty and violence, and there is no way to have one without inviting the other. Both spring from the same well of passions. The world is not divided between poles of good and evil, but wound around a single, tight core of human motive, where even the spirits of liberty and violence can be difficult to distinguish.

Capitalism is not what Karl Marx and generations of Marxists believed, a system of relentless and unjust exploitation whose dynamism builds up to self-destruction. Neither is it what libertarians have imagined, by itself the best arrangement of human affairs, a formula for securing freedom to all and bringing wealth to those who deserve it. The free market remains the most powerful human practice for creating wealth, and a great source of individual liberty, just as Adam Smith wrote. It fosters potent sentiments of liberty and humanity, some of them at odds with the raw workings of the market—a fact as true at the time of Smith's "if" as in today's Benetton politics. The free market also produces factory towns that, although they offer better lives than those in some Cambodian and Indian villages, are defined by desperation and vulnerability. Capitalism creates economic crises such as Indonesia's, with its terrible consequences for the country's political life, from crisis-driven reform to conspiracy theories such as the story of the Illuminati.

Political democracy is neither the bourgeois sham that the left once denounced nor the horrific chaos that the European right used to fear—and which is now, in supreme irony, the favorite nightmare of China's nominally communist rulers. Neither, though, is democratic politics the peaceful panacea that some Western liberals imagine, a form of alchemy that turns fractious peoples into disciplined and peaceful nations. One of the effects of Indian democracy, in a country of sweeping diversity, vast poverty, and widespread illiteracy, has been to embed corruption and religious bigotry so deeply in public life that commerce—from Narayana Murthy's Infosys to a Bombay shopkeeper whose prudence disciplines his prejudice—may be the more powerful force for freedom and tolerance. In Indonesia, the sudden arrival of democracy brought reforms that have crippled the country's economic and political life since: just the sort of popular spasm that the critics of democracy have always used to slur it. At the same time, a deep lack of democracy is the essential failing that threatens to cripple China's lurching reforms and bring the country to disaster. Democracy in its broad sense, including people's confidence that laws will be enforced and workers' right to organize themselves, is the fulcrum that makes Benetton politics, such as the anti-sweatshop fight, either effective or futile. Most important, even though democracy does not make a liberal society, a country without democracy today is unlikely to become liberal and less likely to remain that way.

National sentiment makes political solidarity possible, and so helps to clothe our human nakedness. Nationalism comes with modern democracy in more or less virulent forms. Illiberal nationalism is the bane of contemporary politics in much of the world: riots between Indian Hindus and Muslims, civil wars between Christians and Muslims in Indonesia, ethnic cleansing in the Balkans, and genocide in Rwanda. The political solidarity of diasporas, whether literal diasporas such as the Sikh supporters of Khalistan or figurative diasporas such as the Christian solidarity movement, can have violent consequences for distant people. In countries such as India, made up of many nationalities, there is intrinsic violence in yoking people to a single version of being Indian, and the crooked path between that injury and the counter-injury of religious and linguistic particularism is a scar on the politics of modern India.

America is as prominent a principle in world politics as capitalism, democracy, or nationalism. Associated with all three, the touchstone of aspiration and resentment everywhere, it is a magnet for the passions of liberty and violence alike. Some Egyptians hate America in place of their own repressive government or, more intimately, their sense of confusion and displacement in their own lives, into which America can always reach with a tantalizing promise of prosperity, or to snatch away one son and leave another rebuked and lost. They also love America for the freedom and comfort that it represents. For Narayana Murthy as for many middle-class Indians, America is the image of success that guides a wrenching repudiation: success means convincing foreigners that his company is not "Indian" except in its location and wage scale. There are people around the world who want to live in the United States and to see our freedom and prosperity in their countries, but who also—if their words and spontaneous emotions are any guide—imagine that they would be glad to see us destroyed. That sentiment has become infamous in the Islamic world, but it is not alien to China—to take one looming instance. Our inspiration is large, as Walt Whitman said of himself: it contradicts itself, and it contains multitudes.

What we can ask of any situation, then, is not "Is it democracy?" or "Is it capitalism?," let alone "Is it like America?" Instead we can ask: What passions emerge here? Which inclinations toward liberty are excited in this setting, and which ones toward violence? Which motives are the most volatile? Do people see their economy as a transparent map of opportunity or an opaque tangle of conspiracy that sometimes produces terrible disruption? Does this democracy give people control over their collective lives, or does it enable bigotry and other violent passions to seize control of the government, oppress minorities, or wreck institutions? Does our form of national identity help us to stay whole while undergoing great changes, or does it lead us to dwell on old injuries and resent others who share our living space? Since the answer will often be "both," the real question concerns their proportions: Here in India or Indonesia or Egypt or China or the United States, at this time and no other, among this generation of the living, is there more tendency to liberty or to violence?

The answer always lies in the particular circumstances of a time, a place, and the people who are transiently gathered there. We can know the general lines of possibility and danger—which human tendencies help us to live well together and which ones put us at each other's throats. But there is only so much we can do in the abstract. Politics is the discipline of living in history, trying to see what is possible and what is closed to human choice at any single moment.

There is, however, one discipline we can impose upon ourselves for all times and circumstances, to ensure that we do not stop living in history. That is the discipline of memory. Memory is the unity we give to experience. It is the faculty that makes us not just incidents in the senseless rush of time, but seeds and bearers of seeds, the children of one generation of human life and the parents of another. Memory is not just the imprint of events on the mind, like light on film, but also the product of individual attention and collective ritual and storytelling, the selection of elements from the tangled past and jumbled present that will shape us in the direction of the as-yet-unreal future. Memory is how we train ourselves to understand our lives, in relation to those around us, the dead and remembered, and the unborn but anticipated. Memory is our way of weaving a whole from a world that persistently comes to us in fragments. It is not just retention, but a marriage of recollection and forgetting, in which what we erase is as important to our coherence as what we preserve.

A people, like an individual, can perish from either a lack of memory or an excess of it. An amnesiac people, such as today's Americans, is always in danger of forgetting itself: our purposes, the things we must do and others that we must not do, because doing them would mean becoming someone else. The stay against this confusion is the memory of political, cultural, and moral community. Edmund Burke, who was a student of memory in politics, put it this way:

Always acting as if in the presence of canonized forefathers, the spirit of freedom, leading in itself to misrule and excess, is tempered by an awful gravity. This idea of a liberal descent inspires us with a sense of habitual native dignity. . . . By this means our liberty becomes a noble freedom.

To be Americans in this spirit, we should recall the aspirations and the warnings of John Winthrop and the authors of *The Federalist*: that we might be the world's greatest nation, but that the wrong kind of greatness, built on pride and reckless optimism, could make us history's signal failure. We should remember Abraham Lincoln's brooding, haunted patriotism, and also the ecstatic exhortations of Walt Whitman, a poet of both innocence and experience, who loved Lincoln and saw in him a great American soul. We should invite the spirit of these past figures—assembled, no doubt, by the needs of our present exigency—to instruct and judge us, so that we can instruct and judge ourselves. Memory can dignify us by enforcing our own standards and ideals against us. That is the work of a tradition, which requires memory to survive.

Memory, though, also carries darkness and violence. The poet Czeslaw Milosz again: "It is possible that there is no other memory than the memory of wounds." History is a slaughterhouse, in the last century more than in any before, and suffering scores itself on memory. The cultivated memory of suffering, revisited and revised to keep its passions fresh, is the engine of bigotry and vengeance around the world: in Hindu chauvinism, Islamic extremism, anti-Semitic conspiracy theories at Jakarta's national mosque, and the Christian fundamentalism of the Cairo slums. Such memory can become a debilitating curse. It is against these hazards of memory that American amnesia seems so compelling. Our forgetfulness immunizes us against the hateful remembrance that so many peoples carry.

Yet it is precisely because history is full of unredeemed violence and destruction that we are obliged to remember.

Believing in either the *Encyclopaedia Britannica*'s Age of Reason or American innocence enables one to pass complacently over the long record of bloodshed, as though one's own life had nothing to do with that old, all-too-human violence. But there is no immunity. Liberty and violence are contrary human tendencies, but liberalism does not free a people from violence. We Americans might recall that our peaceful, prosperous, and sometimes innocent nation is built on conquest, virtual genocide, and great ecological wreckage, and that what we have done abroad implicates us in millions of deaths. Recalling this should not mean—as left-wing critics and their right-wing enemies both manage to suggest that it would—believing that we are uniquely or even distinctively destructive. Instead it means recognizing that we live in human history, which has been formed everywhere by violence. Violence against other peoples, the bad use of the earth, and the destruction of everything in the past that did not become the present: these are the common heritage of humanity. If we forget them, we forget ourselves.

In the same Nobel lecture in which he spoke of the memory of wounds, Czeslaw Milosz speculated that perhaps there was a reason that Poland and the other countries of Eastern Europe had fallen under a Soviet tyranny determined to distort and erase the past. The cunning of history might have decided "to make them the bearers of memory, at the time when Europe and America possess it less and less with every generation." If memory keeps us whole, and injury gives vitality to memory, then even the darkness in what we remember can be an ironic blessing, like the "fortunate fall" out of Eden that, by destroying innocence, qualified humanity for salvation. We Americans are always dimly aware of the advantages of our liberal principles of personal freedom, democracy, moderate nationalism, and tempered capitalism: they help us to be prosperous and secure, and everything else that women and men can become when they have overcome those first barriers to free activity.

But we easily forget the other purpose of liberal principles: to prevent the worst things that people do to one another. Liberty is a stay against tyranny, the free agreements of markets against ritual humiliation, tolerance against bigoted violence, skepticism against fanaticism, and, sometimes, selective forgetting against the curse of memory.

Liberalism should be a response to the memory of wounds, not so much those inflicted against one people in particular as wounds in general, the relentless human impulse to injure each other in the name of a dozen passions, a thousand causes, and a million reasons for revenge. Memory should train us to see clearly in a world where good and evil spring from the same sources and are often interwoven in a single act. That is the kind of vision that can see both freedom and violence in capitalism, solidarity and dangerous resentment in nationalism, achievement and danger in democracy, and great possibility alongside real peril in America's preeminent place in the world.

Because America has suffered so few collective injuries, because history has been so generous toward a country of refugees and eccentrics, slavers and emancipators, opportunists and idlers, the United States has as good a chance as any nation to cultivate memory without resentment. To be liberal by memory rather than from amnesia, and optimistic by determination rather than from imagined innocence, is America's still unrealized contribution to human civilization.

There is no universal civilization. There are too many legitimate human aims, too many forms of excellence and too many decent pleasures and refinements, for any form of life to achieve them all. There is no escape from partiality and imperfection. No people is exempt from the attractions of self-righteousness, zealotry, and cruelty. The proportion of liberty to violence results from the play of the passions in nations and individuals, and the passions have no golden ratio or stable resting place.

Every age offers a choice among forms of imperfection. Those who live within the least worst human world of their time have a pair of obligations: to avoid believing that the least worst is the perfect, and to stay true to what is best in it. In the end, peoples cannot take responsibility for each other; but they serve each other when they take responsibility for themselves. Part of that work is appreciating their own relationship to the global prospects of liberty and of violence. There is no Age of Reason, and history can have no end that is happy; but in every time, in the space between memory and oblivion, still lives the hope of earth.

—ɯ—

Some of the concepts in this book have long and varied histories. In this section I give an account of how my use of some of them fits into history and scholarship. I also point toward reading that I have found helpful or exemplary. I do not attempt to list everything I have read in preparing this book, let alone all the relevant material on these themes. (A bibliography for certain of them could itself fill a book.) Instead I give starting points and landmarks for those who care to think further about these matters.

Modernity

Modernity is a vast concept caught up in many arguments. The way I use it falls pretty much in the mainstream. The term refers to the social, cultural, political, and economic circumstances that arose in Europe and North America in the eighteenth and nineteenth centuries (and have developed since), and that distinguish those societies from their predecessors and some of their contemporaries. In social life, modernity means mobility, the decline of traditional hierarchy, and increased importance for individual choices. Social modernity might mean, for instance, an end to arranged marriages in favor of freely chosen matches, picking among careers rather than inheriting the family trade, and forming community by mutual affinity rather than geography or bloodline.

In politics, modernity refers to an emphasis on the equal status of each member of the political community. Universal citizenship is thus a hallmark of modernity, even in authoritarian societies, and slavery and the exclusion of women from citizenship are deeply anti-modern practices. Modernity also includes the idea that politics is directed by deliberation and decision, rather than tradition or the arbitrary will of a leader. The American constitution, crafted and ratified by public argument, exemplifies modern politics, while the "divine right of kings" and hereditary rule are nonmodern. Modernity is also characterized by mass politics, practiced through national and global communication, and addressed to as many as a billion citizens at once (as in India). This naturally compromises the idea of politics as a practice of deliberation, and instead tends to make it a plaything of popular passions.

In economics modernity refers to scale, complexity, and independence from tradition. A modern economy is too large to be encompassed within the practices of any community (unlike, for instance, a guild or caste system) and its complexity requires professional specialization and subspecialization that eliminate generalists and traditional craftspeople. Much of the politics of the past two centuries has centered on the struggle between two versions of a modern economy: a socialist one, in which collective politics is supposed to turn economic life into a tool for general well-being; and a free-market one, in which individual decisions are the motor of economic life.

In culture, modernity expresses a new and intense concern with individuals. Such literary genres as the novel and the memoir, with their emphasis on the personal voice and the inner life of emotions; clinical practices such as psychoanalysis, which claims to probe to the core of the patient; and admiration for individuality, uniqueness, and authenticity all express modernity's attention to individual personality. In modern culture, religion tends to become an increasingly personal matter, an individual quest for truth rather than an inherited body of certainties. At the same time, its disruptions make a fertile field for new, popular religious movements.

The reader will see that these descriptions cluster around two facts. On the one hand are individuals cut loose from inherited ideas of who they are and what they should do, who must assemble their identities as best they can from personal decisions and fragmented inheritances. On the other hand stand mass institutions such as national and international markets, national elections and governments, and global entertainment. Modernity tends to individualize, even fragment, experience, identity, and decisions; at the same time, it tends to collectivize them, submitting everyone to the same economic rules, the same political body, or the same movies, music, and political rhetoric. Much of historical and contemporary argument about modernity turns on which of these dynamics one emphasizes. The early Anglo-American theorists of modernity, including Adam Smith, David Hume, John Stuart Mill, and (a French fellow traveler) Alexis de Tocqueville emphasized the individualizing dynamic, and saw modernity as chiefly about the rise of individual social and economic freedom—although Tocqueville and Mill, in particular, also worried about the intellectual and cultural conformity that resulted from the tyranny of public opinion. Tocqueville believed that a despotic government might arise among atomized citizens. By contrast, Karl Marx believed the central fact about modernity was that the rules of the capitalist economy achieved a tyrannical life of their own, dictating the course of politics, culture, and individual lives like a wicked god. Marx founded a European view of modernity that concentrated on the "objective, structural" mass dynamics that subjected individuals to their unyielding logic.

Probably the greatest student of modernity was Max Weber, the German social thinker who died early in the twentieth century. Like Marx, Weber saw modernity as a set of ineluctable social processes that swept individuals and cultures before them; but he was intensely concerned with the role of ideas and the experience of individuals in these changes. For Weber modernity was the consequence of "rationalization," a self-reinforcing process in which scientific discovery and rigorous efforts at consistency in ethics, aesthetics, politics, and religion combined to "disenchant" the world. People who accepted the scientific picture of the world and forced themselves to think consistently could no longer believe that they lived in a meaningful, benign universe designed to express concern about human lives, built to please the human eye, and imbued with natural distinctions between good and evil. Instead, science was merciless fact, ethics was a bloodless code of right behavior, aesthetics was a refinement of purely human perception, and religion was an expression of the psychological desire for salvation and purity. In such a world, the small, personal satisfactions of friendship and beauty were still possible, but magic was gone. The bright colors of the world's youth had aged into gray on shades of gray. Weber defended modernity, because he believed that repudiating the inevitable would only lead to destructive and self-indulgent irrationalism; but his defense saddened him.

One of the most important questions about modernity is whether, and to what extent, it is a Euro-American phenomenon or a universal event. Marx, following in the tradition of universal history pioneered by G. W. F. Hegel, believed he was describing a relentless historical logic that would overtake every part of the world and remake it all in the same form. Following Weber more than Marx, sociologists and development economists in the mid twentieth century developed a large body of so-called modernization theory, intended to describe the general dynamics of societies entering into modernity. This body of scholarship posited a more or less universal path from traditional, hierarchical, religious society to individualistic, increasingly egalitarian, and secular social life.

All of this has come under sharp attack in the last several decades. The most significant criticism has emerged from a band of scholars who are ranged, often unwillingly, under the label "postmodernist." These overlapping figures and schools of thought can be connected by their denial of several ideas about modernity. First, they rejected the idea of "reason" as a universal, impersonal source of truth and dignity, and suggested that this idea is culturally specific and has been achieved only by suppressing other kinds of experience that, in principle, are equally valid. Second, they asserted that universal history was per se invalid, that the variety of human life was more important than its unity and that historical change had no intrinsic direction. They emphasized the ways in which human personality, language, sexuality, culture, and political order are fluid, shifting, and possessed of many possible forms. Wherever these were fixed into one form or another, the postmodernists sought to show how the stability relied on suppression, violence, or more sophisticated and complex forms of power.

The postmodernists fell into a natural alliance with students of European imperialism, a topic that has recently attracted enormous attention. There was really no universal civilization, yet all the imperial powers had justified their rule with talk of bringing their subjects out of darkness into true civilization and universal history. Was this not the supreme example of the violence that the postmodernists glimpsed in all the universalizing claims that their predecessors had made on behalf of modernity?

In many areas of ethics and social theory, the postmodernists have fallen into purely destructive carping, but they began by making powerful points, and on imperialism in particular it was impossible to say that they were entirely wrong. The chief response to their work, unhappily, was a bout of bad conscience and a long silence: most people just stopped talking about "modernization" and left the developing world to the students of imperialism. (They had to share it, though, with the neoclassical economists, who had no time for anyone's ideas about culture, and were not given to fits of bad conscience.) That was a loss, because the postmodernists were powerful mostly in the negative: they issued occasionally brilliant criticisms of smug or sloppy universalism, but they were not much help in sorting out the large picture of changing societies. Since they had established themselves as enemies of large pictures, their unhelpfulness was, in fact, a matter of principle.

Happily, the silence is beginning to break. Arjun Appadurai, a scholar who is sympathetic to many of the postmodernists' concerns, has published a provocative study of globalization titled *Modernity at Large*. Charles Taylor, a deeply learned Canadian philosopher, has begun asking in a rigorous way which aspects of modernity are peculiarly Western and which may be said to be general. There is also much loose talk of "multiple modernities," most of it not rigorous, but some of it also interesting.

In major respects, my view on these questions is close to Weber's. I believe that critical aspects of modernity, such as the capitalist economy and the leading formulations of liberalism and democracy, emerged from European circumstances: Christianity, the Protestant Reformation, and the Renaissance understanding of classical Greece and Rome. Nonetheless, wherever they started, these modern conditions now have a kind of universality because they are pressing everywhere, breaking down other systems and drawing people into their own logic. This is true partly because they make a powerful appeal to basic human desires for comfort, security, and personal liberty, and partly for reasons of power that I discuss in the chapter titled "Empires, Visible and Invisible." It may be true that they are not universal in principle, but "in principle" does not matter very much when they are increasingly universal in practice. The basic social and economic dynamics of modernity are arriving everywhere, along with certain of its cultural and political features.

But still, these changes in social structure and political doctrines have many possible results. Anyone who doubted this would have only to look at the large and growing differences between Europe and America in attitudes toward individualism, government, religion, and violence, to name a few. India's meeting with modernity takes place in a civilization that was ancient when Europe was still pagan, whose idea of the relationship between the individual and the social order is different from both modern and traditional European and American ideas, and whose customs are its own. Do we accept that, for instance, today's American culture has elements of Ralph Waldo Emerson's Romantic individualism, which in turn was descended from the radical Protestantism of early America? If so, then there is no reason not to expect Hindu traditions to have just as much effect on what India makes of its modernity. Much the same is true of China or the Islamic countries. One McDonald's does not make a country a clone of America, and one world economy does not turn the globe into New Jersey. Moreover, culture flows in more than one direction: The influence of Indian and Chinese spirituality, aesthetics, and medicine is growing in the West, and it may continue to change the way that Americans and Europeans understand their bodies, minds, and world. The precise relationship between what is particular in modernity and what is universal cannot be worked out in theory, but it is being worked out in practice all around us.

There are several reasons that one might hope to see plural modernities develop. One is a kind of ecological principle: the more various decent human cultures exist, the more sources we have of answers to questions such as how to maintain spiritual pursuits in a scientific age, what place the ascetic impulse has in a time of plenty, and how to balance tradition and change. Another reason is an idea that Isaiah Berlin spent his life exploring: value-pluralism, the belief that there are many legitimate human values, not all of which can be pursued at the same time. One cannot hope, for instance, to preserve the virtues of the Homeric heroes, the European aristocracy, medieval monks, and the modern middle class all in the same suburb, or, probably, in the same modern country. If the world has several civilizations instead of one, even though they will intersect and overlap considerably, there will be that much more space for competing human values to survive and change. That seems to me to be a richer world.

In my judgment, though, the pressing issue for the moment is the balance between liberty and violence at the entrance to modernity. Much is at stake in today's social and cultural disruption, the reworking of religious and national identities, and the advent of mass politics. Although these developments will not follow just the same course in India, China, or Egypt as in Europe or America, their outlines are identifiably similar, and we do not have another model for understanding them. To have multiple modernities, we would first have to survive the passage into modernity without succumbing to its worst possibilities of violence: irrationalist nationalism and fundamentalism combined with the technologies of mass politics.

Bibliography: For Adam Smith's view of modernity, the discussions of "natural liberty" in *The Wealth of Nations* and the contrast between courtly and commercial society in *The Theory of Moral Sentiments* are most helpful. Alexis de Tocqueville's *Democracy in America*, particularly the shorter and darker second volume, is the best source of his thought on the topic. John Stuart Mill's *On Liberty* contains his reflections on the dangers of tyrannical public opinion in a mass society. Marx's *Communist Manifesto* remains the classic, accessible statement of his view of universal history, and those who want to brave Hegel will find the first volume of his *Lectures on the Philosophy of History* widely available. Max Weber's view of the situation of the soul in modernity is most eloquently expressed in two short essays, "Science as a Vocation" and "Politics as a Vocation," both contained in *From Max Weber*, a collection edited by C. Wright Mills. This collection also contains illuminating excerpts of Weber's views on the "rationalization" of religions. His first major work, *The Protestant Ethic and the Spirit of Capitalism*, concludes with a memorable image of modernity as an "iron cage," but has less nuance than his later writings.

Arjun Appadurai's *Modernity at Large*, with its emphasis on the variety of modernity's faces in a fast-changing world, makes a lively contrast with Charles Taylor's measured lecturer's prose. Taylor's *Sources of the Self* is a stimulating introduction to the deepening and elaboration of the ideas of individuality and personality that have accompanied, and arguably driven, Western modernity. "Two Theories of Modernity," which appeared in *Public Culture* no. 27 (vol. 11, no. 1) in 1999, lays out his criticism of those who see modernity as purely a matter of economic and technological social structures. Here Taylor argues that multiple modernities should in principle be possible. For a taste of the scholarship that has sprung up around the idea of multiple modernities, the winter 2000 issue of *Daedalus* contains many essays on the theme.

Although one can taste Isaiah Berlin's value-pluralism in any of his collections of essays (of which *The Crooked Timber of Humanity* may be the richest), the most systematic and convincing account I know is in a small, instructive book by Berlin's expositor and admirer, the philosopher John Gray: *Two Faces of Liberalism*. For another view of modernity, which emphasizes how it has stripped the world of sacred or self-transcendent concerns in favor of the life of pleasure, health, and wealth, turn to Pierre Manent's *City of Man*.

Globalization

For a time, everybody talked about globalization. Now there is less eager use of the word, and many people prefer "globalism," suggesting not a process but a condition. There is some confusion in both words, because they are empty without two critical details: globalization of what, and by what means?

I do not use "globalization" many times in this book, and when I do I mainly mean to refer to other people's uses of the word. For instance, when I mention "globalization politics," I mean the debates and street protests where people have expressed views about a loosely conceived combination of the free market, economic integration, growing individualism, and cultural homogenization. I am willing to leave it at that, because I have concluded that "globalization" is a word that expresses more about the person using it than about the phenomenon it purports to name. Trying to give a more precise definition is helpful inasmuch as it specifies what one is talking about, but it does not get closer to "the thing called globalization," because, unlike a new star or species of centipede, there is no single thing out there, waiting to be discovered.

For that reason, I have found it more helpful to concentrate on relatively specific phenomena: sweatshop politics, union organizing abroad, branding campaigns, diaspora communities, the attraction and resentment that attach to America in other countries, and, framing them all, the sweeping social and cultural changes of modernity. Some generalizations are more helpful than others, and I have found the idea of "globalization," as a naked word, almost completely unhelpful.

Among those who do use the word, the most precise definition is economic integration by means of the free market. This is the definition of George Soros' *On Globalization*. It is also most of what Joseph Stiglitz has in mind in his *Globalization and Its Discontents*. Other commentators and most colloquial speakers understand globalization as a self-accelerating coupling of economic integration and cultural change, something closer to what I have called modernization and what many people call Americanization (although its supporters tend to deny adamantly that Americanization is the right term). Thomas Friedman took this broad-gauge view of globalization in *The Lexus and the Olive Tree*, as did John Micklethwait and Adrian Wooldridge in *A Future Perfect*. Both books were defenses of the globalization they described, at least in its broad outlines. By contrast, John Gray in *False Dawn* and William Greider in *One World, Ready or Not* gave a similar definition and proceeded to attack globalization.

These arguments are typically extensions of what the authors already think about domestic political economy. Friedman is a liberal supporter of the welfare state who also likes entrepreneurship, and a multiculturalist who draws the line when other cultures shows signs of being different in ways that might, say, impede free markets and liberal democracy. Micklethwait and Wooldridge, like the *Economist* for which both write, are Margaret Thatcher libertarians with a bit of heart, who believe that free markets make people freer in every way, but also accept that freedom might need some cushioning of its rougher-edged effects.

John Gray is an admirer of Karl Polanyi and Isaiah Berlin. Like Polanyi, the author of *The Great Transformation*, he believes that free markets are an artificial, political creation. Once set in motion, they destroy settled social arrangements and produce violent political reactions. Only sensible regulation can keep them from producing disaster. Like Berlin, Gray believes there are many legitimate but competing human values, and different cultures pursue them in different proportions and various ways. For him, the global market promises social and political crisis, while cultural integration threatens a deadening homogeneity as terrible in its way as mass extinction. Greider is a man of the American left: for him, globalization is basically an extension of Ronald Reagan's attacks on unions, the New Deal, and government regulation. It is about corporations finding new ways to exploit the powerless, and the important question is whether the powerless can find ways to fight back. This sums up many left-wing views of globalization, few of them as well informed as Greider's.

Nationalism and Fundamentalism

"Nationalism," writes Ernest Gellner in *Nations and Nationalism*, "is a theory of political legitimacy, which requires that ethnic boundaries should not cut across political ones." As Gellner himself recognizes, nationalism is a great deal more than that. It is a conviction shared among people about what they have in common, and about the origins of what they share. It treats as primordial a community that is often of recent invention, melded from or superimposed on other communities, and which, even when it is in fact old, acquired its mystical status only recently. Nationalism, as we encounter it today, is a response to the "disenchantment" of modernity: it takes one version of a people's history and purports to inscribe it in the natural order, to make it as much a part of the given world as trees, rivers, and soil. The greater one's sense of displacement, the greater the appeal of nationalist myths of stability and permanence. Nationalism tends to have special force among injured, humiliated populations, people eager to elevate a compass to a lodestone: to turn human-manufactured devices into naturally endowed purposes.

If nationalism is an artificial lodestone, fundamentalism is a concocted polestar, locating human purposes in the heavens. Like nationalism, it looks back to a pure version of its doctrine, ignoring the setting in which the doctrine emerged and all the changes between now and then—trying to get at a moment of perfect revelation or unruptured religious community. Although they are superficially different, then, nationalism and fundamentalism serve the same psychic appetite, creating a false wholeness that papers over the fragmentation of modernity. It is no accident that observers do not know whether to call India's Bharatiya Janata Party Indian nationalists, Hindu fundamentalists, or Hindu nationalists. All are more or less right, inasmuch as they refer to politicized myths about the community that have become substitutes for uprooted ways of life. Both nationalism and fundamentalism are attempts to deal with modernity by denying its premises, inventing or adopting anti-modern certainties as a shield for the vulnerable mind.

That, at any rate, is how I am using the words. I find them helpful as a way of ranging together some of the most important cultural and political responses to modernity. I realize that this largely assimilates fundamentalism to nationalism, which I think is right as a matter of social psychology, but ignores the strict definition of fundamentalism as a doctrine based on the literal reading of a revealed text—a definition on which the idea of Hindu fundamentalism, for instance, would be unintelligible. On nationalism, my characterization aligns me somewhat with those who follow Benedict Anderson's *Imagined Communities* in treating national identity as a matter of political and cultural construction. I admit to a particular sympathy for the work of the Indian scholar Ashis Nandy, who in *The Intimate Enemy* and *The Illegitimacy of Nationalism* has documented the ways that third world nationalism emerges from colonial humiliation, yet repeats the patterns of colonialism in new, self-inflicted wounds. My sense that nationalism is intrinsically violent because it erases other identities and forms of community is due in part to Nandy. Although I doubt there is much love lost between him and the scholars I have just named, my impression of the psychology of nationalism has also been basically shaped by V. S. Naipaul, who in *Among the Believers, Beyond Belief, India: A Million Mutinies Now,* and even the lovely *A House for Mr. Biswas* has shown with painful precision how those who are humiliated undertake grandiose projects to achieve dignity, and end by becoming both ridiculous and dangerous.

I cannot agree with those who like to suggest that because nationalism is socially constructed, it must be somehow avoidable. This nice trick of radicalism by definition is popular among postmodernists, who first define human beings as completely socially constructed and then define everything socially constructed as "contingent" and so "politically contestable." (Judith Butler's *Bodies That Matter* and *Gender Trouble* both describe this attitude in the even more intimate area of sexuality. She gives a more systematic account in "Contingent Foundations," a short essay in *Feminist Contentions*, a quarrel about methodology in social theory assembled by Seyla Benhabib and others.) On the contrary, I am afraid that the necessity of creating collective identities to deal with large-scale politics in societies made up of individualists—that is, the fact of modernity—makes nationalism, with all its dangers, difficult if not impossible to avoid. For this reason, I am sympathetic with those, such as Michael Lind, who argue for the value of "liberal nationalism" founded on common political values rather than blood and soil. Lind propounds this idea, really a philosophical defense of patriotism, in *The Next American Nation* and many shorter essays.

The Anglo-American Tradition

I feel that a word is in order about my view of the figures whose thought I have invoked prominently throughout this book: Adam Smith, Edmund Burke, James Madison, and Alexis de Tocqueville. These are all the favorites of after-dinner speakers, so anyone who takes them as guides is under suspicion of being gassy and sanctimonious.

I believe that the admiration in which they are generally held has led to a serious underestimation of all these thinkers. To my mind they are more interesting, more disturbing, more radical, and also in some ways more or differently conservative than is generally understood. I have drawn on them in this spirit.

There is a book to be written on the bowdlerization of each of these thinkers. Burke became the hero of American conservatives because his defenses of common-sense tradition were good ammunition against reformers, his attacks on the French Revolution and its woolly-headed English supporters seemed to presage American debates about communism in the 1950s and 1960s, and he is eminently quotable. ("All that is necessary for evil to triumph is for good men to do nothing.") My Burke, though, is the one who did not mindlessly defend "organic" tradition, but saw the artificiality of tradition: that it is a self-deception that keeps us human, a "social construction" as we would say today that was also a great achievement. For that very reason Burke believed that creating, preserving, and revising tradition were the highest acts of statesmanship. He is the brooding, haunted parliamentarian who believed that the human capacity for violence is always near the surface, and whose every political act was an attempt to prevent it from bursting forth. Moreover, he is the passionate anti-imperialist who collapsed in exhaustion in the House of Commons during a four-day speech defending India against British abuses, and who once wrote to a correspondent that he would continue his unpopular crusade for India "whether the white people like it or not."

Adam Smith has become the patron saint of the free market, beloved of economists and CEOs. That Smith is real, but he is inseparable from the Adam Smith who saw social life as a struggle for status and esteem, and was intimately attentive to the humiliation and invisibility of the poor, the repugnant obsequiousness of courtiers, the preening self-satisfaction of the rich and powerful, and the possibility of dignity in the small merchant or craftsperson. He is also the social observer who could write that it would be better to surrender modern liberty and prosperity than for slavery to survive and grow into an industrial scale—and who believed that if the decision were left to slaveholders, that is just what would happen. In other words, he was a student of the fate of freedom and dignity in both premodern and modern life, and he was on the side of those values no matter what sacrifices they required.

Alexis de Tocqueville has become the national toastmaster, a congenial and perceptive companion with a kind or instructive word for every occasion. He is widely held to have prophesied nearly every competing view of America: as a country of rampant individualism or runaway government, the land of civic engagement or locked-away private families. He is said to have exhorted us to be good citizens, to serve on juries, and to pay attention to our neighbors, lest we be overtaken by too much government, or too little government, or some other undemocratic and un-American fate.

My Tocqueville is the man caught between two worlds, whose heart belongs to the passing aristocratic order, but who has the clarity and honesty to acknowledge that a democratic society is Europe's future. He will not demean or forget the values of the old order. Indeed, he remains deeply and in some measure permanently oriented to them, and one of his guiding questions is how those values can find analogies or successors in the democratic world. Yet his sympathy with the motives of democratic character is almost perfect, and if he is saddened by some of its aspects and warns against its dangers, his criticism never becomes anger or caricature. He does not express doubt, if he feels it, that the new world will be as fully human as the one that preceded it: quickened by hope and fear, shaped by ambition, eased and ruptured by love, and washed and parched like a border landscape by waves of sympathy and mutual indifference. This richness, the material of human life, is the axiom that survives all change, but is invisible to those who rail either against change or against tradition, and so fail to see to the permanent humanity in both.

James Madison is supposed to be our clever tinker, the most gifted of the infallibly wise generation that descended from some American Olympus to create our Constitution. That is much too simple, as a long tradition of skeptics from Charles Beard to Robert Dahl has demonstrated with varying degrees of decisiveness. Our Constitution was not born perfect. Its many perverse features arose out of a political ferment in which preserving slavery was a major consideration, and much of its wisdom has been put into it by subsequent interpretation and practice—and by the radicalizing aftermath of a Civil War that represented a disastrous constitutional failure. What I find particularly compelling about Madison, though, is his diagnosis in *Federalist* no. 10 of "faction," not as a problem of political mechanics, but as a symptom of the soul, a political perversity born of the perversity of human nature.

To speak of these figures as belonging to a "tradition" is right, I think, but it requires more argument than would be appropriate here. Their work was highly individual, they had quite distinct temperaments and different organizing questions, and their basic suppositions about human life were sometimes at variance in important ways. Nonetheless, their overlapping ideas of the passions united them in an indispensable insight: any clear view of social life must give a central place to dark, "irrational" impulses, such as the appetite for domination and the delight in self-righteousness. These are overcome not by reason alone, but by other passions such as honor and sympathy, and above all by incorporation into a social world where all the passions find a place. This shadowed view of human life unites the students of the passions, and defines their realism.

Liberalism

It will be obvious to readers that the liberalism I describe in the fourth and the final chapters of this book is only one of the many forms that the concept has taken. The distinction that most interests me is between liberalism understood as a set of rules or principles, whether those described in the American Constitution, the Universal Declaration of Human Rights, or the International Monetary Fund's policy documents; and liberalism understood as a temperament or a culture. A great deal of academic political thought recently has followed the cue of philosopher John Rawls in exploring the principles appropriate to a liberal society. Rawls' *Theory of Justice* did much to revive normative political thought when it was published in 1971, and his succeeding *Political Liberalism* reinforced a concentration on the principles that make a liberal society legitimate to its citizens. Rawls' work, which I admire, assumes that it is describing a broadly liberal society, and then asks how such a society should be governed. Such work is an elaboration on where we already are, and anyone who attempted to apply it in illiberal situations would either have to conclude that it was irrelevant or, in the extreme, treat it as a blueprint for forcibly remaking the illiberal society into a liberal one. Rawls' work has this in common with much else that is being done today: it is liberalism refined for the already liberal.

Considering liberalism as a matter of temperament or culture provides a vocabulary for a world in which liberal and illiberal sentiments are always competing, and one needs to understand the appeal of both to appreciate their interplay. It directs attention to the fact that no one is ever perfectly liberal, because liberalism draws on certain aspects of human motivation while struggling against others. In that spirit, this book in part is a consideration of how people become and remain liberal. One major idea at work in it is that commerce can produce liberal sentiments: an idea Montesquieu put forward in *The Spirit of the Laws* and Adam Smith argued somewhat differently in *The Theory of Moral Sentiments*. Another, which I associate with Michel de Montaigne and the poet Czeslaw Milosz, is that liberal sentiment can emerge from an encounter with the worst possibilities of human nature and a resulting determination to guard against them in oneself and others. I do not give much attention to another view: that liberalism as it developed in the Anglo-American world emerged from the social attitudes of Protestant Christianity. (Charles Taylor makes this argument, with special attention to the humanitarian impulse in liberalism, in *Sources of the Self*.) Neither do I spend much time with the idea that clever institutional design, by itself, can do much to produce liberal social relations. This is the "mechanical" view of James Madison's *Federalist* no. 10, which I mention in the last chapter, and which seems to me to beg the question of why people would submit to liberal institutions unless they already had partly liberal dispositions. I do not mean my omission of these ideas as a judgment on them.

My observation that "the circumstances of liberalism" might lead to liberal conclusions along different paths in different countries puts me in debt to John Gray. In *Two Faces of Liberalism*, Gray distinguishes between universalist liberalism, which attempts to identify one set of principles valid for all situations, and pluralist liberalism, which recognizes that the many competing human values can be pursued in various liberal (and even decently illiberal) societies. In that distinction, I am a mild pluralist. I would note, for instance, that European social democracy and the increasingly libertarian American system are both compatible with liberalism, and while I have quarrels with both systems, I consider their differences a family dispute within liberal pluralism.

Where I am not a pluralist is that I believe a decent yet illiberal society is probably impossible in modernity. I think this is so because modernity creates demands for mobility and individual liberty that any form of liberalism satisfies, and that, once present, can be suppressed only by increasingly repressive measures. The Iranian attempt to re-create a traditional society is a case in point: young Iranians have rallied against restrictions on personal liberty, and their wish for American-style freedom has spurred the country's theocracy to become ever more repressive in order to preserve its power. Strong pluralists who imagine that the strictures of traditional society could survive in modernity without repression overlook the genuine appetite for individual liberty that arises everywhere. The political options for modernity are repressive traditionalism, the outright tyranny of communist and fascist states, the kleptocracy of corrupt countries, the violent passions of nationalist regimes, and liberalism. So stated, the choice is not hard to make. It is, however, only the first of many choices to come.

ACKNOWLEDGMENTS

The idea of this book emerged from conversations with David Grewal, Sanjay Reddy, Chris Elmendorf, and Vivek Maru. They have been invaluable interlocutors throughout its writing. In the early months of drafting, Asha Rangappa's generous and sensible contributions planted many seeds. Four Yale faculty members were exceptionally supportive in my early explorations of the topic: Jack Balkin, Owen Fiss, Robert Gordon, and Anthony Kronman.

In Washington, where I wrote most of the manuscript, the support of the New America Foundation and the generosity of Edward and Susan Elmendorf enabled me to live and write. My research assistants at New America were good help and company: Cliff Davidson, Irene Hahn, Eric Brown, and Sveta Srinivasan.

The generosity of many people supported my time abroad in the fall and winter of 2001. My brother, Charles Veley, helped me to fund the trip and provided a much-needed rest in the middle. Sanjay Reddy and Keshav Desiraju went out of their way to help me arrange conversations in India, as did Owen Fiss in Egypt and Paul Gewirtz in China. Pratap Mehta's conversation in Delhi restored my sense of purpose. Florian Amereller, Ingy Rasekh, Sathi Clarke, Jairaj, Nitin, Vikram Doctor, Prem Shankar Jha, Katherine Mooney, Vanessa Chien, and Mei Zhao were among the many who showed me special hospitality.

The manuscript benefited from the criticism of several acute readers. My parents, Walter and Deirdre Purdy, read it for familiar mistakes. Michael Lind gave bracing and heartening criticism on an early draft, as did David Grewal, Chris Elmendorf, Walton A. Green, Eric Cohen, Sherle Schwenninger, Edward Elmendorf, and Owen Fiss. At a later stage, Pratap Mehta, Sidney Kwiram, Jeremy Dauber, Quentin Palfrey, and Vivek Maru prompted me to soften mistakes of emphasis and address glaring omissions. Marco Simons was meticulous in his helpful criticism. Sarah Russell and Brady Case read the manuscript with characteristic sensitivity, precision, and imagination.

Several scholars helped me to correct factual oversights in my discussions of the countries they study. Andrew Reding, Andrew Nathan, Ray Yep, and Diane Singerman kindly reviewed chapters.

Acknowledgments

My editors at Knopf, Ashbel Green, Jonathan Fasman, and Luba Osta-shevsky, have shown more confidence in me than can possibly have been rational, and more patience than was reasonable.

Mary Campbell shared me with the manuscript for eight months and graciously adopted it, contributing to it in too many ways for me to identify.

INDEX

abacus, 181–2
Abbot Labs, 136
abolitionism, 47, 60
accounting standards, 35
Acteal, Mexico, massacre at (1997),
    245–6
ACT UP (AIDS Coalition to
    Unleash Power), 127–8, 133,
    230
Adidas, 156
admiration, appetite for, 237–40
advertising, 40, 108
    Benetton campaigns, 226–32
    global capitalism as envisioned in,
        147–9
    Nike campaigns, 223–4
    see also branding; marketing
Afghanistan, xii, xvi, 10, 11, 16, 88
    American offensive in, 10, 11, 26,
        52–3, 98, 183, 200
    mujahideen in, 16, 113
    Taliban in, 85, 88
Africa, 28, 37, 182, 279
    AIDS in, 126, 129–42, 230, 231
    see also specific countries
African National Congress (ANC),
    138, 140
AIDS, 126–42, 279
    activist groups and, 127–8, 132–4,
        136, 141
    in Africa, 126, 129–42, 230,
        231
    in America, 126–9
    Benetton campaigns and, 228,
        229, 230–2
    drug treatments for, 128–38

interpretation and blame attached
    to, 127, 139–42
Mbeki's opposition to effective
    measures against, 138–42
as reminder of unity of humanity,
    126, 134
    see also HIV
Aigon, 185
Alexandria, library at, 24, 25
Allende, Salvador, 53
Amarnath, Ganpat, 103–5
America:
    belief in innocence of, 46–53, 59,
        62, 70
    as commercial society, 64
    cultural influences absorbed in,
        108–9
    global language of dreams and,
        8–9
    historical amnesia in, 64–5, 142,
        299, 300
    immigrants absorbed into, 22,
        63–4, 75, 274, 280, 281
    imperialism ascribed to, 28–42;
        see also empire
    inequalities in, 76, 281
    liberal temper in, 65–71
    as nation of migrants, 62–3
    pop culture of, 32, 40–1
    prominence of, 295, 297–8
    regard for people vs. government
        of, 11
    spiritual corruption ascribed to, 22
    as universal nation, 43–6, 59, 62,
        70
    visibility and power of, 54–61

JENNIFER GOVERNMENT
by Max Barry

In Max Barry's twisted, hilarious vision of the future, the world is run by giant corporations, taxes are illegal, employees take the last names of the companies they work for, and the Police and the NRA are publicly traded security firms. It's a free-market paradise! But life starts to go awry for Hack Nike when he signs a contract to shoot teenagers to build up street cred for Nike's new line of $2,500 sneakers. Soon Hack finds himself pursued by Jennifer Government, a tough-talking agent who is the consumer watchdog from hell.

Fiction/1-4000-3092-7

KRAZY KAT
by Jay Cantor

Krazy Kat is Jay Cantor's inspired reimagining of George Herriman's classic comic strip, a postmodern masterpiece as profound as it is funny. Having just witnessed a 1945 test for the atomic bomb, Krazy Kat is depressed, and to the exasperation of her costar, Ignatz Mouse, she refuses to work. To coax her back to work so that they can regain the limelight, Ignatz subjects Krazy to his own brand of psychotherapy, orchestrates her kidnapping, and tries to seduce her with promises of stardom from a Hollywood producer.

Fiction/0-375-71382-4

M31: A FAMILY ROMANCE
by Stephen Wright

Husband and wife Dash and Dot—possibly descendants of aliens from the M31 galaxy—are the world's most in-demand lecturers on the UFO circuit. They live in a decommissioned church in the middle of America, with a radar dish on its steeple and a spacecraft in its sanctuary. When a couple of UFO groupies show up looking for the extraterrestrial duo, they find instead a nuclear family—or rather, a family gone nuclear—whose comically discomfiting world resembles our own as much as it does another world altogether.

Fiction/0-375-71294-1